RAFFLES

The Story of Singapore

RAFFLES

The Story of Singapore

Raymond Flower

TIMES BOOKS INTERNATIONAL
Singapore • Kuala Lumpur

Books by the same author:

NAPOLEON TO NASSER   The Story of Modern Egypt
MOTOR SPORTS   An Illustrated History
THE STORY OF SKIING   and Other Winter Sports
CHIANTI   The Land, the People and the Wine
CHIANTI   Storia e Cultura
THE PALACE   A Profile of St Moritz
THE OLD SHIP   A Prospect of Brighton
LLOYD'S OF LONDON   An Illustrated History
                              (with Michael Wynn Jones)
A HUNDRED YEARS OF MOTORING   An RAC Social History of the Car
                              (with Michael Wynn Jones)

MEET YOU AT RAFFLES
THIS BUSINESS OF WRITING

[Published by Times Books International,
an imprint of Times Editions Pte Ltd]
Times Centre
1 New Industrial Road
Singapore 1953

2nd Floor
Wisma Hong Leong Yamaha
50 Jalan Penchala
46050 Petaling Jaya
Selangor Darul Ehsan
Malaysia

First published 1984
Reprinted 1988, 1991

Printed by Times Offset Pte Ltd

ISBN 981 204 257 1

Dedicated, gratefully, to
Donald and Ruth Hawley

ACKNOWLEDGEMENTS

The author and publisher wish to thank those listed below for their kind permission to reproduce photographs and illustrations. The sources, referred to by code letters in the captions, are as follows:

ANM   Arkib Negara Malaysia
AOHD   Archives and Oral History Department, Singapore
ATQS   Antiques of the Orient Pte Ltd
BLKW   Private collection of Baby Low Koon Wee
CKT   Private collection of Cheong Kee Toh
EUP   Eastern Universities Press Collection
FRNS   Private collection of Francis Lee
GH   Private collection of Gillian Ho
GWDC   Girdwood Collection
HLEE   Private collection of Henry Lee
ILN   Illustrated London News
IWM   Imperial War Museum
JF   Private collection of Josephine Fong
JL   Private collection of Julian Lauw
JMH   Private collection of Jamilah Mohd Hassan
JOSY   Private collection of Alex Josey
LCC   Private collection of Lim Cheng Choon
LKC   Private collection of Lim Kheng Chye
LWTC   Loke Wan Tho Collection
MG   Private collection of Margaret Goh
NTLY   National Library, Singapore
PY   Private collection of Paul Yap
RB   Private collection of Rahilah Begum
RH   Raffles Hotel Collection
SNPL   Singapore News and Publications Ltd
WR   Private collection of Wilson Richards

◀ CONTENTS ▶

Author's Preface *viii*
Landfall *1*

PART ONE
The Founders

1. Ancient Singapura *5*
2. Light of Penang *11*
3. Enter Tom Raffles *19*
4. Destination Singapore *23*
5. The Flag is Planted *27*

PART TWO
The Pioneers

6. The Imprint of Raffles *57*
7. The Merchant Venturers: Claret and Cricket *61*
8. The Hazards: Pirates and Tigers *67*
9. Secret Societies and the Straits Chinese *73*
10. Daily Life in the 1850s *83*

PART THREE
The Myth-Makers

11. Conrad, Kipling and the 'Savoy of Singapore' *143*
12. Cameos in Mid-History *153*
13. The Palm Courts of Maugham and Coward *161*

PART FOUR
The Agony and the Fruition

14. Armageddon Approaches *225*
15. The Syonan Interlude: Miseries and Illusions *231*
16. The Emergence of Lee Kuan Yew *237*
17. Colonial Twilight *243*
18. An Island State Comes of Age *251*
19. Selamat Tinggal *263*

AUTHOR'S PREFACE

SOME YEARS AGO, AT THE SUGgestion of friends in Kuala Lumpur, I took a slow boat to Sabah. It was the old *Kimanis*, a cargo ship that sailed from Singapore to Tawau and had sixteen double cabins. After much telephoning, I was told I was lucky to get a berth. But when the vessel finally left, about a fortnight after its scheduled date, I found that I was the only passenger aboard. I had the ship to myself.

Most evenings I was invited up to the Chief Officer's cabin for a game of scrabble. He was a Malay, the radio officer Chinese, and the purser a Tamil. Being Singaporeans, they spoke perfect English, and somewhat to my mortification they nearly always won. Naturally we got chatting, and in the course of conversation it turned out that though all of them were well-educated, not one had the least idea of his country's history. They could dream up the most recondite words for the scrabble board, but they had never heard of Francis Light, they thought Sir Stamford Raffles had built the hotel, and if they knew of Rajah Brooke it was only because they had sailed on a ship named after him.

When, between cogitating about words of seven letters that always seemed to begin with a Q or a Y with a Z in the middle, I gave them what amounted to an impromptu tutorial, they were so obviously enthralled that I resolved there and then to write the story of Singapore. Of course, as we all know, there are plenty of excellent books on the subject. The National Library is full of them. But very few tell the tale in the way that, as a newcomer, I should have liked to come across: that is, a narrative picture of Singapore's progress from a spirited little outpost, beset with pirates, tigers, secret societies and opium wars, into a bastion of the British Empire handling half the world's tin and rubber supplies, and finally a nation on its own. Politics and economics, though naturally an important part of the story, interested me less than how people lived, what Singapore meant to them, and how in the course of time, largely through the efforts of a single man who read law at Cambridge while I was reading history at Oxford, they achieved independence and made an astonishingly good job of it.

Over these things I pondered while staying at Raffles, which of all the hotels I know is one of my most favourite. And since Raffles seems to stand not only for all the fables of the exotic East, as Somerset Maugham once declared in an effusive moment, but also as a symbolic link between the swashbuckling old merchant venturers and today's indigenous technocrats, I thought it would be appropriate, as well as aesthetically impelling, to weave the story around this romantic establishment.

Though the faults are certainly all mine, a number of indulgent friends have helped shape my ideas. Sir Donald and Lady Hawley, to whom this volume is dedicated, introduced me to the mesmeric world of Southeast Asia while presiding over the British High Commission in Kuala Lumpur. Cavaliere Roberto Pregarz and his charming wife

Helena made free the archives of Raffles Hotel and gave me every possible assistance, even though the book, despite its title and substance, sprang from a whim of my own, as unsponsored as the wind. John Hill, Chief Executive of the Hong Kong Bank in Singapore, provided some economic facts, Noel Barber gave me some useful tips, Alex Josey some anecdotes, and Ilsa Sharp, the historian of Raffles, willingly shared her extensive knowledge of the hotel. Howard Richards turned up from the *Straits Times* one afternoon and sportingly offered to help with my research, which he set about doing with spirited efficiency. The staff of the Singapore National Library and the State Archives were unfailingly helpful. And Eastern Universities Press took the project under their wing with an enthusiasm that I have rarely had the joy of encountering: an exemplary case of cooperation between publisher and author which saw Goh Eck Kheng quit the sanctum of his desk to hunt for rare pictures and produce relays of esoteric material about Singapore, while Rita Balachander, the editor, perused my increasingly untidy typescript with a sharp but friendly eye, alert for tautology. And no one could have been more generous in giving access to their incomparable collection of Singapore memorabilia than Michael Sweet, Francis Lee, Paul Yap, Julian Lauw and Lim Kheng Chye.

To these, and all other friends who have lightened and enlivened my task, a most grateful word of thanks.

Lt Col V.A. Flower, with whom the author claims a tenuous link, was a partner in the architectural firm of Swan & MacLaren, and had a part in the designing of Raffles Hotel. He was killed during World War I while commanding a battalion in France. (AOHD)

LANDFALL

'IMPALPABLE AND ENSNARING' was the thought that ran through Joseph Conrad's mind when, shipwrecked and exhausted after 13½ hours in an open boat, he caught his first glimpse of Singapore, — 'like a whispered promise of mysterious delight.' And, a hundred years later, the traveller still experiences the same pleasant frisson of anticipation as he peers cosily out of the window of his jumbo.

Certainly I did, for nothing could have been more spectacular than to arrive at the old Paya Lebar airport just after dusk. For a few hours we had been droning along at 30,000 feet above frozen cotton wool puffs, with the sea sparkling far below. Then, in the time it took to sip a whisky and soda the tropical sunset flared, colouring everything with a burst of bronze before darkness fell. On went the seat-belt lights; the plane banked, and slipped through the clouds.

Suddenly, as though on an illuminated stage, the skyline of Singapore appeared, silver and glittering through a veil of sea-mist. There it was: an endless three-dimensional vista of skyscrapers, every window alight. Floating down above a galaxy of super-tankers, freighters and junks, I just had time to spot a few landmarks — the pocket-computer shaped OCBC building; the river, bulging like a snake that has swallowed a rabbit; the Padang with St Andrew's Cathedral and Raffles Hotel beyond — before sweeping at roof-level past a regiment of arc-lit high-rises as the plane touched down. It was as theatrical a landfall as one could possibly desire.

Nowadays, of course, the aircraft circles further out over the sea to come in at the glitteringly efficient new international airport at Changi, where everything is marble and fountains, with acres of carpeting, boutiques and escalators. You could fancy yourself at Los Angeles, New York or Amsterdam. And yet not entirely, for there is an exhilarating atmosphere here — a sense of movement and opportunity and purpose that grips you from the moment you arrive.

After breezing through immigration, old Singapore hands pause only to put through a quick call from one of the tangerine coloured telephones and perhaps pick up a bottle at the duty-free shop before catching a taxi downtown. After a leisurely quarter of an hour's spin along the tree-lined expressway, they are checking in at Raffles Hotel. Where else?

To be sure, there are plenty of luxurious, oversleek hostelries in town, some of a dazzling splendour. The ShangriLa, for instance, is one of the loveliest hotels in the East, offering an instant foretaste of the 21st century. The Pavilion is another. But I cannot help feeling that many of them have that international sameness which makes all countries one, but in the wrong sort of way — distancing everything but the closed world of the expense account executive, of the package tourist. For anyone of a more enquiring turn of mind, anyone who aims to explore the soul of Singapore, Raffles is the place. A relic of imperial splendour, maybe — shades of Conrad and Kipling, Maugham and Coward — but one that retains some of the grace and charm we once took for granted: a leisured elegance that the world is now losing.

Personally, I envy that fast-departing sense of style. Like Kipling's poetry, you can laugh at its philosophy, but its images continue to haunt your thoughts. And what images Raffles conjures up!

From Changi to Raffles: the spectrum is spanned. And to explore its nuances you have only to stroll out of the hotel along a busy thoroughfare lined with trim flowering trees and soaring skyscrapers, to find yourself on the cropped grass of the huge Padang, where cricket matches have for so long been played against a background of colonial architecture on one side, and the sea on the other. The slender spire of St Andrew's Cathedral, together with the slightly forbidding Supreme Court and City Hall are still as they always were, although the sea has now retreated beyond a flower-bedecked esplanade named after Queen Elizabeth II, along which all Singapore strolls.

It is here, behind the gentlemanly facade of the Cricket Club, that the first whiff of the tropics assails you: a thrilling sweet-sour smell compounded of spices, dried fish, warm skin, frangipani, roasting satay, monsoon drains, and who knows what else. Here in the sweltering night air, as the swarming polyglot city spreads before your eyes — huge office blocks ahead, shophouses packed along the banks of the river, electric guitars counterpointed by ancient flutes, young Chinese on Hondas and, over the river, a Hokkien chef splitting chilli crabs in an eating place on stilts, that the tang of adventure strikes, and you know that you have reached the centrepoint of Asia. You are standing on the spot where Tom Raffles landed eight-fifths of a century ago to found this great emporium just sixty miles from the equator. And if you look over your shoulder, you will see that his statue is there behind you, flanked by oleanders.

Following:
One of a pair of two gold bracelets found on Fort Canning during excavation works in July 1928. Dated about 1350, the ornaments belong to the Javanese empire of Majapahit which occupied Tumasik from 1360. (ANM)

Part One

THE FOUNDERS

◀ 1 ▶

ANCIENT SINGAPURA

THINGS MOVE SO FAST IN THIS
city that it is hard to believe that many young Singaporeans were born into a British
colony. And indeed that history began not in August 1965 when Singaporeans found that
they were a nation-state on their own; nor in September two years earlier, when
Singapore, along with Malaya and British Borneo became independent from Britain; nor
even in February 1819, when Raffles planted the Union Jack on a virtually uninhabited
swamp off the tip of Malaya.

From untold ages the Malay peninsula had played its part in world history. First,
when the ancestors of the Australian and Papuan aborigines began their marathons
through the jungle as they migrated to their present homes around 6000 B.C. Next, around
2000 B.C., when the forebears of the Malays themselves trekked down its rivers as they
moved from south-west China to Sumatra and Java.

In fact, the South China Sea was the cradle of ancient and affluent civilizations, to
which even Roman ships sailed from Egypt in search of spices. And all of them, like the
armadas that followed and the supertankers of today, had to pass through the shallow
waters of the Straits of Malacca — one of the oldest and most strategically placed
waterways in the world — at the entrance to which, situated at the extreme end of the
continent of Asia, lay an island the Chinese called P'u Luo Chung. In about 231 A.D.
General Lu Tai of the Wu Kingdom, sent an expedition to the South Seas. Though only
fragments of its findings have survived, scholars believe that one extract refers to
Singapore. It was not very complimentary, either: 'To the east of Kon Li, there is the
people of P'u Luo Chung, each with a tail five or six inches long. They are accustomed to
cannibalism....'

By then both China and India had become maritime powers, and a Malay-Buddhist
empire known as Sri Vijaya established a foothold in the north of the peninsula to
command the Straits of Malacca, together with an outpost at Palembang on the Sunda
Straits. These strategic nodal points allowed their longships to levy tolls on vessels sailing
between China and India; while upstream from the marshy estuaries, various local river-
states grew up, each ruled by a Malay king and his court from forbidding walled palaces.

Tradition has it that in the 11th century the Chula King Raja Suran came to Tumasik,
as the island of Singapore was then called, with the idea of making it the base for an
expedition to conquer China. Hearing of this, the Emperor is said to have sent a ship
manned by geriatrics and filled with rusty needles as a present to the king — the message
being that any journey to China would take the better part of a lifetime.

Raja Suran took the hint. But the Malay Annals relate that some generations later one
of his descendants, a member of the royal family of Palembang named Sri Tri Buana,
caught sight of the long white beaches of Tumasik and decided to investigate. Upon

landing near the mouth of the river he spotted an animal described as being 'very graceful in its movements, with a black head, white neck and tawny body, swift and bold and the size of an old he-goat'. No one knew what it was, but an aged counsellor told the prince that in his youth he had heard that the lion was a beast of that description. Impressed, Sri Tri Buana decided that if the island could breed such animals, it was a good place to settle in. Changing the name to Singapura, City of the Lion,* he proclaimed himself king.

He then sent for his family and asked his adoptive mother, the Queen of Bentan, for help in colonizing the island. People, horses and elephants arrived, and quite an impressive city grew up. According to the geographical handbook written by a Chinese trader named Wang Ta Yuan, the ancient town of Singapura extended from Fort Canning Hill to the river on one side, and to Stamford Canal on the other. The whole area, he states, was enclosed by thick walls about ten feet high. Behind these walls, imposing buildings and temples were pedestalled on terraces cut into the slopes of the hill; a moat ran around the king's palace. Certainly D'Albuquerque noted in 1511 that 'Singapura was a big town with a large population, as is evidenced by the large ruins which one sees there today.' (The Portuguese thought that Singapura might have been Ptolemy's Zaba, and Roland Braddell believed it was the place Marco Polo referred to as Malaiur, but never in fact visited.)

Historians have combed through the old Malay Annals, and archeologists spent many happy hours digging on Fort Canning, but beyond unearthing a tomb which may be that of the founder of ancient Singapura, very little has been discovered about Sri Tri Buana's little realm. It is now known that he reigned for forty-eight years and was succeeded by four generations of rulers. † But beyond hints of tribute paid to China, a suggestion of Siamese influence, and conflicts with the Javanese State of Majapahit, there is not much to be said. 'The history of the war between Singapura and Java is a very long one' sigh the Annals. 'If we related it all the people who heard it would be bored...for a slow and long drawn-out narrative would not be pleasing to people of intelligence. Singapura was not conquered, and all the people returned to Majapahit.'

All the same, let us spend a moment with these old annals. One of their best known tales is that of the garfish — that curious sharp-nosed fish which skims upright along the surface of the sea as if standing on its tail. According to the myth, these fish began assaulting people on the beach. So the king mounted his elephant and paraded the army on the shore, only to have his own robes torn to bits by a garfish. 'Why let the fish pierce your legs when you can use banana trees instead?' remarked a small boy who was looking on. Whereupon the king had a barricade of banana trunks erected in which the garfish got stuck and were caught by the thousands. But the wise men shook their heads. 'If that boy

---

*A less romantic etymology suggests that the name comes from the words *singgah*, meaning stop-over, and *pura*, meaning city.

†The chronology of the Singapura kings has been established as follows:

Sri Tri Buana, 1st ruler, reigned A.D. 1299–1347
Paduka Sri Pikrama Wira, 2nd ruler, reigned A.D. 1347–1362
Sri Rana Wikerma, 3rd ruler, reigned A.D. 1362–1375
Paduka Sri Maharaja, 4th ruler, reigned A.D. 1375–1388
Sri Sultan Iskandar Shah (also known as Parameswara), 5th ruler, reigned in Singapore A.D. 1388–1391; and in Malacca A.D. 1393–1413.

is so clever now, he will become a peril to his betters when he grows up.' The king heeded their warning and killed him on the spot.

A humble religious man called Tun Jana Khatib fared no better. While he was seated under a palm near the palace the tree suddenly split and came down with a crash. The king was furious. 'Is a man like this to come practising his magic because he knows my wife is looking through her window?' So they took the wretched ascetic 'to the place of execution, which was near a cake-shop, and there they shed his blood with a stabbing blow, but his body vanished leaving only the blood on the ground.'

Ancient Singapura seems to have been a violent place. According to the annals, the daughter of the state treasurer caught the king's eye. But jealous rivals in the harem whispered that she was unfaithful to him, and on the king's orders — this must have been Iskandar Shah, the fifth and last ruler — she was impaled alive in the market place. Whereupon her embittered father sent a message to Java that if the Batara of Majapahit wanted to take Singapura he was ready to assist. When the expedition arrived he opened the gates to the Javanese. There was fierce fighting, and 'so appalling was the bloodshed that the soil of Singapura is blood-red even now' — hence, it is implied, the red clay laterite of the ground.

The king fled with the remnants of his followers to the mainland. There he founded the city of Malacca, which over the next hundred years grew up into the richest emporium in the East. Sri Sultan Iskandar Shah was proclaimed King of Malacca by no less an authority than the Chinese Emperor, and ruled there from A.D. 1393 to 1413. But more important still, he converted to Islam, and Malacca became a centre whence Indian and Arab missionaries spread the Moslem religion to the islands of the Archipelago. By contrast, Singapura, which but for its destruction might very well have become a great trading hub in the fifteenth century, disintegrated instead into so much waste land, inhabited only by a few sea-gypsies. Much later, a picture of Singapura in those days was given by Munshi Abdullah: 'On the banks of the river you could see lying about on the sand some hundreds of human skulls: some were old, others were fresh, some had the scale still clinging to them. When the sea-gypsies were questioned about them, they said they were the skulls of the victims of the pirates, Singapura being the place to which the captives were taken for slaughter.'

So the momentum passed to Malacca, and we move on to the end of the fifteenth century. When Vasco da Gama reached India in 1498, he took the opportunity to load up with spices, which throughout the Middle Ages had been conveyed to Europe by caravans through the deserts of the Middle East at such a huge toll in transit fees that a sack of pepper which cost a mere 5 ducats in Calicut sold for as much as 80 ducats on the Rialto in Venice. So huge was the potential of transporting the spices by sea that the Portuguese wasted no time in setting out to capture this immensely profitable trade.

When Diego Lopez di Siqueira sailed from Lisbon to Malacca, he was hospitably welcomed there at first. But disagreements soon arose, and the Sultan imprisoned some of the Portuguese sailors who were ashore collecting cargo for the ships. In 1511 D'Albuquerque came to their rescue. The Sultan countered his first assault with elephants and poisoned arrows. But these were no match for gunpowder: within a week the place fell.

For the next 130 years Malacca remained in Portuguese hands. It was an ideal entrepot for trade with the Spice Islands and the Far East, 'because it is placed and seated at the beginning of many monsoons,' as d'Albuquerque explained in a dispatch to King Manuel I dated 5 January 1515. In those days of sailing ships, the monsoons over the Bay of Bengal played a vital role in naval strategy. Merchandise, d'Albuquerque added, came from China and Quachyachyna (Cochin China), Siam, Formosa and Borneo, including 'cloves from the Malluque, mace and nutmeg from Banda'. Though in theory it was a free port, his supervisor commented that while 'they do not pay duties in Malacca, they hand over a present, which comes to the same thing because the man who has to produce it is told by the *zabandar* what present he has to give.' However, business was brisk. A Portuguese trader enthused: 'Men cannot estimate the value of Malacca on account of its greatness and profit.'

Alas, inevitably they did. Malacca was twice attacked by the Achinese, and its shipping was harried by the first British vessel to reach the Straits — though the *Edward Bonaventure*, commanded by Edward Lancaster, never got home with the pepper, silk, taffetas and venetian glass that she seized. This was, incidentally, around the time that St. Francis Xavier started the first Christian mission in the Malayan archipelago at Malacca.

More disturbingly, though, Dutch appetites were whetted. Since the Portuguese had no direct access to the principal European markets, they sent their cargoes to the Netherlands for distribution down the Scheldt and the Rhine. It was therefore only a matter of time before the middle-men sought to monopolize this lucrative spice trade by securing the sources of production for themselves. In 1602 the Dutch East India Company was founded, and once the Dutch were entrenched in Batavia and commanded the Sunda Straits it was clear that to enforce their monopoly they would have to dominate the Straits of Malacca as well.

In 1641 they wrested Malacca from the Portuguese, and from these two strategic points they were able to develop their vast colonial and commercial interests without serious competition. That is, until the British East India Company appeared on the scene.

Following:

Francis Light, the illegitimate son of a Suffolk landowner, had his first naval commission as a midshipman. His first Far Eastern posting as a trader was with the agency of the Madras association of merchants, Jourdain, Sulivan and De Souza at Acheh.

In 1771, when a rebellion broke out in the Sultanate of Kedah, the Sultan asked for British assistance. The Madras Government rejected the request but Light, acting on behalf of the Madras firm of merchants, responded, for they were eager to trade in Kedah. By the time Light arrived, the rebellion had failed but he nevertheless took the opportunity and established an agency house for the Madras firm. In return for trading rights, the firm was obliged to maintain a defensive force at Kedah and later, this issue of military assistance was to secure the island of Penang off Kedah for the British.

By 1782, the search for a strategic base for British commerce had become urgent. The Sultan of Kedah, fearing involvement in an imminent war between her overlord, Siam, and Burma, offered Penang in exchange for military assistance.

The opportunity was perhaps too timely. The threat of war influenced the Sultan to allow Light to occupy Penang tentatively even before the agreement for military assistance and compensation was finalised. And before a decision was reached, Penang had become British and a base from which the East India Company would extend its influence to Singapore. (ANM)

◄ 2 ►

LIGHT OF PENANG

JOHN COMPANY — THUS NICK-named from the native way of pronouncing the title Hon.ble Co., as it chose to describe itself in documents and proclamations — was the 17th century equivalent of today's multinational, with a good deal more clout. In fact it was probably the most extraordinary mercantile enterprise that ever existed, possessing its own armies and warships, diplomats and currencies. But though originally founded to acquire spices from Malaya after the merchants of Amsterdam had suddenly doubled the price of pepper (which was vital for preserving meat, for the roast beef of Old England had to be highly seasoned to be palatable at all) John Company soon discovered that the Dutch competition in Southeast Asia was too strong for its liking. In 1623 it decided to abandon Malayan spices for those from India — and, having gone there to do business, went into politics to bolster its trade. Within little more than a century, the East India Company became the paramount power in India, while to all intents and purposes remaining independent of the British government.

Nor did it take long for its officials at Madras, and then in Calcutta, which they virtually created, to assume the airs and graces of an Anglo-Indian aristocracy. Not always a very aristocratic aristocracy, it must be admitted, though they lived in great style and maintained a high *esprit de corps* — along with a propensity for feathering their own nests. But below this slowly cohering upper crust were plenty of other folk who made the four-month trip out in search of fortune. Deserters and bishops' sons, Honourables and wanteds, free-booters and buccaneers were all attracted by the lure of adventure and the desire to become rich.

Among these assorted empire-builders came three audacious men who, by leap-frogging, as it were, over each other's acquisitions, made a logical pattern of their incursions into Malaya. In order of appearance they were Light, Raffles, and Brooke.

Francis Light, was the natural son of William Negus, a great Suffolk landowner with a penchant for saddling up with the women on his estates. His mother, from whom he took his name, was a certain Mary Light of Dalinghoo. Illegitimacy carried little social stigma in those days, and like the other sons of the local gentry, Francis was sent to Seckford's Grammar School at Woodbridge, where the only relic of his school-days is a signature scratched on a pane of glass* in one of the mullioned windows of the old school building.

In 1759, young Light joined the navy as a midshipman, and saw service on HMS *Arrogant*, which was engaged on convoy duties against the French between Portsmouth

---

*Now seen in the Penang museum.

and Gibraltar. But when peace was concluded in 1763, the *Arrogant* was paid off. Along with James Scott, the relative of Sir Walter with whom he was to be closely associated during his career in the East, Francis Light found himself unemployed. But adventure beckoned, and by June he was aboard the East India Company's ship *Clive*, bound for Madras.

There he was given command of a country ship — that is, a locally-owned vessel trading in eastern waters — belonging to Messrs. Jourdain, Sulivan & de Souza. This firm headed a syndicate of merchants interested in establishing agencies in the East Indies, for whom Light sailed to Achen to scout out the land.

And here a whiff of romance creeps in. The identity of the Eurasian lady who, purporting to be an emissary from the Sultan of Kedah, brought him the offer of a trading station in return for assistance against the Sultan's enemies, has historians guessing. It was curious, to say the least, that in a land where women were kept behind the curtain, an Islamic prince should have entrusted her with such affairs of state. Significant, too, that Light later set up household with a Eurasian woman named Martina Rozells.

Be this as it may, he went to Kedah and was soon on cosy terms of friendship with Sultan Mohammed Jewa. He found the old sultan, who like most Malay rulers held a monopoly of the trade in his kingdom, in a quandary, for his neighbours to the south, the Bugis of Selangor, had captured the royal capital, Alor Star; while his overlords to the north — the Siamese — were demanding assistance in their war against Burma. Mohammed Jewa had already written to Madras to seek help from the British so the arrival of this engaging young Englishman, representing the Madras firm, must have seemed like an answer to his prayer.

For his part, Francis Light was only too eager to establish a commercial foothold in Kedah. He could see the makings of a most satisfactory agreement. In August 1771 he reported to his principals that the Sultan would give his seaport, and indeed the whole coastline up to Penang, in return for help against Selangor; and that furthermore he was prepared to share his trade monopoly with the British.

Since military aid was beyond the scope of a trading company, the East India Company decided to send a mission of its own. John Company needed a port of call somewhere in the Malayan archipelago where its ships could harbour and refit while waiting for favourable winds (for the monsoons controlled the timing of voyages); and if the Kedah trade prospects were as tempting as Light seemed to think, it was quite prepared to elbow him out and pounce on the concession itself. There was also the attraction of possessing a naval base on the eastern side of the Indian Ocean.

A young official, the Hon. Edward Monkton, was therefore sent with a mission to Kedah, only to find that the Sultan's demands for an offensive alliance went beyond his terms of reference. What's more, the young man from Head Office seems to have been sadly inexperienced. Though Light — who was forced to remain a passive spectator during the abortive negotiations — did his utmost to retrieve the situation, and even helped secure a draft treaty which Madras subsequently repudiated, the mission failed once it became clear that the Company's support would not include aid against Selangor. Things might have turned out differently had negotiations been left to the man on the spot; instead the Madras Council castigated Light for having been the author of the fiasco.

'The offer the Sultan made me on my first arrival I thought so advantageous that not to have accepted it seemed downright folly', he complained on 17 June 1772 to Warren

Hastings. But Hastings was too preoccupied turning John Company's possessions in India into an empire to have much time for the trade or politics of Malaya. Not for another fifteen years was Light able to realize his dream of securing a British settlement in Malayan waters.

It was only after the Peace of Versailles in 1783 that Hastings began to take positive measures to find a strategic harbour to victual ships engaged in the China trade. Various projects were considered: a mission was sent to Achen, and another under Captain Forrest to Rhio. Both were foiled by the Dutch. But Forrest also surveyed the island of Penang, and thought it a good site for trade.

Light saw that the time for action had come; he was determined to gain possession of Penang. Despite the failure of the Monkton mission, he had continued trading with Kedah and was on good terms with Sultan Abdullah, the successor to the old king. Now, on his own initiative, he asked for the island of Penang in return for British protection against the Sultan's enemies.

The upshot was surprising: in a reversal of the previous negotiations he found himself appointed as *wakil*, or representative, to deal on the Sultan's behalf with the Company in Calcutta. The Sultan's demands were simple. He wanted protection from his enemies and an annual payment of 30,000 Spanish dollars a year to compensate for the loss of trade — a figure that Light considered negotiable, knowing as he did that the 'trade' did not exceed 10,000 dollars a year.

After expressing a handsome tribute (which made some amends for its previous censure) the Company appointed Francis Light chief of the mission to occupy Penang. But instead of a formal agreement to the Sultan's terms, he was given a vague undertaking that the Company would station an armed vessel at Penang and 'take care that the King of Kedah shall not be a sufferer by an English settlement being formed on the Island of Penang.' Doubtless they felt that the Sultan's *wakil* would be able to smooth matters over on the spot — though with the knowledge and connivance of John Company, the sailor empire-builder was sailing very near the wind, to say the least.

Heading a force of three ships (including his own vessel *Speedwell*), 100 native marines, 30 lascars, 15 artillerymen and five officers, with 30,000 rupees for expenses, Light sailed in May from Calcutta to Kedah. There, true to form, he managed to convince a somewhat dubious Sultan to accept the guarded phraseology of the Treaty.

On 16 July 1786 the little expedition arrived on the north side of Penang.

Today much of the island is an urban sprawl, about to be joined to the mainland by a huge bridge; traffic from the airport is so jammed that the drive into town takes almost as long as the flight from Singapore. True, Georgetown still retains a hint of past glories, with a sprinkling of elegant white colonial buildings that offer an elusive glimpse of what Singapore was like in the thirties. But even these are fast disappearing.

So to see what Penang looked like when Light's expedition landed, you must hop sixty miles north to the Langkawi isles, which have miraculously remained untouched by the hand of man. There, dense jungle covers the hills and extends to the edge of translucent green water, which at sunset and dawn becomes suffused with myriads of sparkling silver glints. Still largely uninhabited, the Langkawis are the haunt of placid fisherfolk with a few brilliant green paddy fields. To the single village street, flanked with attap-roofed wooden houses, the population converges on Saturday evenings for the weekly market, and the youth of Langkawi disports itself noisily on a clutch of motor-scooters.

For in 1786 Penang was also uninhabited, apart from a handful of Malays engaged in collecting gum-damar. To land the troops and equipment meant it was necessary to clear the jungle skirting the sea — a task not made easier by torrential rain and timber that proved 'so exceedingly hard that the tools doubled like a piece of lead.' In the end Light got so impatient with his 'ignorant and unworthy marines who made frequent complaints of the hardships they suffer in being obliged to work' that he resorted to ruse. Loading a cannon with bags of coins, he fired it off periodically into the jungle. There was no complaint of inaction after that.

On 10 August, two Company ships, the *Vansittart* and the *Valentine*, arrived from Madras and anchored off shore. It seemed as good a time as any to make a formal gesture. Light noted in his diary: 'August 11th, at noon assembled all the gentlemen under the flag, who unitedly hoisted the flag, taking possession of the island in the name of his Britannic Majesty, and for the use of the Honourable East India Company, the Artillery and ships firing a Royal Salute, the marines three volleys.'

The new settlement took off like a brig with the wind in its sails. Within a few days Chulias from the mainland had opened a bazaar, and soon Asiatics and Europeans were flocking to the island, eager to trade under the British flag. Within a matter of months a visitor from Bengal wrote 'the shops in the bazaar, which is now pretty extensive, are principally kept by Chinese; at present there are sixty families and many more are expected to settle on the island soon.' Ships made use of the new harbour and merchants from all over the Malay archipelago made the long journey through the Straits of Malacca to be free from the Dutch monopoly.

But it was tough going. Since the flat area around the cantonment was swampy and liable to flooding, extensive drainage work was required. Fresh jungle had to be cleared to create space for the rapid influx of settlers, and roads had to be made. Today's town-planners will note, with a professional eye, that the network of footpaths laid out by Light still exists almost unchanged. But the buildings were mostly bungalows constructed of timber with palm thatched roofs, raised Malay-style on posts for protection against flooding. What is more, the cultivation of rice besides 'great quantities of fruit trees, coconuts, pepper, gambier and sugar cane,' was encouraged to render the settlement self-supporting.

All of which was normal pioneering development, to be sure. But it had to be planned and controlled with the help of a single secretary, so that Light became a sort of one-man municipal band, coping with emergencies such as a fire that destroyed much of the bazaar, and maintaining law and order — a serious problem from the start, for the settlement had attracted some pretty unruly characters.

Yet these were the least of his troubles. From the word go, he was left to stew in his own juice by the Bengal authorities. Despite his frequent reports, no word came from the Company until finally Lord Cornwallis, who had succeeded Macpherson as Governor-General, broke a ten months' silence with the request for an accurate financial forecast so that 'we may be enabled to judge whether it will be prudent to continue or to withdraw altogether.' One can sympathise with the harassed superintendent's feelings at this less than enthusiastic support from headquarters. Worse still, the Hon'ble Company seemed bent on revoking the agreement with the Sultan of Kedah. Lord Cornwallis could hardly ignore Abdullah's claim for monetary compensation, for it had already been agreed in principle (and left for Light to deal with as best he could). But Cornwallis refused to sanction any measures that might involve 'the honour, credit, or troops of the Company' in the Sultan's political affairs. In other words, military protection was out.

When he realised that he had been duped into handing over Penang for what was turning out to be a worthless agreement, and that for all the soothing words of his erstwhile *wakil*, possession was nine-tenths of the law, the Sultan began intriguing with the Dutch and the French, offering Penang as a bait. But here too, he was out of luck. The Dutch were concerned with securing British help to preserve the independence of Holland from French designs, and the outbreak of the French Revolution had halted, for the time being, any French actions to expand in the East (beyond assisting Tippoo Sultan against the British in Mysore).

Despite Light's desperate efforts to appease the irate Sultan with a promise to send 10,000 Spanish dollars, Abdullah resolved to retrieve the island by force. Early in April 1791 he concentrated an army of some nine thousand Malays on the mainland, supported by a fleet of Lanun prows. The Malays on the island were secretly urged to turn against the British, and offered a share of the plunder if they did so while the Chinese were promised that no harm would come to them so long as they remained neutral.

Across the still waters of the channel Light could watch these preparations, and hear the creaking of tackle, the neighing of horses, the hoarse voices of command. Realising that any delay would imperil the existence of the settlement, he decided to strike first.

It was a bold decision, and it worked. While four gunboats attacked the prows, Light's little body of men landed under cover of darkness and soundly thrashed the Sultan's army. Within a few days of this summary defeat, Abdullah sued for peace, and, acting again on his own initiative, Light offered to pay him 6000 dollars a year so long as the English were left in possession of Penang.

This offer was embodied in a draft Treaty and accepted by the chastened Sultan without any further mention of military assistance. It was subsequently ratified by the Bengal government, which at last gave legal sanction to the acquisition of Penang. 'Force had succeeded where evasive diplomacy had failed, and force had cost a mere trifle....One wonders what Light felt about it all before he died!' comments Winstedt.

Light gave a hint to an old friend in England. After nearly thirty years in the East, he was yearning to go home. 'To plough your fields is a thousand times preferable to governing,' he wrote, adding that he had 'a longing desire to become the owner of Golsberry Farm' in his beloved Suffolk, which he had not seen since he was a boy. 'Yet I have an inward sensation that though I may linger a year or two I conjecture that I shall not have the happiness to see you', he concluded wryly. An epitaph to ambition!* For by now he was already a sick man. Successive bouts of malaria had already weakened his tough physique, and finally finished him off on 21 October 1794. Yet his foresight and boldness in searching Penang for the East India Company not only checked the Dutch, but laid the foundations of British influence in Malaysia and Singapore. Had Francis Light

---

*Nevertheless his eldest son, William, after distinguishing himself in the Peninsular War, became renowned as the founder of Adelaide — now appropriately twinned with Penang.

not taken the first step, Stamford Raffles would not have had the chance to found Singapore, and the Straits Settlements might never have existed. In a sense, his career was a blueprint for that of his successor. Each in his own way was patriotic, visionary, and deeply committed to Malaya. Each took a pragmatic line to the problems that arose, and despite the ingratitude of the dunderheads for whom they worked, both are still remembered with affection and pride by the communities they created.

Following:
Thomas Raffles, born at sea aboard a West Indiaman, was to become a personage of heroic proportions in the East Indies. Raffles' childhood was harsh. And at fourteen he was obliged to work for his keep in a clerical position at the East India Company. Ten years later, the young man was recognised by this same company and sent to Penang as assistant secretary to the Governor. Another decade passed and the resourceful Raffles was to take Java from the Dutch, make himself known as a zoologist and historian and receive a knighthood. However, all this was but a prelude to his crowning achievement.

On 28 November 1818, Lord Hastings, the Governor General of India, wrote to Raffles instructing him to seek out and establish a station south of Malacca. All eyes were on the Rhio islands, but Raffles, with foresight could write, enroute to his mission, to a friend thus: 'We are on the way . . . . in the hope of doing something, but I much fear the Dutch have hardly left us an inch of ground to stand upon. My attention is principally turned to Johore, and you must not be surprised if my next letter to you is dated from the site of the ancient city of Singapura.' (AOHD)

◄ 3 ►

ENTER TOM RAFFLES

IN THE YEAR THAT THE BRITISH army surrendered at Yorktown and America became independent, the West Indiaman *Ann* sailed from Jamaica in a convoy of some 200 vessels, most of which — having carried slaves from Africa to the Caribbean — were now returning to Liverpool loaded with rum, cotton, and tobacco. Four days out, a baby son was born to the ship's master and christened Thomas Stamford Bingley Raffles (the middle names were in honour of his two godfathers).

Though Captain Benjamin Raffles was involved in this lucrative trade, he died heavily in debt, leaving the boy to support his mother and sisters. Tom had to leave the Mansion House boarding school in Hammersmith and was lucky enough, through the help of his godfather Stamford, to get a job at East India House with a salary of £70 a year. Among his colleagues were Charles Lamb, who wrote many of his essays while at East India House, and Charles Wilkins, the pioneer orientalist. No doubt the young clerk knew them well. Certainly he made his mark as a conscientious worker. In his free time, he taught himself French and studied literature and science, often staying up so late at night that his mother complained at his extravagance with candles.

During the ten years that Raffles spent at East India House, momentous events were taking place on the international scene. In 1793 France declared war on England and occupied Holland, whose colonies became available for the French bases to attack British trade and territory. As a result, the British took possession of the Dutch ports in the East Indies, often with the connivance of the local Dutch authorities who knew that the occupation was only a temporary measure. Indeed Malacca would have been restored to Holland after the Peace of Amiens in 1802 had war not broken out again in Europe, and since it was well understood that the port would have to be handed back sooner or later, the East India Company ordered the town's fortifications to be destroyed. This act of appalling and quite unnecessary vandalism, was carried out by the British Resident, who rode up on horseback to the old walls of the Portuguese fortress with a torch, lit a fuse, and rode away. 'After about ten minutes the gunpowder exploded with a noise like thunder, and pieces of the fort as large as elephants, and even some as large as houses, were blown into the air and cascaded into the sea.... The fort was the pride of Malacca and after its destruction the place lost its glory, like a women bereaved of her husband, the lustre gone from her face', relates Munshi Abdullah, who later became Raffles' secretary.

Hardly was Light in his grave, moreover, than the East India Company began to have second thoughts. Realising the need to strengthen the China trade route, the directors decided to establish a naval station at Penang, and in a burst of enthusiasm that would have amazed its founder, they promoted the little Malay island into a fully-fledged

Presidency, ranking in importance with Madras, Bengal and Bombay.

It was this decision that gave Raffles his chance. The young clerk's merits had not gone unnoticed at East India House, and when the Hon. Philip Dundas was appointed Governor of the new Presidency he chose Raffles to accompany him as Assistant to the Chief Secretary. The appointment carried a salary of £1500 and within a week Raffles got married. His wife, the widow of a surgeon on the Madras establishment, was ten years older than himself, and there were gossips who whispered that the price of his job had been marriage to the discarded mistress of one of the directors — though it was clear that Tom and Olivia Raffles were deeply in love.

They needed to be. The five months' journey out on a creaking East Indiaman was hardly a pleasure cruise. No more than bare living space was provided aboard, and passengers had to make do with such essentials as they had brought themselves. Yet somehow, the indefatigable Raffles managed to learn Malay during the trip, which was more than anyone else on the staff at Penang had any intention of doing.

Although the settlement had grown fast since the early days, the European community was still very small. Including wives, it hardly numbered more than a hundred and twenty souls, whose outlook and habits differed little from those of any small, isolated English port. Had Jane Austen been there, as one of her sailor brothers was, she would have found the same sort of people in Penang as she wrote about at home.

'The Fort and Government House are the first objects which present themselves to attract attention', observed John Leyden, an oriental scholar who arrived from Madras about a month after Raffles. 'The town lies low, and is in a great measure concealed by wood.' He was obliged to put up in a 'kind of naval tavern where all around me is ringing with the vociferation of tarpaulins, the hoarse bawling of sea-oaths, and the rattling of the dice-box' until rescued by the Raffleses, who invited him to stay with them. Leyden had been ill, and Olivia Raffles nursed him back to health. Finding that they shared the same interests, they became firm friends, and later it was Leyden who introduced Raffles to Lord Minto, the new Governor-General in India.

Meanwhile, in contrast to his colleagues, Raffles had set about his job with unflagging efficiency. There was an enormous amount to be done; docks and an arsenal had to be constructed, teak imported from Burma to build ships, municipal amenities extended, houses erected. On top of this he had to handle a mass of correspondence, not only with the authorities in India but also with the local nobles on the mainland, which he was able to conduct in Malay. 'Being of a cheerful lively disposition and very fond of society,' remarked Captain Thomas Otto Travers, 'it was surprising how he was able to entertain so hospitably and yet labour so much.... not only in his official capacity, but in acquiring general knowledge of the history, government and local interests of the neighbouring states, and in this he was greatly aided in doing by conversing freely with the natives who were constantly visiting Penang at this period, in their own language.' According to Travers, Raffles carried the whole burden of the administrative machine. The other 'pompous and ignorant dullards' were quite content to sit back and let him do the work. Although they thought him too big for his boots, and disliked the way he cultivated the friendship of the Malays, they could not deny that he was a first-class secretariat man. Eighteen months after his arrival, Raffles was given the job of Chief Secretary.

To celebrate this promotion, and a leap in salary from £70 to £2000 a year in just over eighteen months, Tom and Olivia moved from the little bungalow on one of the foothills called Mount Olive, a name that has stuck until now, to an elegant brick house they built themselves on the north beach.*

Raffles was now a key figure in Penang, and his wife one of the leaders of society. Her engagements were noted and her clothes described by the weekly *Gazette*. Yet despite the heavy daily grind, Raffles continued to persevere with his oriental studies; during a spell of convalescent leave at Malacca he embodied his views in a comprehensive review of Southeast Asian affairs. His report was well above the heads, and the competence, of his immediate superiors. But John Leyden was able to bring it to the attention of Lord Minto, and Raffles, sensing that this was the cue for his next leap forward, decided that the time had come for him to see the Governor-General in person.

---

*Until the roof caught fire and the building was burnt to the ground in 1901, 'Runnymede' survived just as it had been in Raffles' day. The shell was then incorporated into a handsome, colonial-style hotel, which has now been taken over by the military.

Following:

Col. William Farquhar: Resident of Singapore from 1819 to 1823. He saw Singapore through her first crisis, a threatened Dutch attack, and was also responsible for the early development of the town and trading post. (AOHD)

◄ 4 ►

DESTINATION SINGAPORE

ONCE NAPOLEON'S DESIGNS TO threaten the East India Company by means of an expedition through Persia had been thwarted, Lord Minto then began to consider how the French could be cleared out of Java. And so Raffles' knowledge of the area and his personal contacts with the local rulers were just what the Governor-General sought. The old Scottish landowner and the young official got on like bacon and eggs. As a result, Raffles was instructed to blueprint the invasion of Java.

His staff work was impeccable. An expedition of some ninety ships left Malacca in June 1811 under the personal command of Lord Minto, and took six weeks to reach Java, passing Singapore — a swampy island off the coast of Johore — on the way. By 4 August the whole fleet lay off Batavia, and after a purely token resistance the Dutch flung their French cockades away. It was one of the shortest campaigns on record, and in recognition Raffles was apppointed Lieutenant-Governor. Minto felt convinced that he would govern Java in the interests of the Javanese. 'Let us do all the good we can while we are here', were the Governor-General's parting words to his protege as he re-embarked for Bengal.

Raffles needed no prompting. During the four and a half years that he ruled Java — an island the size of Britain — he strove to replace the vicious old mercantile monopoly practised by the Dutch, with a more liberal free-trade system that allowed Javanese cultivators to sell their products on the open market and to have legal redress against any injustice. He hoped all along that the British occupation of Java would be permanent, and contribute both to the prosperity of the great island as well as to Britain's trade with China. But time was too brief for the change to pay dividends. Had Java remained under British rule, Raffles' policy would surely have proved a sound investment.

Unfortunately, the Court of Directors in London could only take the shortest view. They knew that when peace came, Britain would find it politically expedient to give Holland back her overseas possessions. In the meantime, Java was not paying its way. The deficits had to be made up by grants from the Indian revenues, and once Minto had retired the authorities in Bengal became critical of Raffles' administration. He was too much of a visionary, too unpredictable for their taste (and a bit of an upstart, in their view, perhaps?)

To add to his troubles came the successive deaths of his friend John Leyden, his beloved wife Olivia, and his patron Lord Minto. In 1816 Raffles was recalled. The Dutch returned to the East Indies and quickly reimposed their restrictive trade policies.

Raffles took back to England two hundred cases containing his collection of oriental carvings, textiles, plants, stuffed animals, folk art and notes for a history of Java. Once this was published he found himself lionized. He was made a member of the Royal Society and introduced to the Prince Regent's daughter; before long Queen Charlotte, wife of mad old George III, was asking to see the treasures Raffles had brought back from the East. Diplomatically he had dedicated his *History of Java* to the Prince Regent, and on 29 May 1817 he was commanded to a levee at Carlton House. There, after congratulating him on his book and his administration in Java, the Regent told Raffles to kneel, and gave him a knighthood.

Thus with the flick of a sword Tom Raffles became Sir Stamford, and the starchy establishment at East India House could no longer ignore a figure who so conspicuously enjoyed the friendship of the Royal family and the esteem of England's leading men. Yet the job that they offered him was hardly a promotion. Indeed it is strange that he should have consented to return to the relative obscurity of Bencoolen. With Princess Charlotte pulling the necessary strings, he could have had any position he wanted in England; it was even hinted that he could look forward to a peerage and the Governor-Generalship of India when she became Queen. What is more, that winter he had met and married his second wife, Sophia. Yet, with every inducement to the contrary, he was determined to go. Bencoolen was only a springboard. 'My Elba', he called it.

Before leaving London Raffles submitted a paper to George Canning entitled 'Our Interests in the Eastern Archipelago' in which he emphasised that the China trade, so important to Britain, could only expand if English power and influence were convincingly established in the Malay Archipelago. With Malacca now back in Dutch hands, both Penang and Bencoolen were too remote to curtail Dutch activities. Another settlement was vitally necessary astride the passage from India to the Chinese seas. He recommended occupying either Rhio or Singapore at the mouth of the Straits, before the Dutch got there first.

The argument, of course, ran counter to London's policy that nothing should be done which might in any way upset its allies — a mood that the Dutch were happy to exploit. But back in India, Lord Hastings (the same despotic Governor-General who had bundled Raffles out of Java) was less inclined to be fooled by allies who, having had their island empire restored by British arms, were now playing havoc with British commerce. It was clear that the China trade had to be protected, and that Raffles was the man to do it. He therefore summoned Sir Stamford to Calcutta, and on 28 November 1818 instructed him to found a British settlement at Rhio, and negotiate a commercial treaty with Acheh. The Penang government was to supply stores and troops; Colonel William Farquhar, ex-Resident of Malacca, would be Raffles' assistant. As an afterthought Hastings added that should it turn out that the Dutch were already at Rhio, Raffles might try Johore instead. This alternative choice was more significant than he realised.

One can visualise the zest with which Raffles hurried out of the Marquess' study, cocked hat under his arm, to catch the first available ship to Penang. His instincts told him that there was no time to lose. And his instincts were right: had he remained a moment longer in Calcutta the expedition would have been aborted. For hardly had he sailed than news came in that the Dutch had already occupied Rhio and were claiming treaty rights over the remaining islands. But by then it was too late to stop him. While sailing through the mouth of the Hugli river he confided in a letter to his friend William Marsden: 'We are now on our way to the Eastward in the hope of doing something, but I much fear that the Dutch have hardly left us an inch of ground to stand up on. My attention is principally directed to Johore, and you must not be surprised if my next letter to you is dated from the site of the ancient city of Singapura.'

So his objective was clear. But it was a race against time — and official obstruction. At Penang the local Governor, irritated at Raffles for poaching, as he saw it, on his territory, refused to supply troops and assistance, arguing that further instructions from Bengal were necessary now that it was known that the Dutch were in Rhio. It would be better, he suggested caustically, if Raffles returned to Bencoolen.

But Colonel Bannerman misjudged his man. Pretending to comply with the colonel's wishes, Raffles agreed to remain in Penang until an answer from Hastings was received — which might take a matter of months. In the meantime he persuaded the mollified Governor to let Farquhar proceed with a frigate and some small ships to survey the Carimon islands. Then, the day after they had sailed, in pleasantly cloak-and-dagger fashion, he slipped aboard the merchantman *Indiana,* leaving a message to be delivered (once he was safely over the horizon), that he was going to keep an eye on Farquhar's activities. Off the Carimons he caught up with the little fleet, and despite Farquhar's insistence that they were suitable for a settlement, Raffles nevertheless ordered the expedition to sail for the island of Singapore.

There the ships anchored about half a mile off the mouth of a river. A few sampans and *koleks* floated idly on the calm waters; some Malay boys were playing among the coconut trees that fringed the sandy beach. It was 4 p.m. on Thursday 28, January 1819. The following morning, Raffles went ashore.

Following:
The last page of an additional agreement signed in June 1819 by Raffles, Farquhar and the Temenggong. (AOHD)

بهوا ابن فد چناكى مكا اداله سلطان حسين محمد شاه ... ان انكو نمڠكو عبد الرحمن دان توان بستر كو بر نور د نڬرى دان توان مجيد د پلبر فركور
مكا اداله توان ٢ بڬتو سبوة اين موافقت منووكن حكم دان فرنتهن دان كمڠن م اورڠ نمفت دوق ملبق م ... اين بڬمساة دان كنيتين

فصل بڬتو تله ٢ اداله سنادان دان بڬ د الرلبمران كمڠي بات كبله بار دلوى تنجع سني تنجع كانوق دان كك ارين ساكى قلور
مريم داري لوجي بركليڠ مكا اداله بڬد دالرسنادان بڬتو سبت اين مان نمفت رومه م فركمغتن سلين اورڠ بهق ابت دلوى كمڠو سلطان دان نمڠكو
ملكن د بان حكمن كدين دان سنة لانع دان كبون ٢ بڬ كود ... د اتوبڬ اكن د انع بوله نمڠكو كا كي فد كماف كسو كاسنه د مولو جوك اكن نتاف
هند قله ممبرك تاهو كفد ... بر كدين

فصل بڬ فلكد دانكو هند كله سلا جناه بر فنند كسبڬ ممبوق كمڠو اريك ح جبانن بسر ممها و اكبلير دان اسلا ملابوا اورڠ انكو ... د غلن
بر كمڠو كسبڬ دلوى جبانن بسر ممها كهو بوكوتى

فصل بڬ كبق بر غسوا ة حال احوال بجار د الرنكرى ابن هند قله موافقت دان مثوري د مولو توان بڬبر تيك ابيل كود ... نتف فنقة مك بعرد الله بوى
اورڠ موكل جائع اتو منڠل فلك تاه سلين اورڠ د الرنكرى ابن

فصل بڬ كامت افبيل باغمنة هاى تيت ٢ هاى انتين جمفو كا غوله بوله سلطان ... مؤن نمڠكو ان سدين بر كفنود د رومه بجار دان جكلو اد عذر سلطان
انو نمڠكو بوله د كيلت دانع كرومه بجار ابت

فصل بڬكلام هند قله سلين انو فنڠمو لو نواڠ كمڠو انو دوكن دانع كرومه بجار ممبرك نا هو سلا احوال فكر جة
بڬتله تر بوق د الرنكرى ابن انو مغاد وكن كسبڬ كسو سمن دان فر دعوان كفد توان ٢ ... الرنمفت بجار كفد هاى اسباى ابت

فصل بڬ كامت كسبڬ بڬسريڠ اداله د الرنكرى ابن جكلو نيا دكبلا حكمن كمڠي انو فنڠمو لون انس اورڠ ايت مك هند قله اد رڠبت دانع مغاد وكرومه چلار
ريكبد بن بوله بر سدين د الببت فرڤس بيكمان حكمن بغانت

فصل بڬ كنو جود سكالى د نيا بوله مغبل حاصيل انو جوك انو ... فا جغكن كسوا ة الرنكرى ابن چك تيها اد مغن كسو ... توان سلطان دان نمڠكو
دان ممبرد فركور ا اورڠ كسبڬ بر نبكو ابت اياد الله بوله جدى كسبڬ فكر جاان

سبب شكو دڠن بتاڠن سكل اموك اداله توان كجر تيك ممبو ٤ جف دباق شطر ابن ذكارڠ د سوڠ ابن د الرنكرى كا سيغافور اكفد م هاى بوله م رمضان سنة ١٢٣٤

◄ 5 ►

THE FLAG IS PLANTED

EYE-WITNESSES COME IN USE-
ful, even if small. Wa Hakim was only fifteen then, but fifty years later his memory of the
scene was still vivid. 'At the time when Tuan Raffles came, there were under one
hundred small houses and huts at the mouth of the river', he recalls. The Raja's house
was the only one of any size, standing back between the sea and the river. About twenty
families also lived at the wide part of the river, some ashore and some in boats. 'I
remember a boat landing in the morning. There were two white men and a sepoy in it.
When they landed, they went straight to the Temenggong's house. Tuan Raffles was
there, he was the short man. Tuan Farquhar was there, he was taller than Tuan Raffles
and he wore a helmet. The sepoy carried a musket. They were entertained by the
Temenggong, and he gave them rambutans and all kinds of fruit. Together with the
Malays and Orang Laut I followed them to the edge of the verandah. Tuan Raffles went
to the centre of the house. About four o'clock they came out and went aboard again....'

Had Wa Hakim been inside, he would have heard Raffles explain that he wished to
make a settlement on the island. The trade would help the inhabitants, and he would pay
a good rent. Obviously the prospect of 3000 dollars a year coming out of the blue
appealed to the local chief. But Singapore belonged to the Sultan of Johore, and only he
could give the necessary consent. Meanwhile, said the Temenggong hospitably, the
expedition might come ashore.

For the time being, this was enough. By dusk tents had already been pitched on some
empty ground, and a palm-leaf thatched house was being erected for Raffles. Twelve
guns were brought ashore to a bastion near the freshwater creek, and Raffles chose a site
on rising ground behind the village for a fort to be built. He was taking no chances. With
this tiny force, he was carrying out the coup of the century.

The weakness of his position, as he knew very well, was that the actual Sultan, being
bound by treaty to the Dutch, could not grant any rights at Singapore to the British. But
Raffles was also aware that the throne of Johore was itself in dispute. On the death of the
previous Sultan, the younger son — who acted as regent and enjoyed Dutch support —
had seized the crown. What better, then, than to outwit the Dutch by restoring the
legitimate heir, Tunku Long, and secure the concession from him?

As it happened, Tunku Long was living quietly in exile on Bujong, a small island near
Rhio. And so two Malays were given 500 dollars each to fetch him immediately 'by hook
or by crook, even if he had only one shirt to his back'.

Four days later the 'rightful heir' duly arrived in a small boat, having given out that
he was going fishing. Clearly he was terrified of what the Dutch would do when they
discovered that the British were making him Sultan of Johore. 'But Mr. Raffles then
began to speak, smiling with infinite charm in deference, his words sweet as a sea of

honey', relates Raffles' secretary Abdullah. 'The very stones would have melted on hearing his words. As men of a sudden see the full moon shining in all its lustre on the 14th day of the month, so was the honesty and sincerity of Mr. Raffles apparent to Tunku Long.'

But for all the honeyed words, it was probably the offer of 5000 dollars a year that convinced Tunku Long to accept the throne, while the Temenggong and the villagers played their part by acknowledging him as sovereign.

An installation ceremony was held on 6 February. The ships were decked with flags and, escorted by a guard of Malays, Tunku Long walked up a red carpet, between sepoys lined up at the entrance, to a tent where Raffles conducted him to his chair. The Treaty was then sealed, gifts (mostly opium and arms) were distributed, and the Union Jack was hoisted. A banquet was served, and numerous toasts were drunk. Raffles concluded the ceremony by proclaiming Farquhar as Resident and Commandant, under the authority of Bencoolen. But, most significant of all, he declared that Singapore was hereafter to be a free port — an article of faith which has brought prosperity to the island ever since.

Of course there was a rumpus. The Dutch were incensed; both Thyssen, the opium-growing Governor of Malacca, and the Governor-General of Java, Baron van der Capellan, voiced vehement protests. Thyssen even threatened to sail to Singapore and bring Farquhar back in chains. What is more, they found an unexpected ally in the egregious Colonel Bannerman, who repudiating Raffles' action, reported to Lord Hastings that Tunku Long's title was worthless, and that Raffles had left Farquhar in a dangerous situation — 'like a man who sets fire to a house and himself runs for his life.' Worse still, he refused to send any reinforcements to Singapore, and recommended that the settlement be abandoned at once.

Had Thyssen's threat been carried out, Farquhar might have been forced to leave — though he swore he would make a fight for it with his 340 men and 12 guns. But fortunately Capellan relied on diplomatic action, protesting to Hastings that since Johore was a dependency of Malacca, Raffles had seized a Dutch possession by taking Singapore. What with the weakened state of the Netherlands, he probably realised that threats of military retaliation were idle, and preferred to put his faith in negotiation.

In the end, Singapore was saved by the slowness of communications. Dispatches took weeks to reach Calcutta, and it was not until September that the news of Raffles' coup broke in London. By then a host of Chinese, Bugis and Malays were swarming in, and the harbour was full of ships. The Chinese in particular were quick to seek shelter under the Union Jack, safe from the commercial restrictions of which the Dutch were so fond. 'Singapore at the time was like the sun when it has just risen, waxing stronger and stronger as it gets higher and higher', observed Abdullah, never at a loss for a poetic simile. 'Merchants came from different countries, and a brimming tide of goods flowed in.... and all kinds of products were sold cheaply by auction in four or five different places each day.' The port, he said, was crammed full of ketches, sloops, frigates, two-and-a-half masters, schooners and junks, from China, Annam, Siam and Borneo. Even Raffles was astonished when he returned in May to see how his settlement was getting on. He could hardly believe his eyes at the transformation that had taken place in just four months. There was now a population of about five thousand. A delighted Raffles wrote to his friend in England that the harbour was filled with ships from all quarters, everyone was comfortably housed, provisions were in abundance, and the troops healthy.

Lord Hastings may have had some misgivings when he read Raffles' account of his action, and when the Dutch protests reached Bengal. But commercial opinion was delighted. The *Calcutta Journal* declared that the founding of Singapore was an event of the greatest moment. The editor wrote:

> *We believe and earnestly hope that the establishment of a settlement under such favourable circumstances, and at a moment when we have every reason to fear that the efforts of the Dutch had been successful in excluding us altogether from the Eastern Archipelago, will receive all the support which is necessary to its progress and that by its rapid advance in wealth, industry and population.... it will attest hereafter the wisdom and foresight of the present administration, and its attention to the commercial and political interests of our country.*

Singapore, he felt sure, would prove a fulcrum for the support of the Eastern and China trade.

All of which prompted Hastings to give qualified support to Raffles' enterprise, though he could foresee trouble with both London and Holland. 'The selection of Singapore is considered highly judicious, and it is intended to maintain the port for the present', he conceded, sending blistering orders to Bannerman not to meddle but to send money and reinforcements to Singapore immediately.

Even by the time that the *Calcutta Journal's* leaders was reprinted in London, it was becoming evident that Singapore was something unprecedented in colonial history. True, the Secretary of the Colonies dismissed Raffles as a mere trade agent who had caused embarrassment to the government, but *The Times* hailed the event in a leading article that might have been copied word for word from the *Calcutta Journal.* And if Whitehall and the City saw the matter in a different perspective, the commercial approbation was again too strong to be ignored. Even the thickest heads at East India House were penetrated with the idea that their man might possibly have hit on something good in Singapore; and though they could not resist expressing displeasure that Raffles had exceeded his instructions, Hastings was advised that they did not propose to annul his action — for the time being, at least.

Following:
Singapore could have well looked like this when Raffles landed but here, the flag is American and the river Juruno (Jurong). (ATQS)

The nucleus of the modern city
of Singapore is still as Raffles
had planned it. He had no
doubts that the town would
develop and 'become a place of
magnitude and importance.'
(GWDC)

A curious early lithograph of the Singapore River Basin. Three bridges are in the scene: the masonry one in extreme right corner is clearly Coleman bridge; the middle one is the old Elgin Bridge but the third seems to be a figment of the artist's fertile imagination. (ATQS)

The jungle between a barrack-room and the canteen at Tanglin Barracks was cleared, levelled and turfed on the initiative of Major C.H. Malan for a cricket pitch for the 'good amusement of the men'. The turf — 'the only real turf I saw in Singapore' — belonged to an old Chinese gentleman who very kindly gave it for the cricket ground. (ATQS)

An early lithograph commonly titled Temmengong's Village, is also believed to be of Kampong Bencoolen where the Indian community lived. This would identify the hill in the background as Mount Sophia where C.R. Prinsep had his nutmeg plantation. (GWDC)

Coolies coaling by night have
their path lit by little bonfires.
The streets were lit by lamps
for the first time on the
evening of 1 April 1824 and as
if to show how little use they
were, Mr Purvis' godown was
broken into the same night and
robbed of goods worth $500.
(ATQS)

Preceding
In 1822, Raffles instructed his
Town Planning Committee to
allocate 'that part of the town
to the south west of the
Singapore River' to the large
number of Chinese already
settled. The scene shows the
bridge spanning the canal
which cut across Circular Road
in 1837. (GWDC)

Following:
From the very start, Raffles established Singapore as a free port. By 1822, he was able to report that the total value of imports and exports for the year was over 8.5 million pounds. (ATQS)

On 10 May 1876, Hoo Ah Kay, better known as Whampoa, was made a Companion of the Order of St. Michael and St. George, a honour given to those who distinguished themselves in the British Colonies. 'I cannot express in words my feelings on this, to me, ever memorable occasion,' he said after the ceremony. 'Her Majesty may be assured that I shall always continue to be one of her most loyal and dutiful subjects.' (ATQS)

Tennis played before an admiring audience. The first tennis tournament was played in Singapore years before contests began at Wimbledon. (ATQS)

Crinoline-skirted ladies mingle with uniformed men at this ball. It was given in the Assembly Rooms by Lt Col and Mrs Butterworth in celebration of the 35th anniversary of the Settlement on 6th February 1854. (ATQS)

A page from the *Singapore Free Press,* first published on 8 October 1835. John Henry Moor was its editor working off an office on Robinson Road.

Malay youth with parrot in a
rustic setting. (ATQS)

Fort Canning was an important
location in earliest times. Once
named Forbidden Hill, it was
the seat of power of an ancient
empire before Raffles' day.
Here, troops march down its
eastern slope to the growing
settlement beyond. (ATQS)

Sinca Pora is identified on this map drawn by Joannes Theodore de Bry in 1603. Notes indicate that only the eastern coast was charted and it was yet unknown that Singapore was an island. (ATQS)

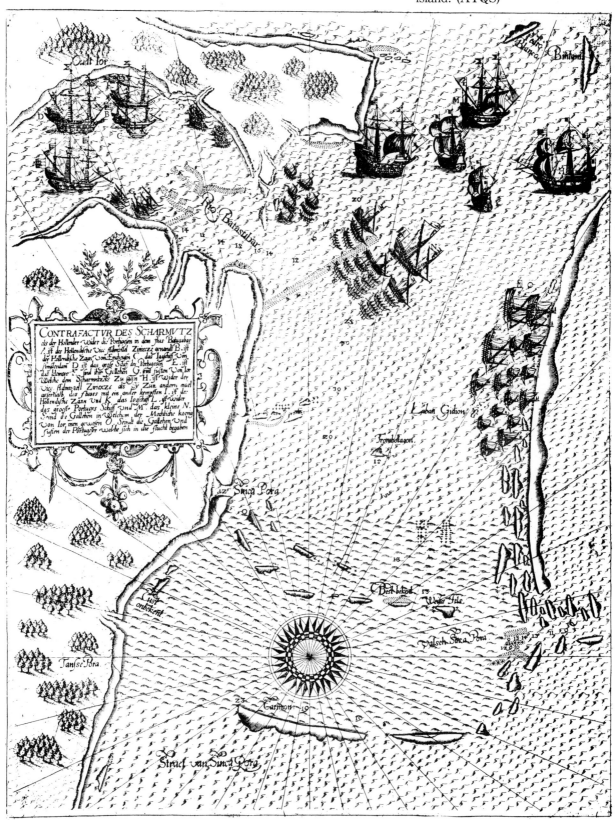

The waters around Singapore are shown in this facsimile of a 15th century Chinese shipping map. The series known collectively as the Wu Pei Chih charts, identifies early Tumasik as 淡马锡.

Preceding:
A western artist's view of a
Chinese festival. In 1840, a
Major Low of the Madras
Army wrote: 'The native
festivals here are, of course,
numerous. If every class was to
have its own way, the town
would be in a continual
clammer by noisy and riotous
processions.' (ATQS)

An early lithograph depicting
Raffles' bungalow on Fort
Canning Hill. (AOHD)

Between races of the New Year
Regatta held after the
Gymkhana, spectators amused
themselves by throwing copper
coins to young men in small
boats. The youths were so
adept at the sport that coins
would rarely reach the sea floor.
(ATQS)

The New Year Gymkhana held traditionally in the Padang was a colourful and riotous social event enjoyed by every community. Menagerie races, greased pole climbing and eating matches were held, and an extraordinary contest where participants ducked their heads into great tubfuls of molasses to fish out half dollars with their teeth. (ATQS)

Following:
A map based on the survey conducted by George Drumgold Coleman soon after he was appointed Superintendent of Public Works, Overseer of Convict Labour and Land Surveyor in 1833. He, more than anyone after Raffles has put his stamp on the appearance of early Singapore. (AOHD)

Part Two

THE PIONEERS

MAP

of

THE TOWN and ENVIRONS

of

SINGAPORE,

Drawn by J.B.Tassin,

from an Actual Survey

BY

G.D. COLEMAN.

◄ 6 ►

THE IMPRINT OF RAFFLES

MEANWHILE, DESPITE THE cloud of uncertainty that loomed over its skies, Singapore thrived. No spy-glass was needed to see that it was cosmopolitan from the start. Malays came from the mainland or Sumatra and settled round the new Sultan's *istana* at Kampong Glam; the Babas from Malacca were joined by an increasing flood of immigrants from South China. And when you said Chinese you uttered a mouthful, meaning Hokkiens, Teochews, Khehs, Hokchias, Cantonese, Hailams, Hokchius and Kwongsais. Though many people in England still thought that Singapore was somewhere in China, in fact China was flocking to Singapore.

They were a colourful lot. Among them was Tan Che Sang, who having made a fortune in Malacca arrived at Singapore in 1819 and built the first warehouse. Tan was a compulsive gambler who slept with his money beneath the bed; besides functioning as agent for the first Chinese junks he helped many of his compatriots to immigrate by guaranteeing the credit of newcomers who wanted to start up in business. Another wealthy arrival was Chua Chong Long, son of the Kapitan China* in Malacca, whose lavish entertainments delighted the Europeans, with whom he acted as a go-between for the Chinese community. In contrast, Tan Tock Seng came in 1819 as a penniless vegetable-hawker, and grew into one of the richest merchants. He founded Tan Tock Seng Hospital, originally a pauper dispensary but now a major medical institution.

There were Tamils, too, such as Naraina Pillai, who accompanied Raffles and became the first building contractor. While among the Arabs, who had played such a vital role in Southeast Asian trade for over a thousand years, were two merchants from Palembang: Syed Mohammed bin Harun Al-Junied and his nephew Omar, who became leader of the growing Arab community. Aristarchus Moses, who settled in 1820, was doyen of the Armenians, a small but wealthy minority which would in due course include the Sarkieses, founders of Raffles Hotel.

All were attracted by the prospect of free trade and jobs under the British flag, unhampered by the taxation, petty regulations and harassment they had suffered in Malacca, Rhio, and other Dutch settlements. Yet the British themselves were slower off the mark, reluctant to settle before they could be certain that this latest gem would be retained in the imperial diadem. But a few took the plunge. Raffles' friend Alexander Lawrie Johnston, a former ship's captain, put up his brass plate in 1820 to become the pioneer British businessman. Another Scot, Alexander Guthrie, arrived from the Cape of Good Hope and founded Guthries. Later that year Captain Pearl of the *Indiana*, the

*Chinese headman

ship that brought Raffles to Singapore, fortuitously sailed in with a cargo of bricks, invested the proceeds in some gambier plantations, and built a country house on the hill that is still called after him. In 1822 John Purvis moved over from China, believing that he could do better in Singapore than at Canton (where his former partner Matheson joined up with Jardine to create an imperious partnership) and in 1823 Hugh Syme started a firm that was to have a long life, even though he himself died at sea seven years later. Notably Syme & Co. became Lloyd's agents in 1829, and their letter of appointment, though sadly dilapidated, is thought to be the oldest commercial document referring to Singapore.

Four months after planting the Union Jack on the beach, Raffles came back for a short visit to lay down the guidelines for planning the settlement. He stipulated that the hill was to become the site of the official residency and that the eastern banks of the river were to be reserved for government use as far as the freshwater stream, beyond which would be allocated the European area; that the commercial centre should be sited on the opposite side of the river, and behind that the Chinese, Malay, and Indian settlements. 'I have had to look for a century or two beforehand,' he wrote before leaving for Bencoolen, 'and provide for what Singapore may one day become.' It was a shapely and simple pattern that was destined to endure, though Farquhar who was left to carry out an ambitious public works programme on a shoe-string budget, found it impracticable to implement. For one thing, the European merchants preferred the eastern banks of the river because the other side was too marshy for their warehouses. Guthrie, indeed, threatened to leave unless given a more suitable location. And many of the Malays and Chinese stubbornly squatted in the area designated for the commercial houses.

Farquhar, an easy-going old hand in the East, was prepared to settle for a more haphazard development than that laid down by his absentee boss. And although he had originally intended to retire in 1820 he soon changed his mind, for he had begun to see himself as the real 'father' of Singapore — a view that was emphatically not shared by Raffles.

When, after a series of personal disasters — three of his four children had died in Bencoolen, and both he and his wife had been desperately ill — Raffles finally returned, 'a little old man all yellow and shrivelled' in October 1822, he was delighted with the progress of Singapore but furious at many aspects of Farquhar's administration. Above all he disapproved of the way the land had been allocated, and was upset by Farquhar's support of legalized gambling and his tolerance of slavery, being a slave-owner himself.

Despite Farquhar's obvious achievements — not least his careful housekeeping through a difficult early period — Raffles proceeded to oust his former friend and appoint a Town Planning Committee, to whom he gave detailed instructions. For instance, being determined that the merchant houses should shift to the west bank of the river, he had a breakwater built to keep out the tide, and ordered that earth from a nearby hill be dumped in the swamp where Raffles Place stands today. Then, to sweeten the pill, plots were auctioned off before the reclamation was completed. In fact Munshi Abdullah affirms that much of the land was given free on the understanding that it was to be rapidly developed.

Raffles intended, moreover, that his brain child be spick and span. The streets were laid out at right angles, with a minimum width for each type of road; it was decreed that shop-houses were to be built of brick and conform to a uniform pattern, each with a covered footway to provide shelter from the sun and rain on both sides of the road. Areas were assigned for churches, police stations and even theatres. Though he was adamant that the different races should be segregated to avoid trouble between them, Raffles was careful to study the needs of each particular community — even the different Chinese ethnic groups were to have separate allotments, and each individual Kapitan was given a prominent site to keep an eye on his people. But as a town planner, Raffles was quite ruthless. The commercial buildings which had already been erected on the eastern bank were demolished or converted to government use, and the Temenggong and his followers were required to move from Kampong Glam to a new location at Telok Belanga.

Law and order were further preoccupations. Up until now Farquhar had left the internal affairs of each community in the hands of the Kapitans, who reported cases so that he and the Sultan could administer justice at the courthouse. But although this system worked tolerably well, there was still no code of law to follow — an omission that Raffles rectified, basing himself on the principles of English justice but modified 'with due regard to the usage and habits of the people'. Basically everyone was to be equal under the law, and — an advanced measure at the time — juries would be composed of Europeans and natives together.

Humanitarian considerations prompted him to abolish slavery, as he had done in Bencoolen. But though he set out to reduce violence by banning the carrying of weapons, there was a puritanical ring to his order that buildings used for gambling and cock-fighting should be confiscated and the participants flogged. Moreover when an Arab ran amok and wounded Farquhar before himself being killed, Raffles had the corpse paraded round the town and then hung up on display in an iron cage. Enlightenment had its limits, to be sure.

Yet the most cherished desire of this complex and dedicated man was to revive the cultural heritage of the region. Immediately after founding the settlement, he had invited Christian missionaries to start a school for Chinese and Malay children, and his last public act in 1823 was to lay the foundation stone of a great college destined to strive 'for the cultivation of Chinese and Malayan literature, and for the moral and intellectual improvement of the Archipelago'.

In all Raffles spent barely ten months in the place he had so dramatically founded, yet which did not legally become a British possession until the Treaty of London and the outright purchase of the island from the Sultan of Johore a year after he left. But for nearly a century and a half the layout of the city, its laws and its ethos bore his signature, and today the National University of Singapore and Raffles Institution are linear descendants of the college he created. Raffles knew his values, and modern Singaporeans are happy to regard his name as synonymous with their own.

Following:
English gentlemen discarding pith helmets for sarongs pose with their men servants of various races. (AOHD)

◄ 7 ►

THE MERCHANT VENTURERS: CLARET AND CRICKET

IN THE PALM COURT AT RAFFLES Hotel, among the hibiscus and the traveller's palms, you can stretch back a century and a half and catch a whisper of how the pioneer merchants — the merchant princes, as they loved to be called — lived in those early days of Singapore. After all, Raffles itself occupies the site of a mansion built by W. R. George, who arrived in 1823 and married the daughter of Colonel Farquhar. There were then twenty large, elegant houses in Beach Road surrounded by flowering gardens, and nearly all of them had a separate building with a billiard table in it.

It was to this line of buildings fronting the beach that a visitor in the early thirties attributed Singapore's attractive appearance. Architecturally, the most striking feature was a broad verandah that ran round each house about six feet from the ground. Pristine columns with moulded capitals supported the roof, which projected several feet to form deep overhanging eaves. All the doors — which were also windows — opened on to the verandah with its neat railings, and in the centre of each house was a huge portico covering the carriageway and a broad flight of steps. Light green shutters and roof tiles weathered to a dark rusty brown contrasted with the snowy white of the walls.

Says a commentator,

> *It is a very fine sight from the beach to see these houses lit up at night. The brilliant argand lamps shedding a flood of light around the lofty white pillars and colonnades of the upper storeys, while the lower parts of the buildings are hid by the shrubbery of the gardens in front. Every door and window is thrown open to admit the cool night breeze, and gathered around their tables or lolling in their easy chairs may be seen the residents, with the strange and often grotesque figures of their native servants flitting around with refreshments. Indeed on a starry night, standing there on the seawall of the bay with the stillness around only broken by the gentle ripple of the wavelets at our feet, it is not difficult while gazing on the houses, the lights, the figures and the heavy leafed shrubbery in front, to imagine oneself amid the garden palaces of the Arabian Nights.*

In fact nearly all these buildings were designed by George Drumgold Coleman, an Irish architect who blended classical lines with a colonial style that was ideally suited to the hot, wet climate of the tropics. Only a few of his buildings still survive, such as the charming Palladian style house in the grounds of the present Convent of the Holy Infant Jesus, at the corner of Bras Basah Road and Victoria Street, and the stately two-storied mansion built in 1826 for Raffles' merchant friend from Java, John Argyll Maxwell, which served as the Supreme Court until 1939, and has now — though modified and enlarged — become Parliament House and the Assembly Chamber. Coleman's own splendid residence, with its stables and outhouses, in which he maintained 'an establishment of horses, grooms and carriages second only to the Governor's', remained relatively unaltered, though occupied by a succession of hotels and shops, until it was demolished in 1969 to make way for the Peninsula Hotel and shopping complex.

Sadly this has been the fate of all too many gracious old buildings so that, in the words of Chow Chue Heong, Singapore's modern landscape barely gives a hint of its wonderful past. 'Much of what was old and unique remains but a memory', he laments. Yet just as the modern landscape gives a foretaste, or at least a conjecture, of how our great-grandchildren may live in the future, so the piazzas and colonnades of Raffles Hotel evoke the spirit of the past, enabling one to take a trip back in history to the time when Singapore was young. When dining by globelight in a corner of the verandah you can sense what it would have been like to have been your own great-grandparents, had they happened to come out here. (An experiment in genealogy over the curried prawns, perhaps?)

Of course one is unlikely to have the same caloric intake as they did. Singapore has always been fond of its food, and the old memoirs abound with tales of gargantuan feasts.

In those days the settlement was a cheerful, friendly place, with none of the caste-conscious aloofness that characterised the British in India. On the contrary, the seventy or eighty European residents were all on excellent terms with each other, and mixed freely with their Asian counterparts.

Dining out, conducted to a comfortable and unvarying routine, was their favourite amusement. It was customary on such occasions, J. T. Thompson (then the Town Surveyor) tells us, for a gentleman to dress in white waistcoat and trousers, and a heavy black coat. Thus formally attired, he would be driven to his host's house in a buggy drawn by a smart Achin pony, with a syce running along at the side. But upon arrival he would immediately be invited to put on a cool white jacket which he had taken the precaution of bringing with him, and to help himself to sherry and bitters from the side-table. Then, once the guests had foregathered, there would be a formal move in the direction of the dining room, where various different soups were laid out in silver tureens, and each guest sat with his own servant behind him. For you were expected to bring your servant with you as a matter of course.

After the soup, the host ceremoniously asked the lady on his right to take wine, which was a signal that all the others might begin drinking too. There followed the fish, then joints of sweet Bengal mutton, Chinese capons, Kedah fowls and Sangora ducks, Yorkshire hams, Java potatoes and Malay ubis. By this time the conversation became animated, 'the ladies unbent from their dignity', and there were several rounds of toasts before the table was cleared and the curry and rice appeared, flanked by sambals, Bombay ducks and Campar roses, salted turtle eggs and omelettes — all washed down with pale ale, apparently as much to the ladies' taste as their menfolk.

Now came the moment for dessert: macaroni puddings, 'shapes', and custard galore. And with it champagne. Or, for those whose teeth were not so sweet, a huge round cheese and more pale ale. After this, the tablecloth was removed and a wonderful variety of tropical fruit — mangosteen, mango, pomelos, langsats, rose-apples, papaya and pineapple — appeared on the polished rosewood along with the wine. 'A rosy pink blushes in the cheeks of the ladies', murmurs Mr Thompson, as they retired to the drawing-room leaving the men to their cigars before joining them for coffee and tea. The piano would then be opened and a duet played; those who liked their whist moved over to a cool end of the verandah with brandies and water, and the room was cleared for dancing.

Piano-playing and singing were an essential part of the evening's entertainment; songs ranged from the patriotic to the comic and usually included old favourites such as 'The coy blushing Sylvia' and 'In my youth I was careless and gay'. Dancing was no less popular and often went on until the early hours of the morning. Though a stately minuet might commence a ball, horn-pipes, cotillions and reels were the normal favourites.

To be sure, such blow-outs have a familiar ring, being par for the course in the days of George IV. A bit bluffer, perhaps; yet, tropical conditions apart, the small so predominantly Scottish community can hardly have differed in scale and style from that of any remote town in the Highlands. With the difference, perhaps, that the settlers themselves were adventurous folk who had come out this far to try their luck in a new land. The journey took six months, so there was little chance of going home on leave. They had no option but to try and recreate the atmosphere they had left and make themselves as comfortable as possible until they had made good and could retire in style. On the whole they lived rather better than they could have done at home, and though moments of nostalgia may have crept in, they probably felt no more isolated than dwelling in some outlying community in the British Isles and cut off from the rest of the country by lack of communications.

Some modern historians have concluded that it was a pretty dull life, with nothing to do of an evening but eat and drink yourself silly. Yet these early settlers seem to have been doggedly content with their daily routine, and worked off the effects of over-indulgence by taking plenty of physical exercise.

A favourite pastime was to go riding in the early morning or late afternoon on a sprightly little pony from Achin or Sumatra, finishing up with a few turns round the esplanade and maybe a quick run-off against a friend. For although no proper horse-racing was held until the race-course was opened in 1843, individual challenges over an agreed distance were common enough and carried sizeable bets.

There was also a good deal of snipe shooting in the marshes behind the town, while boat races and sailing matches were held almost daily. On 1 January 1834 the first regatta took place under the auspices of the Singapore Yacht Club, and in 1839 a complete New Year's Day sports celebration was held, linking the regatta to various events such as a pony race, Kling wrestling, and foot races, which were staged on the esplanade, thereafter known by the Tamils as January Place.

Captain Sherard Osborn RN recounts that he played cricket as a midshipman very early on, and in March 1837 the *Free Press* noted that a match on the esplanade on a Sunday afternoon had drawn complaints from some religious-minded folk. But regular fixtures must have fallen off after that, for in 1843 the paper reported itself 'gratified by seeing the manly game of cricket resumed in the Settlement' when a two-day match was played between the officers of Keppel's *Dido* and a Singapore team.

THE
MERCHANT
VEN-
TURERS:
CLARET AND
CRICKET
63

Considering the climate, it is remarkable that the Fives court built in 1836 should have aroused such enthusiasm. It was used early in the morning as an energetic substitute for the usual constitutional, and a dozen or more players often queued for a game between five and half past six in the evening, which argues that some people managed to keep in trim despite all the brandy and claret.

The Billiard Club, established at a meeting held in E. Boustead's house in October 1829 is generally credited as the first of the Singapore clubs, though the Raffles Club, formed to commemorate the Settlement's founder with a suitable celebration, was started in 1825. Neither lasted very long. The Billiard Club committee drafted an imposing set of rules, most of which dealt with fines for non-attendance at meetings — no doubt frequent, for the minute book ceased in October 1830 and the club petered out soon afterwards. Most of the members had a billiard room attached to their houses, anyway.

Among other developments, a boarding house was opened in High Street by a Mr Hallpike in 1831, followed by a hotel at the north end of the square, which apparently boasted a billiard room and a refreshment hall attached. They too seem to have been fairly short-lived. Around this time Signor Masini, a violinist, gave the first public entertainment; yet an English tailor and a European hairdresser enjoyed little success.

More notably, Singapore's first newspaper, the *Chronicle*, began publication as early as 1824, though on orders from Bengal each issue had to be censored by the authorities. So long as the paper was edited — and very largely written — by the Resident, John Crawfurd, this presented little problem, save that it made for a dull little sheet. The *Free Press*, which appeared once what was called the 'gagging Act' had been lifted, was considerably livelier. Though it concentrated on shipping and commercial matters, the editorial columns often had a puckish touch. The first issue, which appeared on the morning of Thursday 8, October 1835 advocated the cultivation of sugar-cane in Singapore, with the suggestion that large trees should be left to attract moisture from the clouds and to prevent the soil from becoming parched by the sun.* To give a literary flavour, there were glowing reviews of a book on the Indian Archipelago by John Henry Moor (who happened to be editor) and a less than enthusiastic notice on Captain Begbie's recently published *Malaysian Peninsula*. 'If the author were not so much in the clouds himself, he would not speak of "everlasting clouds cooling the wind",' sniffed Mr. Moor, under the pseudonym of Agricola.

Elsewhere a visitor expressed surprise at the extent of the Singapore marshes, and Sir Humphrey Davy proved that a mermaid cannot exist. Among the advertisements, John Purvis offered v. superior brandy in hogsheads at $1.34 cents a gallon and genuine Isley whisky at $10 a dozen. Gin — not selling well — was available at $3.50 a case from A. L. Johnston, who offered both Champagne and Château Gruand Larose at $10 a dozen; Sauternes, St. Emilion and Medoc at exactly half that price, and English sausages at $1 a pound. A bewildering variety of bric-a-brac was purveyed by Rappa & Co., including telescopes and spy glasses, toilet glasses, mirrors in mahogany stands, Morden's patent gold and silver pencil cases with spare pencils, fashionable drab and black Beaver hats, magic lanterns, flutes, charts, metal dish covers, biscuit cannisters,

*Later the American Consul, Balestier, followed this advice with disastrous results.

boys' cloth caps — attesting to the domestic predilections of an expatriate community.

Inevitably, writing letters to the papers became a favourite pastime, and the *Free Press* soon carried contributions from 'Pro Bono Publico', 'Ironside' and the rest. Moreover, since the British love a joke, the inauguration of a Temperance society in 1837 had John Gemmill advertising: 'The Temperance Society is making such rapid strides in this Settlement that it is useless to advertise brandy for sale, although I have got some very good old stock which I wish to get rid of.... I have also received a superior stock of very old Malmsey Madeira that I can confidently recommend, also a fresh batch of genuine old port wine for sale.' Later, however, he made amends by building a clear-water fountain* in the square. But, like elsewhere in the British Empire, the sundowner never flagged in Singapore: for was it not believed that the moment of sunset was the time of the malarial mosquito, and that strong drink taken then was a good prophylactic?

---

*Now sited near the National Museum.

Following:
Statistically, such a small island as Singapore could not provide adequate room for the number of tigers which were shot between the years 1830 and 1940. Perhaps, as some amateur zoologists suggest, they swam to the island from Johore for a happier hunting ground.
(AOHD)

THE MERCHANT VENTURERS: CLARET AND CRICKET

◄ 8 ►

THE HAZARDS: PIRATES AND TIGERS

AFTER THE TREATY OF London — which had aimed at strengthening Anglo-Dutch friendship in Europe by settling the territorial squabbles in the East — Penang, Malacca and Singapore were joined together administratively into what became known as the Straits Settlements. At first its headquarters were at Penang. But within ten years, Singapore's geographic position had annihilated Malacca's commerce and halved that of Penang. Equidistant from Calcutta and Canton, with the flags of Britain, France, Holland and America intermingling with the streamers of Chinese junks and the fanciful colours of the native prahus offshore, the settlement had become an emporium to which ships flocked from every direction; for some, the end of the western seas, for others the eastern. And as Singapore became known as 'Queen of the Further East', the seat of government was moved there in 1832.

The town was still quite small. The swamps near the commercial centre had yet to be filled in, and, save for a few hundred yards from its mouth, the river ran through mangroves. But the seafront to the west and the commercial square were already lined by the handsome buildings of European merchants; while smoothly plastered white shophouses gave a light and elegant, almost 18th century appearance to the busy streets behind.

Across the river, a smooth road ran along the shore for about a mile and a half to Kampong Glam, before turning briefly inland and sweeping back towards the town. It was around this circular road, passing the esplanade, the ruins of the Singapore Institution (which after Raffles departed had been allowed to fall into decay) and the large white houses of the merchants, that the inhabitants took their evening drive — a pleasure denied to those who lived over in the commercial area, because the wooden bridge was in such a rickety state that only pedestrians were allowed to cross it.

The mercantile flavour of the place was emphasised by a lack of government buildings of any importance, apart from the jail — a square white edifice in a swamp at the back of the town — and a small stone hospital just off the circular road. Even the courthouse had originally been built as a merchant's dwelling before being rented by the authorities, and Government House itself, on top of its hill, was constructed of poles filled up with boards and venetian blinds, and topped by an attap thatched roof in which lizards and creepy-crawlies could sport unmolested. At the foot of the hill, the botanical gardens which Raffles had planted with such care were now overrun by weeds, though the ground behind was laid out into tidy fruit and vegetable gardens by the Chinese. Further back were a few pepper and gambier plantations, also owned by Chinese.

Gently undulating and densely wooded, with an isolated barren hill known as Bukit Tima near the north coast, the interior of the island was still virtually unexplored by Europeans, although some way inland was a small Chinese settlement to which Bengal convicts were employed making a road.

Midshipman Osborn remembers the huge junks, glittering white and red and green and black, which lay out to sea, while nearer to shore a swarm of prahus stretched into the harbour. 'Unearthly cries, resembling swine in distress, issued from these ponderous arks', he recalls. Boatmen clustered around his ship, touting for fares, as load after load of officers and bluejackets went ashore into what they called the Babel of Sincumpo, to be fleeced right and left. 'It was pleasing to turn from all these loud noises and strong smells of the commercial part of Singapore to the opposite side of the river, where nestling among the green trees, lay the residences of the wealthy European merchants. There all was as dreamy, quiet and picturesque as anyone could desire.' And hot, for the sun was pouring down without shadow or breeze. 'The sepoy sentry seemed to be frizzling in his leather shako and hideous regimentals — a military martyr lashed to a British musket instead of a stake.'

Yet behind this bustle and ease was a frontier-post atmosphere and a good deal of lawlessness that the police force, only eighteen strong, was unable to control. Murders were frequent. Even if most of the violence occurred in Chinatown or among the Malays, it could also sometimes threaten the European community.

One night in 1831 the Rev. Samuel Milton, who lived with his wife and two children in a corner of the derelict Raffles Institution, was attacked by a gang of thieves who ransacked the place and were only driven off when the neighbours turned up with shotguns. A little time later, burglars entered the house of Dr Oxley, the government surgeon, who shot at one of the thieves as he jumped out of a window after stabbing the doctor's servant with a *kris*. It is said that next morning, on going to the hospital, Dr Oxley found a man with a lot of shot to be picked out of his back. Knowing just how it got there, he made a meal of removing the pellets.

A more serious menace were the pirates, whose fleets of heavily-armed prahus preyed on the local shipping and boldly attacked vessels within full view of the seafront, waylaying passengers in the roads as they were ferried out to ships. It was no secret that the Sultan was behind the trade in arms and loot: for centuries piracy had been a traditional way of life for the Malays of the Archipelago, considered almost an aristocratic occupation calling for skill in combat and good seamanship. 'Just as Elizabethan seamen such as Drake and Raleigh were glorified for their piratical (*sic*) voyages in the West Indies, so Malay romances were full of the exploits of heroic piratical princes and nobles', says historian Tan Ding Eing, adding that many indigenous traders in the East Indies, such as the Sambas and the Bugis, were forced into piracy by the restrictive Dutch monopolies.

Abdullah relates how Raffles once asked Sultan Hussein if he could not stop the piracy that had bedevilled the coastline for so long.

'But what would they do for a living?' objected the Sultan.

Raffles, knowing who was behind it all, suggested that there were fortunes to be made out of trading, and remarked that he would be glad to arrange for the Sultan to have a stock of the best European goods at his disposal.

The Sultan was horrified. Certainly not, he replied haughtily. A sultan and a sultan's son couldn't trade! Whoever did he think they were?

Raffles was taken aback. 'Is it better to be a pirate than a trader, then?'

'Certainly', said the Sultan. 'We have always been pirates. The pastime is inherited, and so is no disgrace. But trade...?'

The swampy and sheltered rivers of Borneo and the Malay Peninsula provided natural shelters for pirates who roamed the seas during the south-west monsoons in fleets of 56-foot long prahus, each mounting half a dozen guns and crewed by up to 200 men. Though their main targets were native craft, they also attacked European ships. In fact during the 1830s piracy became such a hazard along the Malay coasts that Singapore merchants gave up selling goods on credit, for fear that they would be seized by the pirates who were literally swarming around the port. In 1835 a public meeting agitated for the suppression of piracy, and in answer to the merchants' petition HMS *Wolf* was dispatched to the Straits along with the East India Company's ship *Diana*. If nothing else, this provided some comic relief. In an account of their first encounter with the pirates, the *Free Press* relates:

> HMS Wolf *was a sailing vessel, so of course the little steamer went ahead; and the pirates in six large prahus, seeing the smoke, thought it was a sailing ship on fire; so they left the Chinese junk which they were attacking, and bore down on the steamer, firing on her as they approached. To their horror, the vessel came close up against the wind, and then suddenly stopped opposite each prahu and poured in a destructive fire, turning and backing quite against the wind, stretching the pirates in numbers on their decks. A vessel that was independent of the wind was, of course, a miracle to them.*

For nearly two years the *Wolf* and *Diana* worked together, chiefly on the East coast of the Peninsula, before Harry Keppel began his dashing exploits against the pirates of Borneo with the *Dido*, while encouraging his friend James Brooke in Sarawak. Indeed it was not until 1849, when the *Albatross*, under Captain Arthur Farquhar, destroyed a fleet of a hundred prahus, manned by 3500 men, in the largest anti-piracy engagement on record, that the Malay marauders were finally smashed. Even so trouble flared up again within a few years, this time with Chinese pirates attacking shipping from Formosa and Cochinchina. The *Free Press* spoke of ships being plundered 'within the sound of our guns' and feared that only half the Asian craft from the Archipelago succeeded in running the gauntlet to reach Singapore safely. Pirate-bashing remained one of the Royal Navy's chief tasks until the extension of Dutch power in Sumatra and the growth of British influence in the Malay States finally put paid to this menace – which nevertheless continued to crop up from time to time.*

And as if the violence of men was not enough, there were the hazards of beasts. In Raffles' day there had been a plague of rats — which Colonel Farquhar overcame by offering a reward of an anna for every dead rat brought in — and this was followed by an invasion of centipedes. Rewards were again offered, and as Abdullah says: 'The Lipan (centipede) war also ended, and people ceased to mourn from the pain of their stings.'

Tigers, however, were a more serious matter. The first mention of one was in the *Chronicle* in 1831, when a Chinese and a Malay were both killed on the outskirts of the

---

* Indeed a pirate ship was caught off Langkawi yesterday, just a few miles from where I sit writing these words.

town, probably by the same animal. At that time the whole island was covered with prime jungle containing enough deer and wild pig to keep tigers away from human habitations. It was only when the jungle was cut back to make way for gambier and pepper plantations that the tigers became dangerous. By 1840 the loss of life among those working in the jungle averaged a man a day, and when the government offered rewards for every tiger killed, tiger hunting became a favourite sport. Traps were dug, and the *Free Press* describes the shoot after a tiger had fallen into a 24-foot-deep pit three miles up the Bukit Timah Road.

Rushing out in vehicles of every description, hunters found the tiger lying at the bottom of the pit in about two feet of water, and the firing began. 'There was considerable excitement; the chief police magistrate forgot to cap his gun; the chief surveyor fired away his ramrod.' When the smoke cleared, it looked as though the beast had been badly wounded or killed. 'As he did not move, a dapper little man, Mr W. H. Read, got a long bamboo and gave him a prod. There was a terrible roar and a great stampede of nearly all the sportsmen helter-skelter through the brushwood in all directions.'

Rather more presence of mind was shown by a Roman Catholic priest, Father Conellan, who was pounced on by a tiger as he was walking to take the service at Bukit Mertajam. He escaped by opening his umbrella in its face, upon which it seems that the tiger ran one way, and the priest the other.

The rewards offered by the government for killing tigers, and the value of their skins, provided a livelihood for professional hunters, notably a French-Canadian called Carrol, who wore a large gold ring around his beard. *Punch* commented on 27 October 1855:

> *Two deaths by tigers every week are read of in the papers, just about as much a matter of course as the arrival and departure of the P & O Company's steamers. It is notorious that during the last 15 or 20 years many thousands of men have lost their lives from this cause. Yet the only measures adopted by the government, so far as we know, to prevent this enormous sacrifice of life, have been to dig tiger-pits in various parts of the island.... If the population of Singapore is really being converted into food for tigers, and the inhabitants are departing as regularly as the steamers it is high time that something should be done to save the remnant of the populace. Considering that the tigers have evidently got the upper hand, we think they show a sort of moderation in taking only two inhabitants a week, and there is consequently no hope of any further diminution of it, for it is clear that the brutes are already on what may be considered a low diet.... The Singapore journalist expresses his fear that the evil will go on increasing — or in other words that the population will go on diminishing — and we fully sympathise with his editorial fears; for even should he be so lucky as to escape till after every other inhabitant is disposed of, it would be but a sorry consolation to find oneself constituting the last mouthful at a feast of tigers.*

Fortunately these fears proved unfounded. The last tiger to be shot in Singapore was under the billiard table at Raffles Hotel in 1902. But this one had strayed from a circus.

Following:
A Triad Society member's diploma. These membership certificates are of many kinds and may be big or small and white, red or yellow in colour. Most likely printed on cloth to make them more durable, each has nearly always the name of the member written on the back.

The documents are extremely difficult to decipher because the Chinese characters are written in various unorthodox and obscure ways. In this example, for instance, the order of the original Chinese verse has been indiscriminately jumbled up to confuse the uninitiated. Similarly, esoteric composite characters are used as codes.

THE HAZARDS: PIRATES AND TIGERS

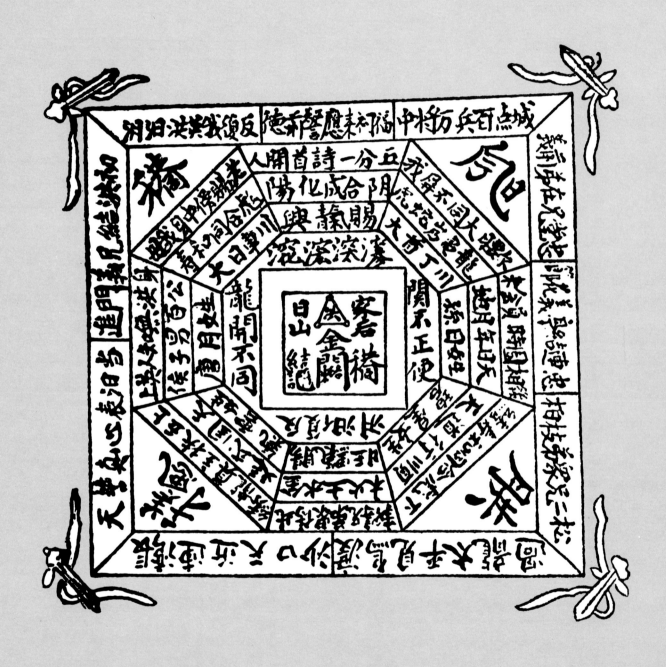

◄ 9 ►

SECRET SOCIETIES AND THE STRAITS CHINESE

The candidate for admission is led blindfold to the hall where sit the officers of the Society; all the doors are guarded by men dressed in rich silk robes and armed with swords. After a few preliminary questions, he is taken to the centre of the hall and the bandage is removed from his eyes. He is then made to worship in silence for half an hour before the oaths are administered. A priest approaches and, opening a large book, swears the candidate in.

'You have come here uninfluenced by fear, by persuasion, or by love of gain, to become a brother. Will you swear before God to reveal nothing that you see and hear this night; to obey all orders you receive from the Society, and to observe its laws?'

When the candidate has solemnly affirmed, the laws of the Society are read out, and each separately sworn to:

'You shall not reveal the proceedings of the Society to any but a brother.'

'You shall not cheat or steal from a brother, nor seduce his wife, his daughter, or his sister.'

'If you do wrong or break these laws, you shall come to the Society to be punished, and not go to the authorities of this country.'

'If you commit murder or robbery you shall be dismissed for ever from the Society, and no brother will receive you.'

'If a brother commits murder or robbery you shall not inform against him; but you shall not assist him to escape, nor prevent the officers of justice from arresting him.'

'If a brother is arrested and condemned, and is innocent, you shall do all you can to effect his escape.'

National characteristics are hard to pin down, and in the voice of translation can easily be misinterpreted. The Chinese are a perplexing people and so immemorial are their traditions, so esoteric their rites, so daunting their stasis, that it becomes difficult to judge the nature of such things as secret societies.

Were they Robin Hoods, or Mafias? Arrows fired from the greensward, or hard-eyed institutionalised greed? Perhaps a little of both: for there is no pat solution to the conundrum of these semi-criminal co-fraternites whose rituals contained elements of Taoism, Buddhism, Confucianism, ancestor-worship and goodness knows what else, whose rules were so immutable that betrayal meant death. To complicate matters further, they were all at each others' throats.

For as long as anyone can remember, there have been Chinese fishing villages in the Malay archipelago, peopled by soft-featured Southern Chinese of Hokkien descent, who were among the first to migrate to Singapore in the very early days of the Settlement. By contrast the Hakka Chinese, a race of hill-farmers known for their initiative and pushiness, turned up in substantial numbers only much later. Many, indeed, came from the families of officers exiled after the Taiping Rebellion. But given that neither Hokkien nor Hakka spoke each other's language and both were at loggerheads from the start, it was not long before the gang warfare between their rival secret societies turned Singapore into an Eastern Chicago.

Yet as apologists have pointed out, these *kongsis* were an ancient form of free-masonry, traceable back to the Hung Brotherhood — the Heaven, Earth and Man Triad — which was originally formed in South China to oppose the oppressive Manchu rule. Since the Chinese have always tended to gravitate together with those from their clan and district, the membership grew and other Huis appeared. They protected their members from bureaucratic cruelty, dealt with their social problems, and dispensed justice without having recourse to the normal legal processes. Though officially banned, they continued to flourish. And when the Chinese from the Southern provinces emigrated to Malaya and Singapore, they brought their secret societies with them.

Many of the immigrants were illiterate lads who had never set foot out of their home villages, and one can imagine their relief at being welcomed into a kind of club. 'The Chinese used to call the new arrival *sin khek*' explains Tan Qing Eing. 'The term had the connotation of a country bumkin, new, bewildered and ignorant. As such he was often exploited by the older and more experienced *lau khek*. But if he joined a Hui or Kongsi he would have security because he came under its protective wing.'

The Hui helped him to get a job and settled his quarrels. It looked after him when he was ill, and gave him a decent burial if he died — a very important thing for a Chinese. Should he fall foul of the law, his 'blood brothers' came to his rescue. They collected funds for his defense, bribed officials, threatened witnesses. In short, they did everything possible to keep him out of jail. But by the same token, they expected him to do as much for others who were in difficulties.

This code of honour would probably have passed muster had the Huis been content simply to keep order among their own people. The British, after all, had developed the Old Boy network into an art form themselves. The trouble was that members were expected to fight for the interests of their own Hui against those of rival groups. And since these interests grew to embrace protection rackets, opium smuggling, prostitution and exploitation of the coolie trade, the various secret societies were inevitably on a collision course. Much of the crime and violence that plagued Singapore in the early days was due to gang rivalry.

Not surprisingly, the Europeans became worried by the disruptive activities of the secret societies (which, incidentally, opposed the conversion of Chinese to Christianity, not so much for religious reasons as for the threat the Church represented to their own authority) and urged that the Huis be banned, or at least controlled. But this would have required a stronger police force than Singapore had at its disposal. Officials were alarmed, too, at the way the societies interfered with the administration of justice when rival Huis were involved.

For example, three men were charged with murder on the testimony of an eye-witness. When the trial opened, the principal witness stepped into the box, declared that he had seen the murder committed, and repeated the evidence word for word as it had been taken down by the investigating magistrate. But at that moment the magistrate himself came into court, and after carefully scrutinizing the witness, said that he did not believe this was the same man who had appeared before him at the police station.

Poor wretch! In the end he broke down and told the truth: the man who had actually seen the murder and given evidence to the police had run away, so he had been told to take his place and say what he had said. No doubt one Hui, on behalf of the prisoners, had got rid of the original witness; and another, to avenge the murder, had sent in a substitute. This unfortunate fellow was given six dozen lashes, which may have relieved the magistrate's feelings, but not much else.

By such insidious methods, the Huis kept the authorities guessing. There is no doubt that the majority of the Chinese population supported them: the Tan Tay Hueh alone was believed to number nearly 6000 adherents. On the other hand the Babas and Chinese merchant class tended to stand aloof, or at least gave the impression of disassociating themselves, from such arcane activities.

At which point it should be said that there had emerged in the Straits Settlements a unique and powerful community affectionately labelled the 'Queen's Chinese'. The Babas were quite distinct from the mainland Chinese, and anthropologists knew that their ethnic progenitors were Chinese immigrants and local Malay women.

The Babas themselves would explain, over a convivial brandy and soda, how some centuries earlier, in a sort of 'cultural' exchange, the Chinese Emperor had sent one of his princesses to the Sultan of Malacca, together with a retinue of five hundred handmaidens. These were given as brides to the local menfolk, and when the Chinese immigrants began arriving they married their Chinese-Malay descendants. Successive generations intermarried to form a caste that characterized itself as being 'Chinese in spirit but Malay in form', and was immensely proud of being British subjects.

Their language, since they sent their children to English schools, developed into a curious hotch-potch of Chinese, Malay, and English, often interlarded with *pantun* — quatrains made up of both a proverb and a simile — for Babas could never resist breaking out into improvised verse.* The Nonyas — that is, female Babas — devised their own secretive equivalent of cockney rhyming slang by speaking Baba Malay backwards or by changing the vowel-sounds.

They had a life-style of their own. Rich Babas tended to live in deep, narrow, terraced houses decorated with *batu* (stone) ribbon† set off by green or Tuscan Doric columns, and filled with distinctive Shanghai porcelain designed exclusively for them. The men retained their Chinese costume — mandarin dresses, thick-soled shoes, conical hats for special occasions, and above all pigtails, despite the fact that queues were still badges of servitude. But the Nonyas wore Malay-style jackets and sarongs, and were as fastidious with their clothes as they were around the house: sarongs had to be perfectly starched

---

* Here is a little *pantun,* written by Felix Chia's mother: *Budak budak main dadu/Dadu di main mata suasa/ Ada meriam tidak peluru/ Habis kuat degan kuasa.* (Children playing dice/ Dice of gold and copper spots/ The cannon without cannon-ball is disdained/ For it has lost its might and mane.) Commenting on it, Felix Chia points out: 'The want of money is reflected in a cannon without a cannon-ball. Money talks!'
† *Batu* ribbon — an example of how Babas mixed English with Malay.

and neatly creased along the folds, beaded slippers and handkerchiefs had to match. A richly but badly dressed woman was looked upon with scorn: it was not what one wore, but how one wore it that counted.* They evolved, too, an exuberant cuisine, mixing Chinese tastes with Malay spices; and their culinary skills were never more apparent than at the Tok Panjang, or Long Table, an elaborate set menu of a dozen or more dishes, without which no special occasion was complete. Baba weddings were spectacular affairs. The bride and groom, gorgeously decked out, were conveyed from temple to home in sedan chairs, and the celebrations lasted for at least twelve days. Yet the Babas were not particularly devout, though they often practised ancestral worship, Taoism, Buddhism and Christianity at the same time (while venerating Admiral Cheng Ho on the side).

Their daily lives were full of superstitions. Children were told they risked getting pock-marks on their faces if they left any grains of rice at the end of a meal; a sudden itching of the eyes meant that an unpleasant surprise was in store; itchy ears foretold unexpected news; itchy palms heralded a windfall. To be hit by a broomstick spelt eternal misery, as well it might.†

The Chinese themselves had plenty of strange beliefs. Should they be disappointed in love, or have a hatred to vent, or simply feel ill, they would call on a spiritualist, and even medical practitioners veiled their prescriptions in a mist of superstition.

New-born mice, swallowed alive, were considered to be an infallible remedy for asthma; if drowned and fermented in brandy they were a certain cure for paralysis. Dog's meat, much prized as an aphrodisiac, was also the recipe for malaria; crocodile-flesh boiled with *wai sang kok*, was good for venereal diseases and coughs; cat's soup was considered to be such a powerful elixir that each helping gave a ten-year span of new life. But it had to be made with old cats; kittens were no good. Which is why there were so few old cats in Chinatown, says Sit Yin Fong. They had all been eaten.

In contrast to the Babas, many of the wealthy Chinese, who had originally come over from China in small open junks, their labour mortgaged to pay for the passage, managed once they became free to borrow money and start on their own. Some made fortunes mining tin in Malaya, while others went in for growing tapioca on land that the government virtually gave away free. They too were lucky, for though tapioca was hardly a profitable crop, when rubber became important the authorities introduced legislation compelling farmers to plant half their land with rubber trees, and many former *sin kheks* became millionaires overnight.

One of them was the original sponsor of Nanyang University. Another was so illiterate that he could not spell his name. When his son put him right, the millionaire began signing cheques correctly — only to have them returned as forgeries. 'You see!' cried the money-bags 'that's what learning does for you.' Another illiterate tycoon refused to give his son a proper education. When asked why, he pointed at his office staff, 'The clerks and secretaries I employ are all educated people. I'm not, but I'm the boss. So what's the use of education?' Some self-made men believed that education deprived a person of his sense of independence and made him less enterprising. There were those who relied on

---

* Though what Nonyas wore beneath their sarongs was as debatable as what Scotsmen wore under their kilts.
† The Babas have tended to disperse in the last half century by intermarrying with other sections of the population, and often there is some uncertainty nowadays as to just who qualifies as a Baba. Dr Goh Keng Swee is a Baba, and Lee Kuan Yew's mother wrote a treatise on Nonya cooking.

fong sui, a form of Chinese geomancy, or sought inspiration from the temple deity, and others who hatched their plans when smoking opium.

Behind most of the great fortunes lay stories of luck and initiative. For instance, one of Singapore's biggest motor distributors came into being when a British engineering firm handed over its cycle-repairing department to one of its mechanics. Indeed the majority of Chinese trading companies owed their success to a British connection. For if the British were the imperialists, the Chinese were the colonizers.

The benefit was mutual. Of course the agency-house system gave an upper hand to the British: after all, British goods were carried in British ships to a British Settlement. Yet if the British firms were connected by national ties with the manufacturers at home, the Chinese *hongs* had equally important racial links with the customers who bought these goods in the East. What is more, the Chinese supplied the produce from Southeast Asia that was exported from Singapore. Which meant that though the Chinese had to keep on good terms with the British, the British needed their Chinese connections every bit as much. The one race complemented the other. What the Chinese lacked, the British provided, and vice-versa. It was a logical, unbeatable combination.

For all this, there was a fundamental difference in their trading philosophies, summed up in the old Chinese tag: 'Englishmen have five dollar, make one dollar business; Chinese have one dollar, make five dollar business.' Being gamblers by nature, the Chinese merchants took far greater risks and frequently became a good deal richer than any *tuan besar*. Yet few of their firms grew to be more than purely family businesses, operated for the exclusive benefit of the founder and his kin. Unknown shareholders held no attraction for the Chinese. But this did not prevent some of their concerns from expanding on a massive scale.

Of these Antonios on the Singapore Rialto, sadly few records remain. Cham Chan Seng and Tan Tock Seng both made substantial donations to found the Chinese hospital in 1844, and Tan's son contributed further funds to enlarge the building, named after his father, a few years later. One of the most substantial merchants was Kim Seng, though if he is remembered today, it is chiefly because of the ball he gave to celebrate the opening of his new godown.

It was the first Chinese entertainment of this kind, and Song Ong Siang quotes a cheerful account of this notable bash. The guests had been invited to turn up in their respective national costumes, and many were the resplendent though eccentrically-matched couples who whirled around the floor: an elaborately dressed young Bengal lady got 'fearfully entangled' while doing a Schottische with a Chinese mandarin, whose waist-length tail flew alarmingly around, until one of his red shoes came off and he rushed hurriedly off to retrieve it, his tail trailing like a comet. Elsewhere on the floor, the tails of two Chinese got hooked together: as they butted their heads forward like rams to dissolve this unwilling partnership, their chosen partners ran into each others' arms and danced on without them. Behind the pillars, safe from such hazards, other Chinese lay full length on sofas smoking opium, while Hindoos pondered over hookahs and a solitary Turk contemplated the proceedings with infinite disdain. When supper was served, it was found to include bird's-nest soups, puppy ragouts, and pilaws of kangaroos' tails.

But of all the early Chinese, the one who loomed largest was Hoo Ah Kay, always known as Whampoa. His father had been one of the first immigrants, opening a grocery shop in Telok Ayer Street; Whampoa expanded this into a thriving provision and ships-

SECRET
SOCIETIES
AND THE
STRAITS
CHINESE
77

chandling business, and since no one loved an evening out better than the Royal Navy, much of his success can be attributed to his lavish hospitality.

Captain Keppel, who was later to become the smallest admiral in the Navy and after whom the New Harbour was named, wrote in 1848:

> *Our worthy old purser, Simmons, departed this life while staying at Whampoa's country house. Whampoa was a fine specimen of his country, and for many years had been contractor for fresh beef and naval stores. His generosity and honesty had long made him a favourite. He had a country house and of course a garden: also a circular pond in which was a magnificent lotus, the* Victoria Regia.... *When it was in bloom, Whampoa gave sumptuous entertainments to naval officers: although our host, he would not sit with us, but sat in a chair slightly withdrawn from the table. At midnight, by the light of a full moon, we would visit this beautiful flower, which faced the moon and moved with it until well below the horizon. Amongst other pets he had an orang-utan who preferred a bottle of cognac to water.*

With its miniature rockeries, its artificial ponds and aquariums, its curious dwarf bamboos and plants trimmed into the shape of animals, its paths bordered with brightly coloured shrubs, its brilliant show of flowers from South China, its menagerie and its aviary, Whampoa's garden was indeed a magnificent sight. And during the Chinese New Year season he threw it open to the public. Then something like a country fair would spring up on the lawns, with stalls and booths, merry-go-rounds and joy-wheels. It was a thoroughly democratic scene, too, for in Chinese fashion the towkays' children played with the poorest of *kranis*, and everyone had a whale of a time.

Whampoa became a legislative councillor of the new Crown Colony in 1869, and also an extraordinary member of the Executive Council. In 1876 he was made a C.M.G., and was simultaneously Consul in Singapore for Russia, China and Japan. When he died in 1880, the *Daily Times* wrote of him; 'Speaking English with the accent and idiom of a well-bred and well-read English gentlemen, he.... still remained true to his own nationality and sometimes jealous in asserting it.' A characteristic that Keppel had already noted: 'Dear old Whampoa's eldest son was sent to England for education, and while there became a Presbyterian. When I was in Singapore years after, the young man returned, and had the assurance to reappear before his father fresh and well, but minus a tail, and consequently was banished to Canton until it regrew and he consented to worship the gods of his fathers.'

If Victorian parents were stern, Chinese fathers were sterner. They it was who decided when and whom their children would marry, and a son who disobeyed was instantly disinherited. There was no gallivanting around in search of a bride, no courting, no Sunday afternoon strolls. A professional marriage broker was called in to produce a suitable girl. Her personal details would be noted down on a slip of red paper, those of her intended mate on another, and then taken to an astrologer for their horoscopes to be matched. If the stars were not propitious, no marriage was possible. What was the use, when it was foredoomed to failure? But if the omens were favourable, presents were exchanged and the couple betrothed. Very seldom, however, were they allowed so much as a peep at each other until the wedding day, and even then the bride was so heavily veiled throughout the ceremonies that the first time they met face to face was in the nuptial chamber (when the groom's feelings can be imagined if she turned out to be hideous.)

Yet a whisper of romance crept into these cold-blooded proceedings, if the *toong-fong* tales are to believed, with their descripion of how the groom paced through the night with a lantern in his hand, how knocks from without were answered by knocks from within, how poetry was recited in a display of culture which had to be answered appropriately before the groom could remove the heavy red veil from the face of his bride . . . As Sit Yin Fong delicately puts it, 'A thousand signs of tenderness were demanded before the bridegroom said: "Lady, I have perforce to be rude with you", and she replied "You may do with me as you wish." '

Civilities ceased abruptly if the groom came storming out with the news that his bride was not what she should have been. In this case she would be driven from the house and compensation claimed — with tremendous loss of face for her parents. Though they could, had they faith in their daughter, demand what was known as the 'lemon test'. For the Chinese believed there were 'white virgins', and the juice of the lemon was supposed to restore the correct hue and save the girl's honour.

What a lottery it all was! The drums were beaten, the cymbals clashed, the bugles were blown, the fire-crackers exploded. There was no escape. Yet far from being numbed into despair by such an inhuman procedure, most marriages seem to have worked out well enough. As a rule the Chinese women were faithful, and the men devoted to their children; from whom they expected, especially the males, the greatest attention in life, and the customary rites at their tombs — upon which, it was believed that the peace of their souls would depend.

True, there was little social intercourse between man and wife, for women were still treated as inferiors a century ago. They took their meals with the children in a separate room, while the men ate alone and even sons were not permitted to sit at the same table as their father when guests were present. And whereas a woman's adultery was punishable by death, the menfolk were allowed to have as many wives and mistresses as they could afford to maintain. Indeed it was a matter of pride for a Chinese to keep a large establishment. As the saying blithely ran, a teapot must have many cups.

In their spare time the women made things for the house, often with great skill and originality. They were fond of taking the children out on picnics, and even fonder of gambling at cards. *Wha Whay* — a card game at which bets were placed on 36 different animals, the prize being thirty times the amount of the stake — was their special favourite. The men gambled separately at cards, dominoes and chess, but mostly mahjong. So great a lure was the clacking of the mahjong cards that fully four-fifths of Singapore's adult Chinese played the game, even if they had to borrow or steal to do so. Some remained glued to their seats all day long, gaming fortunes away. It was a drug almost as addictive as opium — from which the government, operating through opium-farmers, drew much of its income. The drug was adulterated by pouring dissolved sugar into the opium water before it was boiled, noted J. D. Vaughan while Assistant Resident during the 1870s, adding that an inveterate smoker would consume half a tahil (i.e. about 1½ ounces) or more at a time. 'The immoderate use of the drug for a few years completely destroys all a man's energies' he continued in the best pedagogic style. 'On the other hand a moderate use of opium seems to injure no more than any other poison temperately used like alcohol or nicotine.'

As the British Empire grew in grandeur, so did the Straits Chinese. They clung to their customs and traditions, their queues and their dress; they eulogised the colonial government while offhandedly speaking of its magistrates as 'barbarians' and the police as 'big dogs'; and if to resident Englishmen the rich Babas still seemed archetypically Chinese, to the other Asiatics they must have seemed almost as inalienably westernised, bent on recreating the atmosphere of Surrey in Singapore. Though the Chinese towkays mingled on an equal social footing with the Europeans, few of their closest English friends knew anything of their private lives. And while none of them would admit to having any connection with the secret societies, it was thought very likely that quite a few of them, including Whampoa, were *Hui* leaders.

Today, of course, the tails have gone and the towkays head corporate rather than secret societies. Even so, a vestigial remnant of the old Huis lingers on, despite all the authorities' efforts to crack down on them. Some months ago, the Malaysian police arrested a group of Singapore Chinese youths in a Johore cemetary while they were engaged in an initiation ceremony. Not long after, a number of the Sio Loh Kuan society members were arrested after attending the funeral of a well-known gangster. They had been careless enough to write their names and addresses, together with secret society quotations, on the wreaths that they sent

Altogether some 650 gangsters have been jailed during the past few years, most of them working in the protection racket; and Parliament was told recently that some thirty-seven secret societies were still active with, according to the police, between 1500 to 2000 members. It is perhaps a consoling thought that they never cause trouble to visitors, or indeed to Westerners living in Singapore. But obviously tradition dies hard.

Following:
By the 1850s, Singapore truly emerged as a trading centre. Steamships, independent of monsoons, provided regular communication and the port began to be seen as the mail packet of the East. Spice planting gave way to business and industry. Imports and exports reached 60 million Spanish dollars in 1857.

It was also during that time when clammer for the transfer of Singapore from the East India Company to the Colonial Office began. This, however, was not to be realised till a decade later.

All through that period, social life remained colourful and active. A new agri-horticultural society was formed at what is now the Botanical Gardens. The Cricket Club was started at the Padang. Robinson started his "showroom" and Whampoa, an ice factory. A telegraph link, which soon broke down, was laid between Singapore and Batavia. The police got their first uniforms.

And when the decade passed, the population was over 80,000. (AOHD)

◄ 10 ►

DAILY LIFE IN THE 1850s

IN 1838, LIEUTENANT THOMAS Waghorn opened what was to become known as the Overland Route. Having sailed ships around the Cape, he was convinced that the best way to the East was through Egypt: though impecunious and rebuffed, 'not only without official recognition, but with a sort of stigma on my sanity' he succeeded, by using a Nile paddle-steamer and relays of camels, to organize his own transit service across the Delta, thus enabling shipments from England to reach India in just forty days.

'O Waghorn! *Hae tibi erunt artes.*' cried Thackeray, paraphrasing Virgil. 'When I go to the Pyramids I will sacrifice in your honour, and pour out libations of bitter ale and Harvey Sauce in your honour.' And now this same enterprising sailor went on to propose extending the service to China. By using the Red Sea route, he argued, it would be possible to convey mail from Canton to London via Singapore in under eight weeks.

On 28 May that same year, the arrival at Singapore of the British schooner Royalist, *Captain Brooke*, 142 tons, was briefly noted in the shipping report. This aroused little interest, apart from the fact that a steward who had been paid off opened a public house in the Square, which he called the Royalist Hotel.

Then in May 1840 the first vessels assembled at Singapore in anticipation of what came to be known as the 'opium war'. For weeks the esplanade was covered with tents, and Governor Bonham kept open house. Finally, 'presenting a fine and animating spectacle as they steered out of the roads in three divisions, with one of Her Majesty's warships at the head of each' the fleet set sail for China, hoping to convince the Celestials that trading in opium would be to everyone's interest.

Those who lifted a wet finger to the breeze may have sensed that the world was contracting. For Waghorn anticipated de Lesseps by some thirty years, James Brooke was to bring Sarawak into the British orbit, and Hong Kong, born from the unlikely conjunction of opium and tea, would become Singapore's great partner and rival.

At first the founding of Hong Kong and the Chinese Treaty ports filled Singapore with gloom, as more and more of the junk trade and capital were diverted there. Many merchants felt that the Settlement had had its day. 'I think the trade of Singapore has reached its maximum, and that the town has attained to its highest point of importance and prosperity', forecast one businessman gloomily.

As it turned out, he was wrong. The expansion of commerce between India and China gave an enormous fillip to Singapore's trade. Ships of all flags called to load up with Straits produce; within the next fifteen years the turnover more than doubled, and in due course Bousteads were appointed agents for the Hong Kong Bank, or Wayfoong, as it was universally known.

Yet as trade between nations expanded, and distances contracted, the old easy-going atmosphere of the place began to alter, and with it the general tenor of society — a change that the old-timers viewed with misgivings. The town grew larger, property values increased, and rents rose accordingly. Previously convicts from India, of which there were about a thousand employed doing menial jobs kept costs down so that a comfortable two-storied house with dining-room, drawing room, and four to six bedrooms could be had for between 35 to 60 dollars a month. A large house might cost 10,000 dollars to build, while a smaller one could be put up for as little as 3000.

Even so, Major Low of the Madras army found Singapore more expensive than India. His own 'moderate family' employed a butler at seven dollars a month, two underservants at five dollars each, a maid (or ayah) at six dollars, a tailor and a cook each at 8 dollars, as well as an assistant for the latter, a washerman, two grooms, a grass-cutter, a lamp-lighter, a sweeper, a scavenger, and a waterman. For all these put together, the wage bill amounted to about 70 Spanish dollars a month. 'But it must not be imagined that comfort is ensured by the keeping of so many servants' he noted in his journal. 'On the contrary, a family is worse served by these than it would be in England with one-fourth of the number.' And now, with so many new people surging in, the cost of living was increasing even further!

The informality of social contacts increased Major Low's grumpiness. In particular he was irritated by the lackadaisical manner people treated the ceremony of calling (a crime usually committed between eleven and one). As there were no knockers on the doors of the houses, or indeed names on the gates, and servants vanished into the bazaars after breakfast, a stranger had difficulty in not landing up at the wrong address. Then, having finally arrived, there would be no one to announce him. So unless he made 'a disagreeable use of his lungs, he must be the porter of his own card upstairs, or have half an hour of leisure to admire the prints and articles of bijouterie with which most parlour tables are plentifully garnished' before anyone was aware of his presence. Not the sort of thing that went down well with the Indian Army sense of etiquette, to be sure. Box-wallah stuff!

Some Europeans were still living in their godowns around the Square and Battery Road. A. L. Johnstone, the doyen of the British community, stuck firmly to his quarters at the head of the river — a strategic point from which to waylay ships' captains as they sailed in, his competitors complained. Yet there were plenty of opportunities for the old chap with his narrow, humorous face to move away from the bustle of commerce and shipbuilding yards, whose racket made litigation in the neighbouring Courthouse more unintelligible than ever. For instance, the great Palladian house that Coleman had built in Beach Road for the lawyer, David Sheen Napier, was in his hands for sale. But rumour said that it was haunted, and it remained empty until one day John Purvis, himself an early settler, asked Johnstone what the price was. A limit of 3000 dollars, he was told. Was there anything wrong with it, he asked.

'Nothing at all, except some nonsense about ghosts.'

Purvis said he would have a look at it and give an answer the next day. Having checked that the roof was sound, he closed the bargain, and subsequently bought the adjoining house for about 6000 dollars. Half a century later, when Raffles Hotel opened next door, the two properties were worth over a quarter of a million dollars.

Coleman's own palatial mansion in the street that bears his name was rented to a Frenchman, Gaston Dutronquoy, who converted it into the London Hotel. Not content with this, he advertised that he was 'complete master of the newly invented Daguerreotype, enabling ladies and gentlemen to have their likeness taken in the astonishing short space of two minutes'. And for good measure he also rigged up a stage in one of the hotel rooms, which he called optimistically, 'The Theatre Royal'. At the first performance there in 1844, a group of amateurs played *Charles the Second.*

Subsequently Dutronquoy moved his hotel to Edward Boustead's elegant house facing the esplanade. But shortly after this he disappeared, having been murdered, it was rumoured, while digging for gold. The place was taken over from his widow by another Frenchman, Monsieur Casteleyens, who had previously run an establishment in Beach Road called the Hotel de l'Europe. With him, he brought the name. Such was the genesis of the famous hotel which quickly became the centre of social activities, and remained a formidable rival to Raffles until it was demolished in 1934 to make way for the Supreme Court.

J. T. Thompson recalls the delightful appearance of that part of Singapore in the forties, describing 'the long rows of piazzas, the white-sashed buildings covered with tiles, the low but cool and comfortable bungalows, the princely mansions in the suburbs, the fine esplanade, the umbragious arsena and tall casuarina trees....' And, as he says, the town was already beginning to move inland. Charles Carnie of Dyce & Co had built the first house in Tanglin on Cairn Hill, and the medical profession was acquiring a taste for what was still the open countryside. Dr Martin had a house at Annanbank in River Valley Road, Dr Little had another at Bonnygrass, while Dr Oxley lived on the hill away from town. The furthest out was Thomas Hewetson on Mount Elizabeth, indeed a bit too far for safety. It was notorious for tigers, and when attacked by a gang of 200 Chinese during the secret society riots in 1846, the Hewetsons only escaped by scrambling through a trap-door into a loft at the top of the house.

By that time the *Straits Times* had been founded. The first issue of this now prestigious newspaper appeared on 15 July 1845, with R. C. Woods from Bombay as editor. Later the editorial chair was taken over by John Cameron, a former ship's captain, who has left a pleasant picture of how a European spent his day during the mid-19th century.

Practically everyone lived within hearing distance of the 68-pounder which went off every morning at 5 a.m., and this was the signal to show a leg (though some of the younger folk stayed in bed a bit longer). Still, by six o'clock most of the men were dressed and about, for nothing could be more delicious than a two-mile walk or a ride down the country lanes as dawn broke and the sun appeared through banks of clouds. You could be sure of meeting a companiable soul from whom to catch up with the gossip of the previous day or the latest news from Europe and China. And during the training season, it was a good opportunity to size up the race-horses being taken on their rounds.

Back home, a cup of tea with biscuits and fruit would be waiting, and the next couple of hours before the heat of the day set in would be spent very pleasantly reading or simply lolling about on the verandah in a dressing gown.

At half past eight the gong sounded to get dressed for breakfast. 'A gentleman's toilette in this part of the East is not an elaborate one, and half an hour is ample time for its completion,' remarks Mr Cameron.

First came the local equivalent of a shower. Each bedroom had a dressing and small bathroom with a brick-lined floor, in which stood a 'Shanghai jar', otherwise known as a *tong*, holding sixty or seventy gallons of water. You stood on a small wooden grating close to this jar and dashed the water over your body with a hand bucket — apparently a better way of showering than it sounds, for 'the successive shocks to the system which are obtained by the discharge of each bucketful of water seems to have a much more bracing effect than one sudden and continuous immersion.'* Meanwhile next door, a native 'boy' was laying out your clothes, and a Hindu barber waiting to shave you.

It was when another bell summoned the whole household to breakfast at nine o'clock that the ladies made their first appearance. Though substantial enough, comprising fish, curry and rice, and eggs washed down with a tumbler or two of claret, which Mr Cameron considered made a very fair foundation on which to begin the labours of the day, breakfast was quickly disposed of, and by ten the carriages were at the door. Since everyone had his own 'turn-out', there was a fine old traffic jam at the two bridges for the next half hour. For most businessmen, the first stop was in the Square — very much of a Singapore habit this — for steamers came in almost every day bringing information that ranged from the state of affairs in China to the progress of the war in America.

By ten-thirty everyone was at work and a buzz filled the offices until tiffin time came, which did not mean 'the luxurious abandonment to the table that it does in Java', but simply a plate of curry and rice and some fruit, or just biscuits and a glass of beer. And as the daily newspapers came out at this time, some people slipped over to the Exchange to read them, while others had a short siesta before returning to their desks.

By half past four, or five at the latest, most Europeans had downed tools to play fives or cricket, even though the temperature was usually still well in the eighties. But on Tuesdays and Fridays a regimental band performed on the esplanade, which attracted 'the beauty and the fashion of the place'. This was the moment for the womenfolk, who seem otherwise to have been left out of most outdoor amusements. The band played until it was dark, and a long string of carriages made for home.

On other nights the men would be home by six for a quick glass of sherry and bitters before dressing for dinner, which was not the light airy meal which one might have imagined went with the climate. Quite to the contrary: 'The everyday dinner of Singapore, were it not for the waving punkahs, the white jackets of the gentlemen and the gauzy dresses of the ladies, the motley array of native servants, each standing behind his master's or mistress' chair, and the goodly display of argand lamps, might be mistaken for some special occasion at home.'

The menu never varied: soup, fish, and then 'the substantials' followed by curry and rice, from which there was no escape. *Plus ça change....* But our chronicler had a special word for the cheese: 'very good...., obtained in fortnightly supplies by overland (*sic*) steamers. And as good fresh butter is always to be had, this part of the dinner is well enjoyed, accompanied as it is by excellent pale ale'.

'The people of Singapore set their faces against any sort of entertainment which does not include a dinner' concludes Mr Cameron. 'They are by no means inclined to place too

---

*Primitive though it sounds, the *tong* was a device that visitors quickly learned to appreciate. 'One of the great delights in one's daily routine, morning and evening, was to douse oneself over with those lovely streams of cold water from a wooden scoop of large dimensions known as a *gayong*' says the American mining engineer Norman Cleaveland, who was shocked to find one in his bathroom at Raffles Hotel. Like many a newly-arrived innocent, Cleaveland mistook the jar's purpose. 'I thought you were supposed to get in it, so much to the distress of the servants, I got in and bathed in the Shanghai jar. I thought it looked a little tight, but it was kind of cosy.' Also, in the days before refrigerators it had another useful function: 'We used to put our beer in there.'

narrow restrictions on their libations. In the experience of older residents, a liberality in this respect conduces to good health and long life.'

Following:

Standing on the site of the present Elgin Bridge was the iron bridge imported from Calcutta and named for Lord Elgin. He was enroute, as British High Commissioner and Plenipotentiary to China, to Peking and is said to have paced the long verandah of Raffles' Government House on Fort Canning when the Indian Mutiny broke out. Seen vaguely on Fort Canning is Singapore's first lighthouse which was merely a bright light fixed to the flagstaff of the signal station. (ATQS)

Esplanade — Singapore.

Landaus being prepared by their drivers and grooms wait by the beach at Tanjong Katong to take their Tuan and Mem to town. (JL)

The Esplanade, shaded by a canopy of angsana, cooled by the light breeze from the Singapore Straits, was the ideal place for a stroll or ride in evening hours, circa 1909. (PY)

At its founding, Raffles made Singapore a free port, thus attracting trade and an ever-growing community to the island. People, of course came and went by sea and wharf side scenes like this one were not an uncommon sight. (JL)

Mail arrives: bringing much
awaited and appreciated news
from home to Englishmen in
the East. (ATQS)

Mail leaves: taking sons and
fathers homeward on furlough
to the damp and cold of the
British Isles. (ATQS)

w Year Regatta, Singapore.

Koleks, Malay coastal vessels with their dart-like sails, line up for the start of their event at the Regatta, watched by a crowd of spectators lining the sea wall by Fullerton Square. (PY)

At ten o'clock, Gymkhana Day, the official party took their positions and the signal was given for the sports to commence. On the verandah of the Cricket Club would be Sir Charles Brooke, second white Raja of Sarawak and H. H. Abu Bakar, the Sultan of Johore, among the many dignitaries who came to support and enjoy the spectacle of tug-of-wars, foot races and novelty games. (PY)

Following:
By the 1870s, the city area of Singapore was already built up. This view from Fort Canning has the Cathedral of the Good Shepherd standing as a landmark and the Christian cemetery in the foreground. At the turn of the century, historian C.B. Buckley noted that inscriptions on the tombstones were becoming illegible, and no wonder, for on a visit, he found the caretaker using an old tombstone as a curry grinder. (ATQS)

Crowds watching New Year Regatta, Singapore.

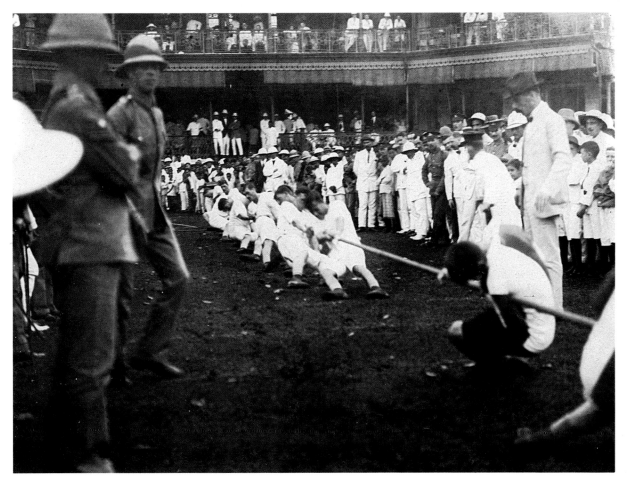

Chinese Fruit Shop.

The Chinese have always been known for their entrepreneural abilities. This stall holder was no exception, having diversified from fruits to incude brooms (left) and footwear (right). (JL)

Coolies working long, hard and irregular hours were happy to snatch a quick meal bought from passing hawkers. A few coppers paid for a bowl of gruel or rice, and perhaps some salted stuff. (JL)

A busy market-place in the
1900s selling an assortment of
goods ranging from deck-chairs
and tinned food to fuel and
haberdashery. (AOHD)

From the hinterland of the
southern Malay states came
fruits like the pineapple to meet
the city's demand for fresh
fruit. (AOHD)

Though posted in Cochinchina, the scene on this picture postcard depicting street trades of the Chinese, was typical also of Singapore. (AOHD)

A quick, strong, heady brew of coffee from this Indian hawker would certainly pick up one's senses dulled by the hypnotic damp heat of the tropics. (LKC)

The original caption reads 'Malay Bread'. More accurately, it is *Kuih Keria,* an unleavened sweet-potato doughnut. (PY)

Chinese Cake Seller
Singapore.

Though captioned 'Cake Seller', this street hawker more likely sold bowls of stomach-filling, energy-giving rice to labourers and rickshaw pullers. (AOHD)

Bullock Carts in full loading, Singapore.

In Singapore, if you were told not to think your five cent coin as big as a bullock cart's wheel, you can be sure that you were being put in place for over-rating the value of your possessions. (PY)

Twakows, deep draught work boats, having been sheltered by Boat Quay for more than a century and a half were moved to their new mooring place off Tanjong Pagar in September 1983. (PY)

Preceding left:
'Always pleased to have a visit
from the above at any time.
CBJ, 26th October 1905.' (LKC)

Preceding right:
Some parts of Singapore don't
seem to change, like this five-
foot-way along Hasting Road
off the Indian shopping area of
Serangoon Road. (PY)

With a fez on his head, a
confectioner plys his cakes from
a trishaw complete with horn
and light while his Chinese
counterpart goes about selling in
more basic style. (JL)

Singapore Sweet Meat Seller

Market Scene,
Singapore

Orchard Road market — a hive
of activity. Men squatting
beside hawker baskets for a
quick snack, amahs haggling
over the price of fresh fish,
children playing about and
adding to the sounds of a busy
market place. (PY)

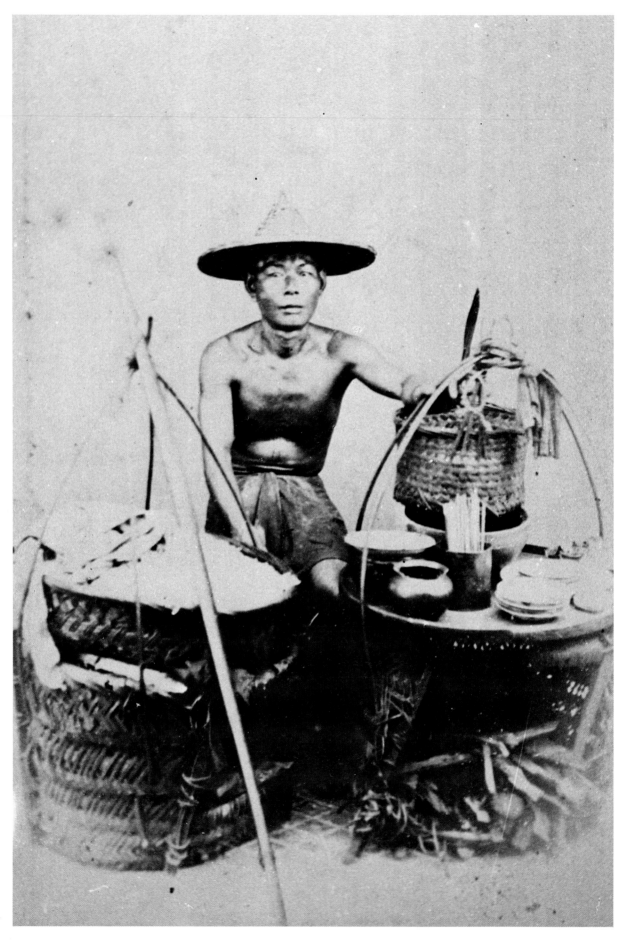

'The Chinese', says J.D. Vaughan in 1879, 'are everything: they are actors, acrobats, artists, musicians, chemists and druggists, clerks, cashiers, engineers, architects, surveyors, missionaries, priests, doctors, schoolmasters, lodging house keepers, butchers, porksellers, cultivators of pepper and gambier, cakesellers, cart and hackney carriage owners, cloth hawkers, distillers of spirits, eating-house keepers, fishmongers, fruitsellers, ferrymen, grass-sellers, hawkers, merchants and agents, oilsellers, opium shopkeepers, servants, timber dealers, tobacconists, vegetable sellers, planters, market-gardeners, labourers, bakers, millers, barbers, blacksmiths, boatmen, book binders, boot and shoemakers, brickmasters, carpenters, cabinet makers, carriage builders, cartwrights, cart and hackney drivers, charcoal burners and sellers, coffinmakers, confectioners, contractors and builders, coopers, engine-drivers, and firemen, fishermen, goldsmiths, gunsmiths and locksmiths, limeburners, masons, and bricklayers, mat, kajang and basket makers, oil manufacturers, and miners. To which we may add painters, paper lantern makers, porters, pea grinders, printers, sago, sugar and gambier manufacturers, sawyers, seamen, ship and boat builders, soap boilers, stone cutters, sugar boilers, tailors, tanners, tinsmiths and braziers, umbrella makers, undertakers, and tomb builders, watchmakers, water carriers, wood cutters and sellers, wood and ivory carvers, fortune tellers, grocers, beggers, idle vagabonds or samsengs, and thieves.' (ATQS)

CHILDREN OF DIFFERENT NATIONALITIES AT SINGAPORE.
THE S.P.G. began work in the district of Singapore in 1861.

Chinadolls with English straw hats sport distinctive Ching period hairstyles. (AOHD)

The fashion of her clothes and the style of her hair suggests a much earlier period than when this portrait was done in the 1880s. A likelihood is that she was an entertainer or perhaps a Pi Pah Chai. (ATQS)

The first church in Singapore was St. Andrew's Church built in 1820 on the same land as St. Andrew's Cathedral. The Armenians built their place of worship by 1835. The Methodist mission arrived in 1885 at which time, Presbytarians, Brethrens and Catholics were already established in the settlement. The Society for the Propagation of the Gospel probably used postcards, popular in those days, to publicise their work. (JL)

Albert Dock: one of the largest dry docks in its day. The other was its sister facility, named for Queen Victoria. In the 1880s, steamers and sailing vessels shared the facilities of Singapore harbour. (AOHD)

They meant business when they went under cover in 1860: the first detective branch of the police force worked at a time when street fights and clan clashes were a regular occurrence. (AOHD)

A chip of the niblick brought the
ball into the grounds of Sepoy
Lines and the General Hospital.
(AOHD)

REPAIRING ROAD, SINGAPORE.

Road repairs being carried out by coolies in Chinatown. On 31 May 1818, on his way to Bencoolen from Penang, Raffles brought 5000 pieces of timber, 5000 tiles, 200 *parangs*, 100 *changkuls* and even bullocks for the first Public Works Department in Singapore. (PY)

Orchard Road in this picture looks almost rustic. Obviously the photograph was taken after electric lighting was introduced in Singapore in 1906.

A charming Malay lady, hair slightly greased and bobbed, holds a sprig of Honolulu vine for effect. (AOHD)

The spiky object carried by the
Malay gentleman is the Durian
— emperor of tropical fruits.
The custard-textured pulp in the
tough shell is sensational only if
one has the liking for its
incredible aroma. Many writers
have attempted to describe this
smell without much success.
One, in a desperate attempt,
has said that the experience
was like eating strawberries and
cream in a public lavatory.
(LKC)

It is strange that in spite of the sharp population rise in the 1930s, this is one of the only very few photographs of an expectant mother from that time. (LKC)

A scene like this is timeless. Even in the 1980s, there are kampongs in idyllic settings in the north of Singapore. There, communities of Malays enjoy rare old-time friendship. (AOHD)

Just as the accordian this woman played is not a traditional Malay instrument, a number of folk songs popularly sung did not originate from Malaya. 'Rasa Sayang Eh', for example, is from the Moluccas while 'Dayung Sampan' can be traced to the Chinese. (LKC)

To be sure, Betsy would have been thrilled to have a fancy dress like that. (LKC)

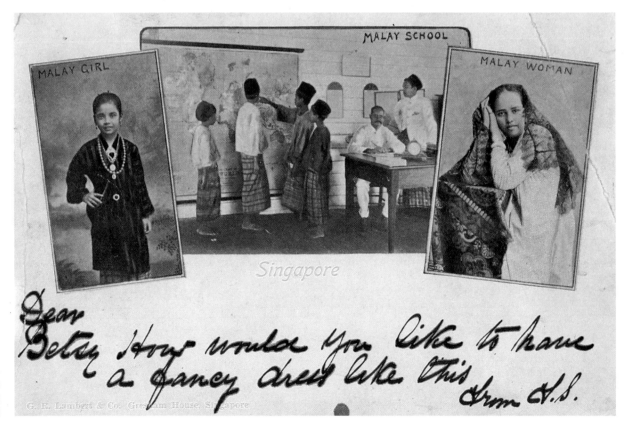

Following:
This now well-known image of the Singapore Chinese Girls' School was first made for a picture postcard. Considering that lessons had to be disrupted and the whole class moved outdoors, it is a fame that is well worth the effort. (PY)

While the Chinese and Babas had no qualms about sending their children to be educated in Christian mission schools, the Malay community was restricted by its religious convictions. The Government thus started Malay schools to provide basic education for young Malays. (JL)

MALAY GIRL'S SCHOOL SINGAPORE

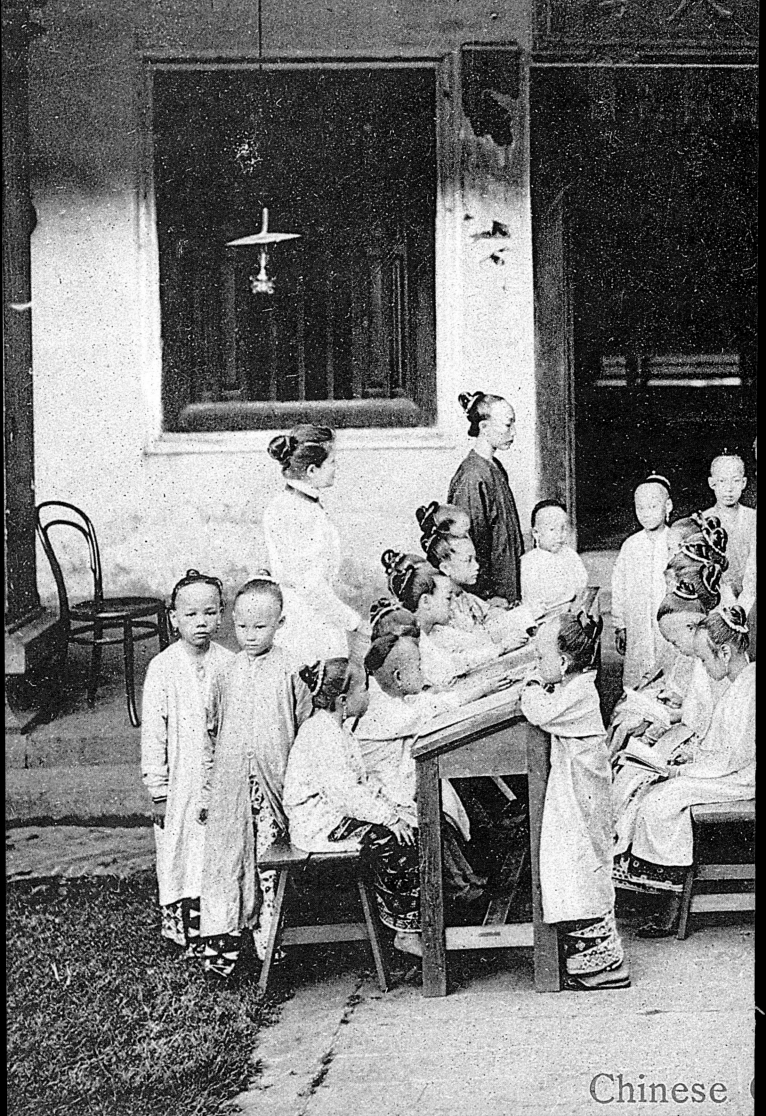

Chinese

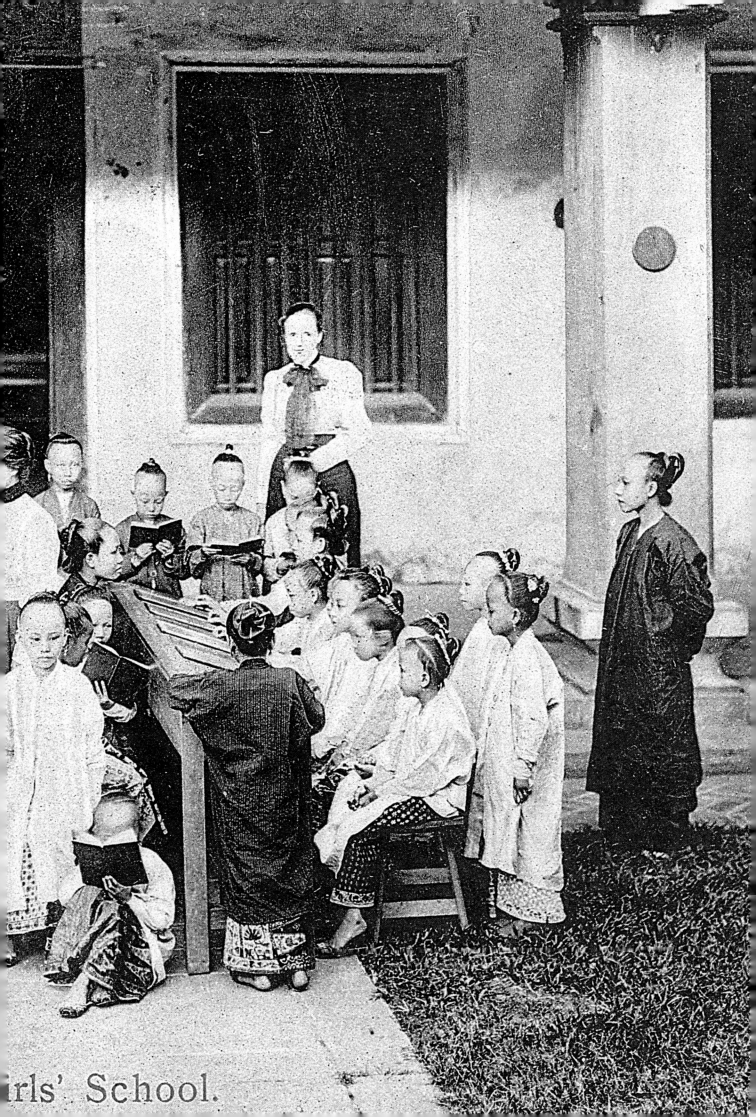

irls' School.

Singapore. Chinese actor.

with love/Al

It was perhaps an actor suited as this one was which gave early British observers their first taste of Chinese culture. Sometimes, the impression was far from impressive. One observer reported that the Theatre Experience involved singing, beating tom-toms, yelling; smoking, playing a kind of flute and in other ways kicking up as much row as one could. (AOHD)

An early photograph of the Temple of the Twin Grove of the Lotus Mountain or the Shuang Lin Temple in Toa Payoh. Reputed to be the second largest Chinese Buddhist temple after the Kek Lok Si in Penang, its founders included the well known Hokkien merchants Low Kim Pong and Yeo Poon Seng. (JL)

Chinese Temple, Singapore

In the quiet setting of a temple garden, a Taoist priest speaks words of counsel to his little disciple. (AOHD)

The merchant house that
sponsored this float for the
year's Chingay procession
thought of everything, including
an extended parasol to shade
the high riding model from the
noonday sun. (PY)

A Chinese funeral procession at
the turn of the century. George
Mansfield once saw a Buddhist
priest in 1886 and was
reminded of the Roman Catholic
religion. 'The hat,' he observed,
'.... was a counterpart in shape
to a R.C. Archbishop's hat.'
(PY)

Singapore. Chinese funeral party.

The most pernicious habit indulged in by the Chinese, so says civil servant, lawyer, editor, talented amateur actor, singer and painter Jonas Daniel Vaughan, is the immoderate use of opium. He could not, in his investigations, ascertain from smokers if the results of the drug were the wonderful visions experienced by the great English opium-eater, De Quincey. He thought not, seeing how the smoking of it produced profound sleep on users. (JL)

Opium Smoking

Singapore. Chinese Doctor. 7/2/06.

NOTICE THE LENGTH OF THE FINGER NAILS. THIS IS A SIGN OF A PERSON WHO IS RICH + DOES NOT REQUIRE TO WORK, THE NAIL MAY BE SEEN SIX INCHES LONG IN SOME PEOPLE + SOMETIMES THEY WEAR GOLD OR SILVER GUARDS.

CHINESE COOLIES AT MEAL.

SINGAPORE

Though used in 1906, this postcard was certainly produced in the 1800s. In the early 20th century, Chinese youth in Singapore were taking the cue from their counterparts in China and were discarding the shaven head and pig-tailed look of the Manchus. (JL)

Coolies having a meal washed down by bottles of strong Chinese wine or a brew of tea kept hot in a wicker basket. (LKC)

It took Henry Ridley ten years to persuade planters that rubber trees were the solution to the flagging coffee industry. When they realised this, they soon saw it was one with a paying future. Exports rose from 432 tons in 1905 to 8,792 tons in the short space of six years. (AOHD)

Thai, the tenth month of the Tamil calendar is a very important one, for it is then that the full moon is in transit through Pusam, the brightest star in the sign of Cancer. The festival of Thaipusam celebrates the victory of Lord Subramania in the struggle between good and evil. Devotees carry *kavadis*, spiked metal frames, as a sacrifice for vows and pledges given. These statues are images which guard temple premises. (LKC)

Following left:
Raffles Square looking north. Phillip Robinson's store first occupied the three-storey building on the extreme right. He was later, in 1939, to move his establishment across the Square. Incidentally, Mr Robinson also gathered at one of the first Christian churches of Singapore, the Bethesda.

Following right:
Raffles Square looking south. Not the opposite side of the Square as in the northward picture, but the view from the opposite end with John Littles in the foregound. (PY)

Preceding:
Built in 1867, Cavanagh Bridge spared commuters who previously crossed by ferry the risk of a ducking in the fetid waters of the Singapore River. For 43 years, hackneys and bullock-carts rolled and jogged its spans. When Anderson Bridge was built nearer the river mouth, a sign was put up banning oxcarts, horses and vehicles exceeding 3 cwt from using the old bridge. (ATQS)

A military band and troops paraded along Battery Road in honour of King Chulalongkorn's visit to Singapore in March 1871. This was the first foreign visit made by a king of Siam and the monarch was warmly welcomed by a gun salute from warships in the Roads. To commemorate the visit, the King presented Singapore a bronze elephant which now stands on a high pedestal in the groups of Parliament House. It originally stood at the site of Raffles' statue in Empress Place. (ATQS)

A cosmopolitan crowd in Fullerton Square outside the Singapore Exchange make their way from Johnston's Pier towards Cavanagh Bridge. The Exchange as well as the old General Post Office were demolished and Fullerton Building was then built. (ATQS)

Place in front of the Exchange Shore. 198.

Part Three

THE MYTH-MAKERS

CONRAD, KIPLING, AND THE 'SAVOY OF SINGAPORE'

OF ALL THE WRITERS IN THE Raffles cornucopia, none ever became so emotionally involved in the Malayan archipelago, none echoed its cadences more accurately than Joseph Conrad. And though he never mentioned the city by name — explicitness, he used to say, is fatal to the glamour of all artistic work — his novels of the East evoke the atmosphere of Singapore with remarkable fidelity. Often, indeed, they were almost autobiographical.

In *Lord Jim* for instance, the hero — like Conrad himself — goes to hospital as the result of an accident, where 'a gentle breeze entering through the windows, always flung wide open, brought into the bare room the softness of the sky, the langour of the earth, the bewitching breath of the Eastern waters....'

Like other merchant seamen, Conrad spent much of his time around the long rambling building opposite the Harbour Office which housed the offices of various shipping firms, and patronised a restaurant known as Emerson's Tiffin Rooms. In one of his books, *The End of the Tether*, an old mariner called Captain Whalley strolls through the city. The Harbour Office, with its 'portal of dressed white stone above a flight of shallow white steps' stood in those days beside the Post Office, then the most important one in the East, at the end of Collyer Quay and on the site of the present GPO. From here Captain Whalley walks down 'a recently opened and untidy thoroughfare with rudimentary sidewalks', at one end of which was a slummy street of Chinese shops near the harbour (the beginning, that is, of Chinatown) and at the other, some two miles off, the gates of the New Harbour Dock.

This was Singapore's first dry dock, constructed in 1854, and Whalley remembers how it had caught fire and smouldered for days 'so that amazed ships came into a roadstead full of sulphurous fog, and the sun hung blood-red at midday'. He recalls that the new road (which a map from 1884 shows extending from Fullerton Battery westwards along Keppel Road to Pasir Panjang) was shunned by natives after business hours because of the tigers 'coming at a loping canter down the middle to get a Chinese shopkeeper for supper'. Returning eastwards he enters a crowded thoroughfare 'as narrow as a lane and absolutely riotous with life' where 'the tightly packed cable tramway navigated cautiously through the human stream with incessant blares on its horn.'*

Then, leaving behind the sweep of the quays, Captain Whalley stops on 'the apex of a small bridge spanning steeply the bed of a canalized creek with granite shores' — which was, of course, Cavanagh Bridge, built in 1866 and still in use — to savour the contrast between the noise and congestion of the commercial quarter, the calm of the government

---

* Steam trams, introduced in 1885, ran every ten minutes down Battery Road.

offices, and the spaciousness of the Esplanade with its avenue of big trees.

The view from Cavanagh bridge is amplified by Conrad in another book, where from the same spot he notes how 'the mass of praus, coasting boats and sampans, jammed up together in the canal, lay covered with mats and flooded by the cold moonlight, with here and there a dim lantern burning amongst the confusion of high sterns, spars, masts, and lowered sails.'

But to return to Whalley: not far off was the yellow portico of what he called 'the Malabar Hotel, low but somehow palatial, displaying its white, pillared pavilions surrounded by trim grass plots' — a pseudonym for the Hotel de l'Europe which fronted on the Esplanade. Then suddenly,

> '...a succession of open carriages came bowling along the newly opened sea road, turning in an open space near the little bridge, in a wide curve away from the sunset.
>
> But one carriage and pair, coming late, did not join the line. It fled along in a noiseless roll...it was a long dark-green landau, having a dignified and buoyant motion between the sharply curved C-springs, and a sort of strictly official majesty in its supreme elegance. It seemed more roomy than is usual, its horses seemed slightly bigger, the appointments a shade more perfect, the servants perched somewhat higher on the box. The dresses of three women...seemed to fill completely the shallow body of the carriage. The fourth face was of a man, heavy-lidded, distinguished and sallow, with a sombre, thick, iron-grey imperial and moustaches, which somehow had the air of solid appendages. His Excellency —'

Yes, Sir Frederick Weld, Governor of Singapore from 1880 to 1887, most of the time that Conrad was there.

The sight of Sir Frederick sets Whalley meditating nostalgically back to his early days in the settlement, which in retrospect seemed so much more pleasant than it was now. He thought of how he had preferred his old Panama hat to the comparatively modern fashion of pipe-clayed cork helmets, and hoped he would manage to keep a cool head to the end of his life without 'all these contrivances for hygienic ventilation'.

His first memories were of 'muddy shores, a harbour without quays, the one solitary wooden pier...jutting out crookedly'.

The then Governor had given him no end of encouragement. 'No Excellency he (George Bonham) this Governor with his jacket off; a man who tended night and day, so to speak, the growing prosperity of the Settlement with the self-forgetful devotion of a nurse for the child she loves....'

Though Whalley obviously prefers Bonham to Weld, to be fair Sir Frederick was a notable administrator who concentrated on extending British power in the Malayan peninsula. But Conrad was right in stressing the changes that had come over Singapore during the lifetime of a mariner such as Whalley. In retrospect, so much had happened.

During the fifties the European merchants had become increasingly critical of the cheese-paring indifference of John Company's rule from Bengal. Finally, when the Indian Mutiny erupted in 1857, they petitioned Parliament in London to separate the Straits

Settlements from India and convert them into a British Crown Colony. At length, after ten years of haggling, the Colonial Office agreed. But Colonial rule brought colonial institutions: an executive council comprising the Governor and senior officials, and a legislative council which included three non-officials nominated by the Governor. Yet although one of his nominees was none other than our friend Whampoa, the merchants who had agitated so passionately for transfer soon found to their dismay that they had very little say in the running of the Colony. What is more, the first Governor, Sir Harry St George Ord, was a pompous dolt, and the hostility between him and the business community continued until a more sympathetic figure, in the shape of Sir Andrew Clarke, arrived in 1873.

To be sure, this initial disappointment was softened by the spectacular boom in trade that followed the opening of the Suez Canal in 1869. Over the next three years turnover increased by more than 50%, from £58 million in 1868 to £90 million in 1873, as Singapore became the chief entrepot between Europe and the Far East, the headquarters of shipping firms and business houses engaged in exploiting the economic development of the Malay states and north Sumatra. Rice, tea, spices, pineapple and opium (to say nothing of human beings shipped as deck cargo from South China to Malaya and Java) contributed to the overall prosperity.

For once bright young men like Swettenham and Clifford had brought order to the quarrelsome Sultans of the peninsula, resulting in the federation of Protected Malay States, commerce and agriculture boomed. And this new political stability — along with the introduction of steam engines and centrifugal pumps — revived the faltering Malay mines; so that with railway communications now leading to its wharves, and ships big enough to handle all the cargo available, Singapore quickly became the focal point for half the world's tin.

Yet that was not all. At the very moment that Karl Benz and Gottlieb Daimler were working on the development of the horseless carriage, Henry Ridley, director of the Singapore Botanical Gardens, was experimenting with some rubber seeds that had been sent out from Kew. Having finally discovered the most satisfactory method of tapping rubber trees, he persuaded a Chinese planter called Tan Chay Yan in Malacca and the Kindersley brothers in Selangor to sow rubber as a commercial experiment, where it transformed the Malayan economy, and the landscape too. Indeed so enormous was the demand from the electrical and motor industries that by 1920, with a million hectares under cultivation, Malaya was producing 53% of the world's rubber. Tin and rubber, added to the other commodities that passed through its hands, were to make Singapore one of the greatest ports on earth.

This was still, of course, a distant prospect when the Colony celebrated Queen Victoria's Golden Jubilee in June 1887. But already, like gamblers on a lucky streak, the local businessmen felt that their commercial power was self-engendering, that they were riding on a wave of destiny which could only lead them on to fulfilment. It was a moment of great excitement and self-esteem. In the span of the Queen's life they had reached a meridian: what could be more fitting than to commemorate her jubilee by erecting a statue of the Colony's founder? And, almost coincidentally, by the opening of a hotel which (though they could not yet guess it) was to become his best-known memorial.

Yet ironically, this pre-eminently British establishment was not the brain child of English entrepreneurs, as might have been expected, but of four Armenian brothers.

There had been Sarkieses in Singapore since 1820. But the story of Raffles Hotel, like that of Singapore, starts in Penang, where Martin Sarkies set himself up as an engineer half a century later. Scenting the need for a first class establishment, he teamed up with his brother Tigran, then trading in Java, to open the Eastern Hotel in 1884. When a third brother, Ariet, joined them a year later, they embarked on another enterprise which they called the Oriental. The hotels thrived, and were in due course amalgamated into the famous E & O. Under the astute management of the youngest brother, Arshak, who entered the partnership when Martin retired in 1891, the E & O soon became the best address in Penang.

If local press reports are to be believed, it very nearly didn't. For the venture had barely started than the landlord abruptly doubled the rent. 'A joke', reported the *Penang Gazette*, 'which Mr Sarkies does not appear to appreciate, and he has consequently decided to seek new, and let us hope happier, hunting grounds.'

Perhaps this was just an astute piece of bluff. But though history does not relate whether the question of rent was settled to their satisfaction, the E & O continued to flourish, encouraging the Sarkieses to expand into a more challenging market.

Even before Joseph Chamberlain coined the phrase 'Trade follows the flag' they had been scouting around Singapore to find the right location for an elegant and luxurious hotel. Which — as in the case of the E & O and the Strand which they founded later in Rangoon — meant a sea frontage with plenty of greenery around, close to the Esplanade but protected from the hubbub of the harbour and commercial quarter. And as luck would have it, a prime site in Beach Road became available.

For it so happened that Captain Dare, who lived in the George family's old mansion at the corner of Bras Basah, had been ruined by the unwise speculations of a business associate. And having the finest cook in town, he decided to turn his billiard room annex into a tiffin room for selected acquaintances. His lunches were the best in Singapore and to add to their attraction you could eat in the garden among the chattering mynah birds at tables shaded by scarlet flame trees, with a view of the sea through the fan-shaped fronds of the travellers' palms.

The house itself was let to the Raffles Girls' boarding school when the Sarkieses acquired the whole property in 1886 and immediately set about enlarging and renovating the premises. Back in Penang, the *Gazette* divulged enthusiastically that the new hotel would contain 48 bedrooms, each with its own private verandah and bathroom. Facilities were to include a large and commodious billiard room capable of containing four tables — as essential then as a swimming pool would be today — and the furniture had been ordered from Europe.

If their selection of a name (suggesting ruffles and raffish?) was the final touch of artistry, it must be said that having taken over an establishment already known as the Raffles Girls' School, slap across from the Raffles Institution and within sight of Sir Stamford's new statue in the middle of the Esplanade, it was an obvious choice.

This was the birth of Raffles Hotel, which Noel Barber considers to be the most nostalgically named hostelry in the world, and which has been known affectionately ever since, in every corner of the globe, quite simply as 'Raffles'.*

* Never 'the Raffles', which sounds like a jumble sale!

When it opened its doors on 1 December 1887, one of the first guests was Joseph Conrad, who finally left Singapore the following March. By then he had become a British subject and had obtained his Master's certificate; and once a command came his way — even if it was only in the modest shape of a barque — he felt he should move from the sailors' rest house in South Bridge Road, where he normally stayed for a dollar a day, into the comfort of a hotel. Though characteristically he omits to give the name, it was probably Raffles.

When he speaks of 'the straggling building of bricks, as airy as a birdcage', the lofty rooms, the draughty corridors, the long chairs on the verandahs, and how periodic invasions of tourists from a passenger steamer 'flitted through the windswept dusk of the apartments', it sounds very much like a description of Raffles in the eighties.

At all events he would certainly have looked in for a meal, as Mrs Caddy did when travelling with the Duke of Sutherland on his yacht *Sans Peur*. After having what she called a Malay lunch, they read the newspapers to find out what the world had been doing and cooled themselves in the verandah, in prosaic contrast to the rip-roar of some young officers, boisterously leap-frogging around the billiard tables.

Around about the same time, 23-year-old Rudyard Kipling, wrote 'Providence conducted me along a beach, in full view of five miles of shipping — five solid miles of masts and funnels — to a place called Raffles Hotel, where the food is excellent as the rooms are bad. Let the traveller take note. Feed at Raffles and sleep at the Hotel de l'Europe.'

The Singapore British he found much the same as those in India: 'The pretty memsahib with light hair and fascinating manners, the plump little memsahib that talked to everyone and was in everybody's confidence, the spinster fresh from home, the bean-fed well groomed subaltern with the light coat and fox terrier.' Sitting around were 'The fat colonel, and the large judge, and the engineer's wife, and the merchantman and his family. But for the fact that they were entire strangers, I would have saluted them as old friends.'

Tigran Sarkies, who was managing Raffles at that moment, got his own back on the precocious idealizer (and occasional scoffer) of Empire by extracting the words 'Feed at Raffles — where the food is excellent' as a useful endorsement. But, being no fool, he knew that criticism of the rooms was justified. Moreover, with the growing number of visitors to Singapore, accommodation in the original building was less than adequate. So in 1890, despite a trade depression and a fall in the value of silver on which the Colony's currency was based, he added two more wings to the central block — a foretaste of the later Palm Court enclosure — and also acquired the adjoining American Consulate house at No. 3 Beach Road.

Contemporary accounts speak of Raffles in those days as a delightfully sunshaded, courtyarded, loose-limbed place, already famous for its cool drinks at the long teak bar with glass mirrors behind, from which issued forth 'corpulent Dutch visitors from Java, strolling in bunches of half a dozen, bareheaded, hats in hand, accompanied by buxom and bouncing Dutch ladies whose shrill laughs occasionally rent the air with their merry glee; while parties of tall Germans strode along with military jaunt and enveloped in clouds of cigar smoke.'

On the face of it, they all seemed to be having a marvellous time, as ship's captains and planters swapped tall tales in the bar. Yet as you thumb through the press reports of the nineties you find hints here and there of Neapolitan hazards: hotel guests who slipped away without paying their bills, and others who were robbed by liveried 'boys'. In June 1895 a member of the Magistrates' Court dropped down dead when playing a late-night game of billiards at Raffles; not long afterwards the manager was summoned out of bed with the news that a gentleman was in the passage very sick. It turned out at the inquest that a new accountant from the Chartered Bank had accidently poisoned himself.

But for the most part nothing more remarkable happened during those early days than at any other hotel that lived by the British Empire and was rising with its fortunes. The management contented itself with publishing an ever-lengthening guest list studded with names from Debrett and Gotha — a roaming Duke or two, some foot-loose Crown Princes, a handful of Maharajahs, local celebrities like Sir Frank Swettenham and Sir Henry Keppel, and a great number of other worthies whose identities have now, alas, faded into obscurity.

If the presence of these celebrities was gratifying to the Sarkieses (for hoteliers are nothing if not snobs, and coronets ranked higher than kind hearts in Victorian days) it was not until they embarked on a complete reconstruction in 1897 that Raffles reached its unique position in the vocabulary of travel.

Raffles' new building was the first major project of the architects Swan & Maclaren, who are still prominent in Singapore today. Until then, most of the city's architecture had been designed by a variety of amateurs and semi-professionals: army engineers, priests, surveyors and contractors, inspired by Coleman and by Anglo-Indian patterns. A. A. Swan and J. W. Maclaren were both engineer-surveyors themselves. Their distinctive 'Neo-Renaissance' style, with its deeply coursed plaster work, rusticated columns, and arched pilasters, was developed by an architect named R. A. J. Bidwell, who before joining the partnership had worked with the London County Council and on the Saracenic Secretariat at Kuala Lumpur — whose exuberant idiom he later employed on the Singapore Telephone Building. His assistant in planning the new Raffles, which involved replacing the existing building with a much larger three-storey block, was V. A. Flower (a tenuous link with the present narrator!)

Characteristically, the Victorians had a taste for symbols in architecture — Roman for Justice, Gothic for Learning, Greek for Government, Venetian for Commerce. (Their enthusiasm, it must be admitted, sometimes got wildly out of hand.) So it was appropriate that Bidwell should have conceived a form of Neo-Renaissance for Raffles, a cross between a Florentine palazzo and a French château, to which would be added in due course the cloistered verandahs around Palm Court — a colonial metamorphosis of an Oxford college? His meticulously drawn plans were executed in water colours on parchment-type paper to highlight the details, so that when the paper was held up to the light, the colour seeped through in almost life-like depth.

Hardly had the braggadocio celebrating Queen Victoria's Diamond Jubilee died down than the work began, and was completed two and a half years later. When it was unveiled in November 1899, the building was so swanky, and had developed the art of living in a tropical climate to such a pitch of finesse, that it became a sybaritic symbol of Singapore. The historian of Raffles Hotel, Ilsa Sharp, quotes a contemporary description:

A wide, richly decorated verandah ran round all four sides of the building, sheltering the rooms from sun and rain. The frontal approach led to a T-shaped dining hall of great grandeur: its 96 ft by 67 ft floor, with 36 ft wings, was paved in Carrara marble, and galleries supported by ornate columns and arches looked down on the central portion from both of the two storeys above, the whole being crowned by an elaborately ornamented skylight and ventilator that filtered sun and air to the interior. Access to the verandahs was provided by massive carved doors, while at the far end the main staircase, of wood construction with fine mouldings and flanked by bronze statues set on plinths formed by the stair newels, swept majestically to the upper floors. Two private dining rooms, decorated on the same lines as the main hall, were set one on each side of the staircase. The ground floor, which boasted an entrance porch at each corner, housed a reception lobby and the hotel office as well as bedrooms with dressing and bathrooms attached. Similar residential accommodation was provided on the first and second floors, and two of the rooms on the first were set apart for Tigran Sarkies...

Although electricity was still in its infancy, and suspect at that ('electric light is still a toy. What do we want with toys?') Raffles introduced it to Singapore. The whole hotel was illuminated with dynamos capable of igniting 800 bulbs and five arc-lights which lit up the entrance. There were electric fans in the dining hall and other public rooms, and in the bedroom suites too if desired. These were also equipped with 'an arrangement by which the electric light can be turned off and on at pleasure by the occupant'. But not to flout tradition too much, the punkah-wallahs were retained, rythmically moving a sheet of cloth suspended from the ceiling by means of a cord attached to their big toes, even when they fell asleep.

Obviously Raffles was now very grand indeed. Its lofty dining hall, still known as the Tiffin Room, was the largest in the East, served by two European chefs and a squad of turban- and tunic-clad waiters. Its hundred apartments were all suites — complete with sitting room, bedroom, bathroom and dressing room. Palms lined the garden which ran down almost as far as the beach; there were tennis courts, livery stables, a private laundry, a dark room for amateur photographers, and rubber-tyred jinrickshas. No wonder the London *Sphere* called it 'The Savoy of Singapore' — in those days the biggest compliment that could be paid. Although perhaps Senator Stainiforth Smith of the USA went one better by saying, as early as in 1906 that 'Raffles Hotel is more than a hostelry. It is an institution.'

Anthropologists may speculate about the chemistry of a great hotel, but they will agree that it owes its character to the personality of the man who runs it. The Sarkies brothers, especially Tigran and Arshak, were perfectionists in an age that loved luxury and style. Like other legendary hoteliers such as César Ritz, Louis Adlon and Hans Badrutt, they were prominent social figures who not only ran their establishments themselves but were personal friends of many of the guests. Their distinctive touch undoubtedly helped to create the ambience of Raffles.

Arshak, whose cynical worldliness concealed a generous heart, loved gambling and women above all (he had two wives); his favourite party trick was to waltz around the ballroom balancing a glass of whisky on his bald head without spilling a drop. He was incredibly open-handed. Old clients who fell on hard times would find that he had secretly settled their accounts, and in his later days at Penang it was said that he ran the E & O more for the pleasure of entertaining his friends than to make money. 'Stern, red-faced, with a Semitic nose,' wrote George Bilainikin, who as editor of the *Penang Echo* knew him well, 'he spread his freemasonry sparingly but men who were his friends knew a generosity difficult to match. Arshak had a curious pride, a curious impertinence that one may ascribe to his Semitic origin. He never asked visitors whether they had been comfortable or had enjoyed themselves. He told them firmly that they had enjoyed themselves, had been comfortable, and anticipated, accurately, that they would reply that they had been made happy by his staff. Then, silence.'

One wonders what he made of a certain gawky young Wandervögel who stayed at Raffles in 1911. Though Hermann Hesse is now considered the peer of Thomas Mann and Stefan Zweig, and has achieved something of a cult status in the West, he was still unknown outside Germany when he joined the Swiss painter Hans Sturzenegger for a trip out East. On the last leg of their journey they spent ten days in Singapore, where Sturzenegger's brother had a business; and from Hesse's diary, which has only recently been published, we get his views of the place, warts and all:

Wednesday 25 October: *Tired arrival. Mail at last. At dusk walked along the magnificent avenue of the esplanade and through High Street, where we visited Chinese, Japanese and Indian shops. I like Singapore better this time, we are staying expensively but well in Raffles Hotel. The food is bad here too. In the shops, treasures of all kinds, a delight for the eyes. I bought toys and photographs. In the evening unpacking and writing, the gigantic hotel is horrible acoustically and echoes like a drum in its vast corridors and staircases. Sleep with Veronal.*

Thursday 26 October. *Sociable lunch. In the evening, trip to the Botanical Garden. Dinner in the hotel, as always with music, the boys are dressed all in white, the supervising waiters all in black. At the next table a jolly drunk amuses us and everybody else, he loses his patent leather shoe and retrieves it with his foot etc. He is an English administrative officer, who has been here for years and sits at his hotel table almost every evening as drunk as this. Trip to the German Teutonia Club, where we joined in an English bowling game until after 11 o'clock, with ten pins and absurdly large and heavy balls, we sweated awfully and became dead tired.*

Friday 27 October: *Excursion by tram and riksha, unending coconut groves with kampongs and European houses, beautiful beach. The Chinese coolies mostly wear blue linen trousers, one leg rolled down, the other rolled up to the knee. Pretty young female Chinese in a riksha. Lunch in the Singapore Club, refined with Hock punch, afterwards buying photographs, all terribly expensive. Rain. In the evening very hot in dinner jacket, because we visited a Chinese acrobatic performance in the Town Hall.*

Saturday 28 October: *Damp and sweltering, early rain... went through Chinatown, alive with glowing nocturnal business, hundreds of hawker stalls lit up with lamps in all the streets, some of the houses here also three-storeyed....*

Sunday 29 October: *Last night in the large stone paved game hall of our hotel there was roller skating until midnight, of which, however, we saw nothing.... Afterwards, when we returned at one o'clock, a few tipsy young Englishmen played around in the hall with the brutality of football players, shattering the shop window of the poor postcard dealer to smithereens and shouted, fooled wildly around and fought with each other half the night like pigs. In the morning we went to Johore by train.... English Sunday: no music during meals, miserable food.*

Tuesday 31 October: *Sunny, piercingly hot. Morning stroll through the nearby Chinese quarter, extremely busy but at the same time almost quiet, often reminding me of Italy, but more active and without the childish shouting, with which in Italy every matchstick boy calls out his bagatelle wares...locksmiths and blacksmiths, basket makers, cooks, and mobile food hawkers too, who carry their stoves around with them, a complete closed world, that doesn't need us. In the afternoon, sudden rain. I also managed to procure, albeit quite expensively, some of the holy joss sticks, letters of indulgence, etc...beautiful, grotesque figures and reliefs, two basis with holy tortoises.... In the evening I wanted to go to the Star Opera with the Sturzenegger brothers, but there was nothing new on, we turned back...when Hasenfratz turned up. As it was the last evening with him we took a whisky together and the three of us returned to Chinatown. These night rides or walks in the Chinese streets are always magnificent. The Chinese brothels, that look very pretty, seem to be only for the yellow people. We were only accosted and invited by the Chinese women; for the white people there are brothels in other streets with Japanese females. Incidentally, the majority of the brothels, which run at a high profit, are supposed to be owned by (Portuguese or French) mission fathers...*

Friday 3 November: *In the evening there was Sturzenegger's big reception in the hotel, elegant dinner with about 20 guests, drinking and unrestrained merriment, afterwards three of us roamed around the brothel streets till three o'clock at night, a fight involving a raving Englishman, many Russian whores.*

And there we will leave him, a slightly bemused figure frowning through his pince-nez not quite at home in his surroundings, wondering perhaps what the price will be, and whether it might not be best, after all, to go back to his Veronal.

Following:
H.N. (Rubber) Ridley, the farsighted botanist who almost failed to find planters to cultivate the rubber seeds he had brought from Kew. (ANM)

◄ 12 ►

CAMEOS IN MID-HISTORY

FOR ALL THE BUSTLE IN THE docks and behind the gleaming plates of the trading firms on the waterfront, Singapore in mid-history was still by modern standards undeveloped. Visitors who sauntered out of Raffles were liable to get covered with red dust from the laterite roads that radiated for about two miles from the centre, and at dusk the Tamil lamp-lighters made their rounds, ladder in hand, igniting each wick.

At half-time in our story, a man such as W. H. Read, born a year before the settlement was founded, who had crossed swords with Governor Butterworth in the forties and played a prominent part in bringing the Malay states under British protection, was busy writing his reminiscences. And on the other hand, there are still a few people alive today who can remember what Singapore was like at the turn of the century.

Life was much easier then than it is now, says Dr Bertram van Cuylenburg, a Singaporean of Dutch origins who was then a schoolboy. Ordinary middle class people like his family — his father worked as a draughtsman in the Survey Office at a salary of 60 dollars a month — employed a cook and an amah; while slightly more affluent households would also have a Hylam 'boy', a Malay gardener, and if they ran to a horse and a trap, a Malay syce as well. Families such as these lived in Queen Street, Waterloo Street or Serangoon Road, gradually moving further afield as the town grew in size. Apart from the Esplanade and the Racecourse there were still few large open spaces, but also very little need for them since every bungalow was surrounded by a garden, and at every corner the sea beckoned.

Despite the swarming masses in the streets — yellow, black, and brown — the place was ineffably British: solid, prosperous, conservative, resentful of change, distrustful of enthusiasms, and above all commercial. Europeans filled all the chief governmental and municipal posts, as well as the professions. Yet perceptibly the early Queen's scholars, recipients of the scholarships to British universities established in 1889 by Clementi Smith, were heralding the emergence of a professional local class. A new breed of doctors and lawyers was opening the way for later generations of ethnic Singaporeans.

Of course there were still no cars in evidence, though C. B. Buckley could occasionally be seen driving a single-cylinder 1896 Benz that he had bought in London for sixteen pounds (it had to be pushed up the gentlest gradient and could be started only by turning the large flywheel at the back by hand, after putting a teaspoonful of petrol in the carburettor and lighting it with a match.) This curious device, which Buckley insisted was 'only a toy and of no use at all', was joined by an Albion, a De Dion Bouton, and Mrs G. M. Dare's two-cylinder Star — which made her the first lady motorist in Singapore. By June 1907 enough machinery had congregated, including the Sultan of Johore's Mercedes Sixty, for a first meeting of the Singapore Automobile Club.

In the meantime the *tuan besars* still rode about in open horse-traps and gharries drawn by Java ponies with a syce. Some of them, when using a ricksha, employed a runner behind, who was useful in helping push the vehicle up hillocks though his head emerged disconcertingly behind the occupant. Cuylenburg remembers the peculiar grating sound made by the ricksha's iron-rimmed wheels, and how his mother's Irish terrier used to run between them when she went out shopping. There was much excitement when rickshas with 'rubber' wheels appeared at Raffles, complete with carbide lamps, and charging three times the usual fare of six cents a mile. But these enterprising ricksha-pullers had their noses put out of joint when a tramcar service started from Raffles Hotel along Serangoon Road, and a ride from Paya Lebar to the terminus at Raffles cost only 8 cents.

That supreme British artefact, the railway, only came to Singapore in 1903, but until the Causeway was built in 1923, the Malay trains stopped at Johore Bahru, and you had to take a ferry over to Woodlands station to catch the connection to the city. The railway track ran parallel to the Bukit Timah road and there was usually someone on horseback who tried to race the train to the Newton Road station, after which it steamed across a bridge over Orchard Road and cut across Oxley to reach the terminal at Tank Road. People who had seen friends off at the station used to hurry to a vantage point and wave again as the train slowly puffed its way above Orchard Road, where any traffic invariably stopped, believing that it was unlucky to go under the bridge when a train was crossing.

Sports, being one of Britain's chief spiritual exports was taken seriously. Cricket was in its hey-day, even if the Singapore Cricket Club's pavilion was still a small bungalow with shady trees, and only assumed an exuberant shape, to Bidwell's design, in 1908. During the nineties the club regularly held matches against the various Malay states, Hong Kong, Colombo and Batavia. In 1906 the SCC did not lose a single game; the scorebooks record that R. T. Reid made 234 not out for the Merchants against the Garrison, J. D. Saunders smacked Lawrie Dougal for eleven in two hits off consecutive balls, and 'Slogger' Parsons regularly dislodged tiles in the Municipal offices. (Since a good batting average spelt promotion, he quickly became a brigadier.)

For luncheon the teams adjourned to the Hotel de l'Europe across the road, and on several occasions batsmen who had been in their stride were out first ball after the interval, having been led into error by the opposition bowlers and swigged too many 'pegs' at the bar.

Lawn Tennis was also popular, and the earliest Singapore championship was held in 1875, two years before Wimbledon and five years before the first Championship of America. In those days the net was five feet high at the sides and only three feet three inches at the centre, which meant that the player who came up to the net had everything his own way, until a stonewaller from the civil service introduced lobbing and took the title four times. But once the Law became proficient, the era of patball was over. R. W. Bradall won eight of the bi-annual championships, and Lance Gaunt five, achieving also the nebulous distinction of being named Asian champion. From 1884 the ladies had a club of their own, with, we are told, a pavilion which, painted and furnished, cost 632 dollars, and a cup presented by the Sultana of Johore.

Football was introduced by the Engineers around 1889 on a ground near Tank Road, and quickly became popular among the Other Ranks of the army as well as with the Chinese and Malays, who formed their own leagues. Rugger, in contrast, was a naval and

Scottish speciality, reaching its climax in the match between Scotland and the rest of the world on St Andrew's Day. Hockey, considered socially respectable, was played on the Esplanade from 1892. Golf started in 1891 on a nine-hole links in the centre of the racecourse.

But above all the British brought their taste for equestrian sports. A swamp on the site of Farrer Park was drained to form the racecourse, with brilliant white rails, sprinkled lawns, and a grandstand big enough to accommodate all the nobs of the Turf Club. The Johore military band usually played in the paddock, and Sultan Ibrahim, horsily resplendent in his general's uniform, was invariably present. For race-days were great social occasions, usually followed by a ball at Government House.

Like royalty at Ascot, the Governor and his wife drove across the lawns to the stand. The National Anthem was played, slightly out of tune, and the races started. But while the grandstand was all frock-coats and parasols, the centre of the racecourse became a huge fun-fair. There were merry-go-rounds for the children, cake-sellers, *goreng-pisang* (fried banana) vendors, *tikam-tikam* (games of chance), card-tricksters urging people to 'spot the Queen', and of course all the schoolboys, clerks and hospital attendants, for every race day became a general half holiday. The air was full of bookmakers' cries, most of them Australians, surrounded by eager crowds of punters. Even the most cautious soul felt bound to have a flutter.

Just as much part of the Singapore scene, were the Chinese New Year celebrations. At their godowns by the river, Chinese merchants competed to see who could light up the longest chain of fire-crackers, festooned in strings from the rooftops to the pavements below. At seven in the evening the cracker-firing started, to usher in their sumptuous New Year's Eve dinners, and went on for hours on end, while hawkers did a brisk trade selling 'dashing' crackers to the kids. These were small cubes, packed eight or ten to a box like lumps of sugar; hurled at any target they made most satisfying bangs which scared the nervous and infuriated the grown-ups, especially ricksha-pullers when youngsters in the seats behind threw crackers on their nether parts urging them to run faster. Other celebrations on the calender were the Indian festival of Chettiar Thaipusam, when an elaborate firework display was held on the Esplanade; and the annual Chingay procession with its lanterns and dragon-dancers, after which the Governor opened the gardens of Government House, then known as The Domain, for Singaporeans to catch a glimpse of pomp and circumstance.

Yet, if Conrad and Kipling used the exoticism of Singapore as a backdrop for their fiction, delighting in the whip of the sail and the scented landfall, there is no doubt that the rationale of the colony was essentially commercial. Culturally speaking it was sturdily provincial, susceptible to the magnificats of Anglican imperialism and the jolly dazzle of Gilbert and Sullivan. True, there were regular visits by metropolitan companies such as the Bandman Opera and d'Oyle Carte, and Sir Matheson Lang played *Carnival* in Singapore before appearing at the New Theatre in London. But most of the productions at the old Victoria Theatre were staged by local amateurs whose taste tended towards prolific performances of a farce called *A Fast Train! High Pressure!! Express!!!* (which ought to have damned it, but apparently didn't) and *D'ye Know Me Now?*, an expression which became a catch phrase among Singaporeans of the day.

Looking back to his youth, Cuylenburg recalls queueing for hours to get tickets, and then the mad scramble up a hundred-odd steps to secure a seat in the gallery, collar torn and coat minus buttons. His happy memories of the *Mikado* and *The Pirates of Penzance*, to say nothing of Miss Ida van Cuylenburg in *The Geisha*, give the impression that the Singapore amateurs managed to put over their stuff pretty well, despite some inevitable backbiting behind the scenes. So seriously did they take their prerogatives that when Pavlova arrived for an engagement they refused to make way for her at the Victoria Theatre, and that most celebrated ballerina was obliged to appear on a makeshift stage at the Teutonia Club.

After the show, and indeed at all times of the day, it was customary to cool off at the patisseries, or 'ice-cream shops' as they were called. Of these the most elegant was at Raffles, in a corner of the hotel now occupied by the new Tiger Tavern, where the sticky cakes were as luscious as those of Rumplemayer or Hanselman in St Moritz. Hitherwards the fashionable crowd and their children would direct their steps after mattins at St Andrew's Cathedral, before moving on to the inevitable Tiffin Room curry lunch. But other well-patronized haunts were Joseph Baker's, Moutani's, and da Silva's Confectionary. Baker's red building still stands at the corner of Bras Basah, though it was long ago taken over by a Chinese concern; oldtimers remember how Joe and his staff of Hylam 'boys' dressed in spotless white suits and pump shoes would produce the most delicious raspberry and vanilla ice-cream sodas. And then there was Kye Ming, next door to St Joseph's school playing field, who maintained a fleet of itinerant hawkers, equipped with fires and burning embers to keep his curry-puffs and minced meat on toast hot and crispy. But Jimmy the ice-cream seller was the children's favourite. Of his special selections, the one they liked best was flavoured with durian. 'When his shrill "Jimmy" call was heard, the kids would rush to him, giving up in the middle of marbles or a kite-flying contest, and soon Jimmy would be dishing out his delicious ice-cream,' Cuylenburg recalls. 'As a medical man I now dread to think how many contracted dysentery or typhoid fever from it, but suffice it to say, Jimmy sold his ice-cream till old age prevented him from hawking his delight.'

Raffles Square has not changed in shape, but only in name — for it is now called Raffles Place — since the beginning of the century. Then it was sheltered by shady flame trees, under which tired ponies rested and ricksha-pullers sipped hot coffee provided by a Bengali hawker, or gulped down ice water sweetened with doubtful syrup, at half a cent a glass. And brokers in their tutups congregated near the entrance to Change Alley as they do today. But Collyer Quay is quite different from the time when the frontages all abutted on the seafront wall, and traffic from town crossed over Cavanagh Bridge. In those days each office had an elongated verandah on the seafront, so that you could walk along and see your friends in another office without going downstairs. In contrast, North Bridge Road has altered little, save for a few new buildings. But even the sites of the old entertainment centres are still 'theatre-land' for Singaporeans — such as the famous Wayang Kassim near Arab Street, where Kairo Dean, the idol of the Babas and Nonyas, held sway during the golden era of Malay opera. Of course the old Harima Hall, a wooden tile-roofed structure that showed silent films of the Russo-Japanese war, was rebuilt as the Tivoli. Probably just as well too, for those early Pathé films (bioscope shows, as they were called) flickered so badly that one could hardly read the sub-titles, let alone see the 'brave' Japanese bayonet the 'decrepit' Russians, all to the tune of a screeching violin played by a Filipino accompanied by a piano. The Gaiety was another popular venue in the days of silent films, until Joe and Julius Fisher built the Capitol and brought in the latest American attractions. The Marcus Show, launched a taste for strip-tease, now banned by the authorities.

For footloose bachelors, who outnumbered white women by about thirty to one, there was The Great World, a huge circular barn of a place with a centrepiece of bamboo and palms, where the band played against a backdrop of garish birds and a gold dragon scrambled about on the ceiling. The Tingle-tangle was another favourite haunt. And of course Malay Street, in its day as notorious as Blood Alley in Shanghai, Jade Street in Peking, and Yoshiwara, Tokyo's suburb of painted ladies. No holds barred!

Here came the tough European girls — Russians, Hungarians, French, Germans — who sat on the doorsteps below their heavily-scented rooms and screamed their wares. In Malay Street, says R. C. H. Mckie, you could be beaten up and robbed for fifty cents, or knifed for a dollar. And since he knew the scene well, let us join him for a stroll round Chinatown, to mingle with the mob streaming along the alleyways beside open-air eating houses hung with scarlet ducks and dripping meat, past drink stalls, knick-knack shops and shooting galleries where you could smash glass bulbs and work off your feelings on nodding, misshapen animals. Beneath a huge sign saying: 'Make sure of your virility — take sunlight pills for men, moonlight pills for women' and under it a diagram in coloured crayon which was obviously intended to represent sexual organs, a gully-gully man wearing a fez tantalized a sleeping cobra with anaemic bagpipe notes on his flute. After being prodded and slapped, the snake eventually puffed out its copper hood and hissed disinterestedly.

Across the road, in the glare of naked lights, the audience at a Chinese theatre — neat pig-tailed amahs, clerks, shopkeepers and a few bewhiskered pundits — argued among themselves, occasionally leaving off spitting and chewing their melon seeds to shout '*Hau*' or some such word to signify their approval. The play was an historical drama, acted by Cantonese whose costumes had been handed down for generations; the leading character wore a magnificent get-up of scarlet silk embroidered with silver and gold designs, and a head-dress like a wedding-cake with two flowing peacock plumes. When he was handed a stick with a yellow tasselled end and put it between his lips, it meant that he was on horseback; when three men stood beside him, he became a general with an army at his back. 'It's like trying to read a novel in code' sighs Mckie. The play, of course, was centuries old, with an historical background of too many generations to count. It can no doubt be witnessed today, no more with the female parts taken by men speaking in a falsetto shriek but still the bad lad of the piece being finally dispatched by a cardboard sword with a golden hilt.

For years Malay Street was the ultimate goal for lonely bachelors and overnight tourists who returned home to boast about their Eastern sex adventures, until its reputation became so lurid that the authorities stepped in. 'One night,' says Mckie, 'early patrons of Malay Street found the houses closed, the girls gone, and in their place came the high-coiffured kimono-wearing Japanese courtesans who had clean tatami-covered rooms, did not scream or throw bottles, bowed you courteously in and out, hoped you would come again, and did not mind if you only dropped in for a few minutes to drink a bottle of beer.' Thence forth Malay Street was the street of the Japanese, with an eastern philosophy towards the lady of the night, and Ricksha Parade took over as the soliciting point. The Parade was less than fifty yards long, on the sea side of Dhoby Ghat and had no houses.

The real brothels were now shophouses disguised as hotels with incongruous names such as the Ritz, where you went through the Gilbertian farce of signing a false name on the formal police sheet. Since the police were strict, the girls were not kept in the house. The brothel-keeper showed you photographs in an album with descriptions — 'A passionately palpitating piece from Peking', 'Malay Magic' — and the object of your choice was then sent for.

Of course there were also the dumps and dives of Lavender Street, clip-joints where the wail of a three-man Chinese band cut through the noise of bawling voices; and squabbles over the taxi-girls could suddenly break into a rough house. After such a muck-raking tour of the town it would be a relief to get back to the brilliantly lit entrance of Raffles as couples in evening dress, the men in dinner jackets and the women in long glittering gowns, were preparing to leave.

Under the paternal eye of Tigran Sarkies and his manager, Joe Constantine, Raffles was sumptuously serene and reassuringly staid — you might even say stuffy. The conventions were rigorously enforced, and right up until World War II only Europeans were allowed on the dance floor.

The joke is that in the evening a crowd of Asiatics would gather on Beach Road, to watch the swankily-dressed Europeans dining on the lawn beneath the tall pencil palms. It was their nightly free show. Mentally they licked their lips at the sight of the white women in their backless dresses. They genuinely thought they were whores.

Following:
William Somerset Maugham, being one of the most popular authors of his day made the colonial world famous through his writings. Soon, Singapore and Malaya were Maugham country and Raffles Hotel, following his remark, became what stood for all the fables of the exotic East. (RH)

◄ 13 ►

THE PALM COURTS OF MAUGHAM AND COWARD

Victoria...Edward VII...George V. Throughout their reigns the golden days continued, a pattern of increasing commercial prosperity and undiminished imperial authority, with no hint of the Armageddon that would occur on Chinese New Year's Day in 1942.

With hindsight, the omens were there, to be sure. Yet the Chinese revolution and World War I — both decisive influences, as it turned out — were too comfortably remote to have much impact on Singapore. In fact the only shock during the war was the mutiny of an Indian regiment about to embark for Hong Kong, when the city was obliged to defend itself against its own garrison. But the mutiny, once it had been quelled with the help of crews from Russian, French, and Japanese ships, was shrugged off as a ten days' wonder (unlike the Singapore Sling, created at Raffles that same year.) And hardly had the Great War ended than Singaporeans were preoccupied with the island's centenary.

Casting his thoughts backwards, the editor of the *Straits Times* reflected : 'The rulers of Singapore have revealed their genius more by abstinence than by action, in other words, their success has been due to their fidelity to the principle of *laissez-faire*.' He counselled against such inaction in the future. The time would come, he foresaw, when the whole island of Singapore would swiftly become one great town, a greater entrepôt port than ever, served by 'ships which will wing the air in swift and graceful flight'. What was needed were 'strong guiding hands, not potterers, to plan for these eventualities and in the growing climate of democracy, to lead Malaya towards a system of representative self-government'.

Prophetic words, but unfortunately the potterers remained. True, a British-Japanese alliance was concluded in 1921, followed by the establishment of a naval base which, when completed, was intended to be the mightiest fortress in the East. There was some concern, too, about the spread of communism by agents from Soviet Russia among the Chinese community. But the authorities judged that the majority of Chinese and Malays were more interested in making money than in seeking political control. However they prudently shelved any plans they may have had for democratic experiments.

And despite periodic booms and slumps, the money was certainly easy to make. Huge fortunes were amassed overnight, chiefly by the Chinese. One thinks of Tan Kah Kee who made over eight million dollars, and his son-in-law Lee Kong Chian who gave up teaching to form the Lee Rubber Company; Tay Koh Yat with his buses and Aw Boon Haw of Tiger Balm fame. Many British businessmen did almost as well, and enjoyed themselves in the process.

Emblematic of this success were the traditional haunts of wealth and privilege, such as the Singapore Cricket Club, the Tanglin Club, and of course Raffles. Everyone who could, made his way there.

Newly arrived from England, Alec Dixon confesses that he was daunted by the regal bearing of the Sikh who opened the door of his taxi as it drew up beneath the wide porte-cochère, and ushered him up a crimson carpet laid as if for a royal progress. The interior of the hotel suggested Government House, even if one's view was restricted by palm leaves curving over the rim of the largest brass bowl he had ever seen.

The tables were filled with men discussing the market, glasses at their elbows, and women whose hats would have been fashionable in the Bois de Boulogne, chatting discreetly. Chinese boys moved silently between the tables, and behind a screen of palms a Filipino orchestra played Mozart. 'Everything in that hotel' thought Dixon, 'from the fans overhead to the ice which bedewed one's glass, ministered to the white man's comfort.'

These impressions appear in a book Dixon wrote about his experiences as a police officer during the twenties. But, for the atmosphere of that period one must turn to William Somerset Maugham, whose most persistently quoted remark (in hotel blurbs rather than in a dictionary of quotations) was that Raffles 'stands for all the fables of the exotic East'.

Maugham made this colonial world his own: soon Singapore, to say nothing of Malaya and Borneo, became known as Maugham country. But curiously he did not spend long in the area — rather less than six months in 1921, and four months in 1925. Yet he seems as much part of Malaysia as Kipling is of India. As his biographer Ted Morgan explains, Maugham was fascinated by the things that happened to Europeans in the tropics. Ordinary people, humdrum enough at home, became dramatic figures. Everyone had stories to tell, and Maugham told them. Of 'Footprints in the Jungle', for instance, which is about a couple who had committed a murder, he wrote quite openly that it was one of those stories that he could hardly claim the authorship of, for it was told to him word for word one evening in the club.

One of his best known stories, 'The Letter', later made into a play and then a movie, concerned a married Englishwoman who killed her lover and then pretended he was trying to rape her. The plot came straight from the newspaper accounts of her trial, which a Singapore lawyer described to him at dinner one evening.

The trouble was that he hardly took any pains to disguise his material. Victor Purcell, a Malayan civil servant, wrote: 'Maugham's passage in Malaya was clearly marked by a trial of angry people. The indignation aroused by his play, *The Letter*, which was based on a local *cause célèbre*, was voiced in emotional terms. It was charged against him that he abused hospitality by ferreting out the family skeletons of his hosts and putting them into books.'

But Purcell added that Maugham's representation of European life in Malaya was 'photographic', which is precisely what gives the tales such a sense of reality. And, to be fair, Maugham was the first to admit that the people he wrote about were exceptions. 'The vast majority who spent their working lives in Malaya were ordinary people ordinarily satisfied with their station in life... They were good, decent, normal people' he wrote. What caught his eye were the local scandals: the baronet who eloped with the sister of a Chinese millionaire; the brother and sister with an incestuous relationship; the distinguished member of the legislative council who was caught *in flagrante*. And out of the gossip of Singapore he fashioned some marvellous stories.

Maugham first arrived in Singapore with his secretary, Gerald Haxton, in March

1921. He was then 47, at the height of his fame, with twenty-one plays and ten novels behind him. For a short while they stayed at the Hotel Van Wijk (which became the Van Dyke in the story *Neil MacAdam*), a favourite haunt of ship's captains. But in April they embarked for Borneo, travelling up the Sarawak river into the heart of the jungle and living among the Dyak headhunters, who gave feasts and dances in their honour. On the way back, their paddle-boat, crewed by convicts from the Simanggong jail, was suddenly overturned by a bore — an inrush of water some ten feet high. Both were nearly drowned.

After this frightening experience, described by Maugham in *A Writer's Notebook*, they returned to Singapore to recuperate. Staying this time at Raffles in Suite 78, Maugham corrected the galleys of his South Seas stories, *The Trembling of a Leaf*, which was published by Doran on 17 September. These seven stories including the famous 'Rain', were set in Hawaii, Samoa and Tahiti, and established his reputation as a short-story writer. Sainte-Beuve's 'feuille tremblante' separating despair from happiness, was to become a favourite theme of his: the plight of people in the tropics who have failed to come to terms with their surroundings.

Also sitting at a table in a corner of the Palm Court among the frangipani and hisbiscus, he worked on a play called *East of Suez* before setting off on a tour of the Malay states. Often he and Haxton arrived at some remote spot with a letter of introduction to the local Resident, who was delighted to put them up, and — as Maugham confessed in *The Gentleman in the Parlour* — gave him plenty of useful material as they chatted over their *stengahs*.

Maugham returned to Singapore in the autumn of 1925 to pick up a fresh crop of stories. Sadly one must discount the legend that he wrote his two best-selling novels, *Of Human Bondage* and *The Moon and Sixpence* while staying at Raffles; both were published long before he ever set foot in Singapore. But while here, he certainly worked on some of the stories in *The Casuarina Tree* which put such a cat among the pigeons that twelve years later an editorial in the *Straits Times* was still discussing 'the prejudice against Somerset Maugham which is so intense and widespread in this part of the world'. Giles Playfair called him 'the national red rag'.

He did not in fact come back until 1959, when at the age of 85 he was on his way to Japan for the opening of an exhibition in his honour. In Japan, Maugham was treated like a god; it was the last and perhaps the greatest triumph of his career. And at Singapore the welcome given him was almost as warm. The press poured onboard his ship and an impromptu banquet was laid on, after which, said Raffles' resident doctor to the hotel's historian, Ilsa Sharp, 'We all took cushions and sat in the patio, and Somerset Maugham said: "I would love to hear some Singapore tales", and out they flowed! From people you never realized had very extraordinary things happen to them. It was when I was driving him back to the hotel that Maugham said that if I didn't write some of the stories down, he would!'

On this occasion Maugham stayed in the suite in the writers' corner of Palm Court that bears his name, alongside that of his friend Sir Noel Coward and those of his earlier contemporaries, Conrad and Kipling. Like so many times before, the room 'boy' placed a table and chair for him in the garden each morning and he wrote steadily until lunchtime. It was tempting to think that some new Singapore tales were in the making. But actually he was busy on his last book, *Purely for my Pleasure*, an account of his collecting, which was published in 1962.

THE PALM
COURTS OF
MAUGHAM
AND
COWARD

163

Inevitably he found Singapore and indeed Raffles changed. Old and crochety, he felt a stranger in the place to which he was so mythically linked. Yet this hardly justified his parting shot at the Tanglin Club, where the manager of Raffles had taken him for a drink. There was a fuss that he was 'improperly dressed' in his bush jacket and Maugham, resenting this tyranny of the tie, gazed contemptuously over his glass at the assembled company. In a voice pitched high enough for everyone to hear, he declared: 'Observing these people, I am no longer surprised that there is such a scarcity of domestic servants back home in England.'

Even so, Singapore treasures his memory.

Lord Boothby once said that in his opinion the four Englishmen who had given more pleasure to more people than any others in the 20th century were Charles Chaplin, Noel Coward, P. G. Wodehouse, and Somerset Maugham. Three of them found a haven at Raffles, and 'Plum' Wodehouse would surely have done so had he come out East.

Noel Coward had just finished writing *Private Lives* when, after he had slipped inconspicuously into Singapore with his friend Lord Amherst aboard a Danish cargo ship in 1929, he ran slap into a heatwave. Sitting on the verandah at Raffles, he remembers 'There was a thunderstorm brewing and the airless heat pressed down on my head. I felt as though I were inside a hot cardboard box which was growing rapidly smaller and smaller. Sipping a gin sling and staring at the muddy sea, I think my spirits reached their lowest ebb on the first evening I spent in Singapore.'

Since Amherst had dysentery, they stayed for about a month, which gave Singapore the chance of a spectacle that had been denied to Broadway audiences. A company brought out from London by Grant Anderson was staging R.C. Sheriff's *Journey's End*, and the actor taking the principal part had fallen ill. As it happened, Coward had already been asked by the author to play the lead in America, and had refused. But he now agreed to act as substitute and in three days learnt the lines. According to critics, he was word-perfect and gave a sensational performance in this moving play set in the Great War, inspiring the rest of the cast and arousing a pitch of enthusiasm at the Victoria Theatre that had never been known before. He himself modestly records that 'The elite of Singapore assembled in white ducks and flowered chiffons and politely watched me take a fine part in a fine play and throw it into the alley.'

Unfortunately some anger crept in too. At the party after the show, one of the 'elite' made a cutting remark and got back as good as he gave. It seems that Coward had disgraced himself by awarding a prize in a contest to a woman 'suspected of having coloured blood'. 'Had I known this' he retorted, 'I should have given her the first prize, even if she had been a Zulu.'

His offstage antics with members of the company caused further raised eyebrows at Raffles. 'Some of the more refined social lights of Singapore looked obliquely at us, as though we were not quite the thing' he recalls, '— a little too rowdy perhaps, on the common side. I'm sure they were right. Actors always laugh more loudly than other people when they're enjoying themselves, and we laughed most of the time.'

But rowdiness in the theatre was quite another matter, he told George Bilainkin when the editor was showing him the sights. If he had his way, he would turn the hose-pipe on noisy first-nighters. 'On a first night, strung up, it is terrible for a man to hear a coarse interruption from the gallery. When he is doing his best, he goes off and does worse and worse.'

Bilainkin was curious to know how he worked. 'I write quickly in longhand, having previously thought out the matter' explained Coward. 'Then I re-write on the typewriter — a habit of typing from the days when I could not afford a secretary.'

Could a quick thinker like himself not write better on the typewriter? 'No, because one begins to scurry through.'

If Bilainkin was impressed by the playwright's knowledge of natural history and biology, he was even more surprised when they visited the zoo. As they walked by the cage of a large and fierce Malayan tiger, someone playfully put a stick through the bars. The tiger snarled and raced angrily from one end to the other, whereupon Coward asked his companions to leave him for a moment. 'When we returned' says Bilainkin, 'the large fierce beast, the terror of the Malayan jungle, was lying down, paws in the air, moving backward and forward, as happy as a Persian cat in a Kensington spinster's room.'

Coward became friendly with Arshak Sarkies, with whom he sat chatting for hours on end. He was remembered at Raffles for his monogrammed silk shirts and blue beret (which someone thought was a torn coat cover.) Later he made Raffles the setting for *Pretty Polly Barlow*, in which the sudden death of one of the characters was attributed to 'having stuffed herself with curry in the Tiffin Room', and the BBC TV film was shot at the hotel.

But if Raffles cherished its literary connections, with the Writers' Bar and a row of suites along the Palm Court named after them, authors were not necessarily the most colourful guests, tending to remain closetted in their rooms or sit gazing vacantly into space as they wrestled with a tricky twist in the plot.

A memorable figure was Peter von Stein Callenfels, the Rabelaisian Dutch archeologist — '24 stone of solid science, Falstaff in the flesh' — who was immortalised by Conan Doyle as Professor Challenger in *The Lost World*, and whose exploits still raise chuckles at the Long Bar.

It is told that when still a colonial cadet in charge of government coffee plantations in a district of Java, he was visited by the local Resident who noticed that monkeys were damaging the coffee crops. A month later he received a pompous note from the official hoping that he was paying proper attention to the coffee plantations.

'Sir,' replied Callenfels, 'I have the honour to report that there have been no monkeys in the coffee plantations since you were here last.'

On another occasion, when an official census was being taken, his written reply to the question 'How many children have you?' read: 'Since I arrived in Java at the beginning of this century, the population has increased by fifteen million.'

Mckie remembers him at Raffles, in curry-stained pyjamas, 'overflowing the chair in vast undulations of flesh which started from his pregnant paunch and rolled downwards, upwards and sideways, his monstrous body heaving and shuddering like a shaken blancmange as he addressed an audience of women in a voice that could be heard a hundred yards away... like the salty tang of a typhoon tearing through an intellectual swamp.'

His gargantuan capacity was a subject of wonder. It was said that he once drank ten bottles of gin at breakfast, and many tales were told of the Professor drinking twenty or thirty bottles of beer at a sitting. It was believed that his record was thirty-five and he was furious when an engagement prevented him from finishing the thirty-sixth bottle which he had just opened. What's more, his appetite for food was no less remarkable.

When a friend bet him a case of champagne that he could not eat every dish on the hotel menu, he not only did so but — watched by every diner in the room — proceeded to go through the menu again in reverse order, just to show that he could do it.

Conventions he scoffed. During an argument about the basis of authority in colonial administration, there was a good deal of palaver about the personality of the individual and his ability to command respect and obedience from the natives under his control at which Callenfels laughed. Authority, he said, rested simply on the man's uniform. To prove the point, he called for his carriage, had his gardener dressed in full dress civil service uniform, sat him in the back, and told the coachman to drive around town. And sure enough at the sight of the uniform, notwithstanding the brown face above it, the populace squatted reverently on the ground as the carriage passed by.

Though he himself had no time for outward trappings, the arbiters of the social scene most certainly did. The management of Raffles might be prepared to overlook the appearance of this monstrous but well-loved character, but other local luminaries were expected to toe the line. Colonial shibboleths demanded suits (usually limp, and stretched in damp creases) during the day time and dinner jackets or short white mess jackets, known as 'bum-freezers' in the evening.

Few Asians, with the exception of Royal visitors and the Sultans of Johore — who frequently slipped over the Causeway from their palaces on the mainland — and of course the Babas (for so long the favourite 'children' of Britain) stayed at Raffles during this colour-conscious period of the Empire. But if they did so it was with panache, like Mrs 'Pansy' Lee Choon Guan, the wife of a member of the Legislative Council, who would turn up wearing a solid collar of diamonds, or a jacket with 12-carat diamond buttons, looking, it is said, like a torchlight in the darkness.

In fact, rifling through the pages of the hotel registers, you come across the signatures of many of the same people you would have found, at the appropriate season, at Claridge's in London, the Ritz in Paris, the Palace at St Moritz, or the Pierre in New York. Dr Serge Voronoff, the monkey-gland rejuvination specialist, who undoubtedly numbered many of these fellow guests among his clientele, was a regular visitor, still accompanied in old age by a spectacularly beautiful blonde who looked like his daughter but indeed was his wife. The proof of the pudding!

Baron Empain, the Belgium banker who founded the suburb of Heliopolis outside Cairo and built the famous Heliopolis Palace Hotel (now President Moubarek's headquarters), frequently arrived on his yacht with a crowd of young people aboard; some thirty boys and girls dressed in sailors' costumes would troop in for luncheon behind the baron in full captain's regalia. And though Frank Buck left his cargo of wild animals in his camp at Johore, he was so often at Raffles, and put Singapore so emphatically on the movie map with his 'Bring 'em Back Alive' films that he came to be regarded as an honorary citizen. Other early movie stars to make an appearance were Charlie Chaplin, Maurice Chevalier, George Arliss, Ronald Coleman, Norma Shearer, Jeannette Macdonald and Jean Harlow. When the little man with the bowler hat and stick stepped off his ship in the harbour he was given a standing ovation by the normally torpid ricksha men; but Jean Harlow's pictures, like those of Mae West's, had been so badly cut by the censor that Singapore hardly realized her capabilities.

On the face of it, they were all having a marvellous time — certainly compared to the teeming masses outside (who were not obliged, however, to doll up like crusaders in mail armour on a midsummer day in the Holy Land). Every night of the week there was a dance at either Raffles or the Hotel de l'Europe, and for the New Year's Eve balls the presents and favours, brought over from Paris along with most of the garlands and festoons, were so lavish that to one observer 'the walls and ceiling glowed like an orchard in full blossom...nothing more resplendent was ever seen at a gala night at Cannes or Monte Carlo'. And at Government House the discomfort of a tailcoat and white tie in a temperature of 85° was offset by a dazzling succession of banquets and balls, swathed in bunting and fireworks.

The formal pomp of these occasions, though not of course their jollity, was embodied in institutions such as the Havelock Road Police Court, whose aura of faded dignity was almost ludicrous, thought Sjovald Cunyngham-Brown, a magistrate during the thirties. Amid crashing salutes and cries of *'Diam!'* for silence, everyone in the courtroom had to spring to his feet as the magistrate swept to his place on the dais behind a huge baize-covered table.

Yet even the law could suffer a dent, as he engagingly confesses in Charles Allen's *Tales from the South China Seas*.

> *Sailing my little boat across the Malacca-Strait I'd got abominably sunburnt. So in the absolute safety and security of my seat, knowing that I had a big baize curtain hanging down over the table's other edge so that nobody could see what I did, I undid my belt; what a relief! I then listened to a long discourse on the part of the counsel for the defendant and opened a few buttons. And when it came to a little further cross-examination with the plaintiff's lawyer, I took a bold step: I slipped off my trousers, lifted my shirt and gave myself a really good and satisfying scratch. I couldn't understand what was happening in court. There had been a certain murmuring from earlier on but now a positive uproar suddenly broke out. I saw small boys standing on tables at the back pointing and screaming, as the three uniformed police were banging on the floor, shouting 'Diam! Diam everybody!' And the Clerk of the Court, turning round to see why there was all this fuss, jumped up with a face of horror, opening his jacket like wings, and said, 'Sir, they've taken the baize away to be cleaned!'*

In the years following the first World War, girls were still in short supply. 'You would merely *hope* to dance' recalls an old-timer, and indeed the passageway at Raffles that flanks the ballroom and the bar was known as Cad's Alley because of the bachelors who congregated there in the hope of cutting in. It was an accepted convention that young Englishmen employed in Singapore were not allowed to marry until they had completed their first tour of duty and had graduated to become permanent members of the staff. They were then given leave and told to find a wife. But exporting one's bride-to-be from home was often a tricky business. 'If you didn't take her through the Red Sea on the P & O yourself, she was almost bound to fall for someone on the ship' we are told. 'She'd come down the gangplank with some shipyard romance on her arm and the beach wedding would be his instead of your's.'

As time wore on, single girls came out to fill jobs in the educational or medical services and found themselves with no shortage of dates. People queued up to take them dancing at Raffles, swimming at the club, or for picnics up the coast. But though it evened out the numbers, the arrival of more and more European wives, who immediately became memsahibs (however humble their backgrounds and limited their accomplishments), accounted for much of the decorative starchiness that began to creep in, as the directing force of social life passed into their hands. 'The white woman has inevitably tried to recreate England, and usually Surbiton, in the tropics' commented an unkind observer, in whose opinion the social niceties were accentuated and maintained by the wives, many of whom became very grand and took themselves very seriously.

An old lady told Ilsa Sharp that it was hard nowadays to imagine the strictness of life when she was a girl going to dances at Raffles. 'It was very formal. We had to check off our dance engagements on little programmes.' And decorous too: waltzes and valitas interspersed with an occasional two-step. The Charleston and the fox-trot did not come in until later.

Such strict preoccupation with the conventions was a far cry from the early days, when concubinage had been accepted as one of life's little solaces. Earlier generations of officials and businessmen had happily miscegenated, bringing a whole caste of Eurasians into being, and incidentally getting much closer to the life and feelings of the people than their successors were ever likely to do. Indeed Charles Brooke, the second White Rajah of Sarawak once publicly suggested that such intercourse was the best way of preserving the Empire. A cross-breed of European and Asiatic, he thought, would be the best population for the development of tropical countries.

It was certainly unthinkable now. The British were the highest in Singapore's caste system, whereas Eurasians, known contemptuously by the word that was used for a small whisky, *stengah*, or half, were considered the lowest. If a European had a Eurasian as a mistress (and many of them were lovely) he was expected to be discreet about it, and under no circumstances to take her to any of the white clubs or into the main hotels. The fact was, remarks R. H. Bruce Lockhart tensely, the British did not believe in breeding bastards. Not at this stage, anyway. And if an Englishman did the decent thing and married her, he would not only be socially ostracised, but probably sent home in disgrace.

This rigid racial discrimination was carried to such absurd lengths that in 1941 when Rob Scott, then Director of Information, escorted an Indonesian princess from a large official party on to the dance floor at Raffles, the band stopped playing and refused to start up again until they had left.

On the following day, which happened to be Sunday, 7 December, the first Japanese bombs began falling on Singapore.

Following, top:
Set among white-washed colonial mansions along Beach Road, Raffles Hotel was once an old family mansion which later became the Raffles Girls' boarding school. (PY)

Following, bottom:
Billiard rooms in hotels were once as essential as swimming pools are today. Raffles Hotel boasted of a four table room, which would, one supposes, be equivalent to an olympic size swimming pool. (PY)

'When in Singapore, eat at Raffles.' The Tiffin Room, circa 1923. (RH)

Rare billiard tokens once commonly used in the pool rooms of Raffles Hotel and Emerson's Billiards Room. (CKT)

Tigran Sarkies

Arshak Sarkies

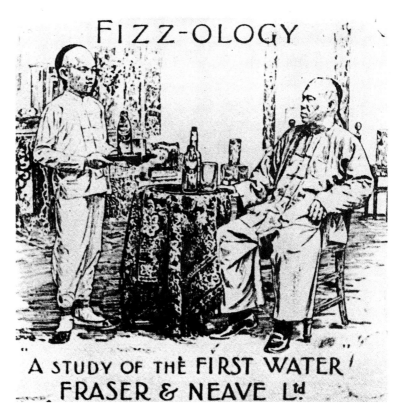

An early advertisement for Frazer & Neave. Perhaps it was with cold aerated drinks in mind that Whampoa imported ice from Boston. One would have thought cool relief would have been welcomed but strangely the business failed. (RH)

Ball Room Raffles Hotel, Singapore
"The Coolest Ball Room in the East"
Telegraphic Address: Raffles, Singapore

4672

While Harry Houdini performed thrilling escapes and Ethel Griffies flickered on the silver screen, they danced ragtime at Raffles. (RH)

Raffles Hotel's signature tune composed in 1903 is still regularly played today. (RH)

Europe Hotel, the grand competitor to Raffles made way for the Supreme Court building in 1936. In its heyday, it boasted of 120 well appointed rooms, a 100 sq. metre ballroom and a roof garden. (PY) (JL)

Following left, top:
'At Tanjong Katong, the sea is oh, so blue' goes a familiar Malay folk song. Here, among the coconut palms of the Sea View Hotel, the lilting melody was perhaps hummed by lovers and village folk alike. (PY)

Following left, bottom:
Somerset Maugham lived in the Van Wijk when he first visited Singapore. He, of course, later moved to more stylish accommodations at Raffles Hotel where a room is now named after him (PY)

Following right:
One of a series of postcards depicting the children of the Empire. (JL)

STRAITS SETTLEMENTS

In Singapore this small girl lives,
The things that come from there
Are india·rubber, sago, rice,
And many spices rare

H.G.C.
Marsh
Lambert

Hoo Ah Kay, nicknamed Whampoa by his British associates after his native Chinese district, was the only local representative in the Legislative Council in 1873. Chief Justice Thomas Sidgreaves sits on the left and Governor Sir Harry St George Ord is on the right. Standing from left to right are: Thomas Scott, Dr Robert Little, Thomas Braddell (Attorney-General), H. F. Plow (Clerk of Council), W. Williams (Colonial Treasurer), unidentified, J. W. W. Birch (Colonial Secretary), Hoo Ah Kay, and Major J. F. McNair (Colonial Engineer). (AOHD)

Two landmarks stood between Read and Coleman bridges when this picture was made. Whampoa's ice-house can be seen on the left while Ellenborough market stood on the opposite bank. (AOHD)

A long felt want: a suggested recreation room and gymnasium for members of the Legislative Council, 1924, to counteract a slight stiffness noticeable at times in their deliberations.

Following:
After the unveiling ceremony of the statue of Thomas Bingley Raffles on 27 June 1887, surprised Malays were overheard as saying: *'Hai-yah! Dia orang hitam macham kita!'* (Great Scott! He's a black man like ourselves!). (AOHD)

Showing off their skill for
posterity, firemen pose for their
camera with their newly
acquired horse-drawn fire
engines in the 1890s. Two
decades later, the horses were
put to pasture with the
introduction of motorised fire-
trucks. (AOHD)

The first racing meet of the
Singapore Automobile Club took
place at Tyersall in June, 1907.
Cars of every description
gathered, from H.H. The Sultan
of Johore's seventy horse-power
Mercedes to Mr. C.B. Buckley's
'coffee machine'. (AOHD)

Charles Burton Buckley, known more for having written *An Anecdotal History of Olden Times in Singapore* than owning the first car, a 1896 Benz, on the island, was a partner of the law firm Rodyk & Davidson. (AOHD)

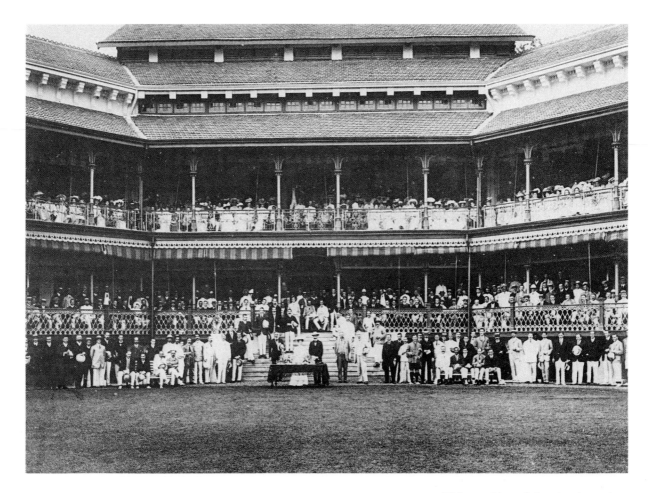

This could well be the formal membership portrait taken at the Singapore Cricket Club on the completion of the renovations to the clubhouse. That was in 1907 and guests at the Europe Hotel across the road could sit in the evening breeze watching sportsmen play fives and, of course, cricket on Raffles Plain. (AOHD)

Fashion of a different clime and place ruled in the settlement of Singapore. The humidity and heat did not deter genteel folk from wearing the latest styles of Edwardian England. (AOHD)

Farces, theatricals, amateur or otherwise, helped occupy the after-work hours of the colonial community. Sometimes, professional actors and actresses fresh from London music halls would arrive to be acclaimed by a full house. (AOHD)

A jinricksha rank on Collyer Quay awaiting arrivals from the Road. A ¼ cent or less paid for a quick ride to Commercial Square. (AOHD)

Electric tram cars disappeared with the coming of war. So did the rickshas. With the advent of peace, the trams ran briefly again but were taken off the tracks permanently at about the time the now familiar trishaws came on the road. (PY)

Kittyhawk. The writer of this postcard tells this story: 'This aviator promised the public a flight of 6000 ft. high but alas he rose to no higher the (*sic*) 100.' (LKC)

Primitive though they may seem, engines and coaches such as this one of the Federated Malayan States Railway provided a speedier and reliable service for goods and passengers between the port of Singapore and its hinterland 'up country'. (AOHD)

The Kalang River reservoir has since been renamed the Pierce Reservoir but the pavilion still stands as it did when the facility first opened. (PY)

Kalang River Reservoir — Opening of new Works 26th March 1912

When Farrer Park was the Race Course, Indian families would stroll from their homes in the neighbouring Indian community to watch the sport. Race Course Road in the vicinity still carries the name from that period. (LKC)

What would Raffles have said if he saw this sight: punters gathering around like moths to fire. The founder objected absolutely when the first Resident suggested that the most painless way of raising revenue was to create, among other vices, gambling farms. (JL)

Cryers at the Race Course, Singapore

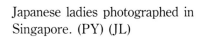

Japanese ladies photographed in Singapore. (PY) (JL)

There seems to have been a sizeable Japanese community in Singapore in the early 20th century. S.T. Yama — operated a photographer's studio on the junction of Hylam Street and Middle Road. Another Japanese must have had his residence a little further down on the left, seeing how carp streamers for the Japanese Boy's festival fly above a shophouse. (JL)

Singapore. Japanese lady.

MALAY STREET, SINGAPORE.

There are several Japanese restaurants on the right of Malay Street which is perpendicular to Hylam Street. It would seem that there was a sizeable Japanese community living in the area. In its day, notorious Malay Street was the ultimate goal for lonely bachelors who wanted a taste of the lurid East. The street was the home of Japanese 'ladies of the night' who were otherwise impeccably behaved. (LKC)

The first Tan Tock Seng
Hospital was a pauper's hospital
in Pearls Hill. It was later
moved to Serangoon Road and
thence to Moulmein Road.
Conditions were far from what
they are now but signs of
comfort and care were present
in this ward at Serangoon:
mosquito nets and an orderly on
duty. (NTLY)

Orchard Road was a haphazard two-way street when motor cars shared the road with bullocks and rickshaws. The old market is on the left, making the scene just at the junction of Cuppage Road. (JL)

The forerunner to chic tea time venues Adelphi and Mon't Dor, Louis Mouteni's confectionary gave way to cinema and the Cathay Building. (JL)

In 1882, the Municipal Commissioners erected a fountain in Fullerton Square in honour of Tan Kim Seng. It was to commemorate his donation towards the cost of the Singapore Water Works. Sadly, by 1923, the fountain was neglected and allowed to run dry. It was only in 1953, as a curtain raiser to Coronation Week, that the fountain relocated on Queen Elizabeth Walk, was working again in its restored splendour. (JL)

Singapore. Hongkong Shanghai Bank (decorated).

Hongkong and Shanghai Bank on ever busy Battery Road is decked out to usher in a new era upon the coronation of Edward VII in 1901. (JL)

Each morning after the lamp extinguishers were about to finish their rounds, the market streets of Singapore would come alive with activity. (JL)

COOLIES UNPACKING POTTERY, SINGAPORE.

This is where I buy my flower pots.   Oct. 6. 1904.

'Many thanks for pretty curios, they are lovely. Dear little island. Hope you will enjoy the trip to B. I will write letter soon. Love all from us both. MTO. This is where I buy my flower pots. Oct. 6 1904.' (PY)

Coolies and *samsui* women were considered 'cheaper labour' by their colonial masters. A story is recorded of how one kind hearted British Major did not see fit to put defaulters on clearing jungles because of stinging red ants. His solution was simple: he put his Malay gardener and other locals to the work. (JL)

For over 170 years, the Singapore River was a working river on which the *sinkehs* found a living, worked hard, but rarely found their fortunes. (JL)

Left:

Representatives of the Singapore Chinese Chamber of Commerce gather at their stand to welcome the Prince of Wales on the opening of the Malaya-Borneo Exhibition, 1922. From left to right are: K. Y. Doo, Chow Kuenam, Lim Seow Kiew, S. Q. Wong, D. Beaty, Lim Chwee Chian, Ong Thye Chee, Lo Chong, See Teong Wah, Ho Siak Kuan, Teo Eng Hock and Kum Cheng Soo. (AOHD)

Left, bottom:

Methodist school boys playing marbles. On the reverse of this card is a letter from a missionary who refers to the boys as 'intelligent' and 'very quick at learning the language'. Undoubtedly, these boys were the early students of the Anglo-Chinese School founded by Bishop Oldham in 1887. (LKC)

As the port grew, there was a need for docking facilities. On 21 June 1913, Governor Sir Arthur Young declared open Lagoon Dock which subsequently was renamed King's Dock and then Empire Dock. (NTLY)

LAGOON DOCK SINGAPORE
ADMISSION OF WATER
21ST JUNE 1913

Quite definitely, the entire
population of Singapore when
Raffles arrived was just a
fraction of this crowd which
joined the celebrations of a
hundred years later at Farrer
Park Race Course. (NTLY)

Following left:
The Jinricksha Question — One of the Possible Disadvantages: being the misadventure of an English gentleman on meeting a deaf ricksha puller. (ATQS)

Following right:
In the 1920s, trolley, motor and privately run Mosquito buses plied the roads. Mosquito Buses were so called because 'they were like the insect that could flit about the streets, dodging amongst the traffic with the ease of a private car, and being a perfect pest to the STC (Singapore Traction Company)'.

Dr Lim Boon Keng and friends pose in their cars outside what might well be Bendemeer House. (FRNS)

When the Empress Dowager was spending public funds for palatial gardens and allowing China to be cut up by foreign nations, Dr Sun Yat Sen rallied loyalists around the world to support his cause for the overthrow of the weak-willed, backward Qing Dynasty. From 1900 to 1911, Dr Sun was to come to Singapore eight times to muster aid. Among his most staunch supporters were Teo Eng Hock (left) and Tan Chor Nam. (FRNS)

While Chinese men felt comfortable in western cut clothes, the womenfolk of the early 1900s were more inclined to cling to their traditional costumes. (FRNS)

This couple looks so much alike that they were perhaps not bride and groom but brother and sister in traditional Baba wedding garments. The young man has his left ear pierced which, according to custom, would ward off evil influences seeking to interfere with his well-being. (FRNS)

The Babas were known for their eclectic culture, its elements drawn freely from their Chinese roots and Malay ties. During the heyday of the community in the 1920s, Babas were naturally the most cosmopolitan and forward looking of peoples in the Straits Settlement towns of Singapore, Malacca and Penang. This family probably lost its patriarch, which serves in this context to highlight the matriarchal dominance in Baba households. (FRNS)

In Baba households, children were often given pet names which indicate their status in the family. Baba was shortened to *Ba* and Nonya abridged as *Nya*; thus the first boy might be called *Ba Besar* (Eldest Baba) and a fair daughter *Nya Putih* (White Nonya). Male and female progeny were numbered separately, therefore homes might have both a *Ba Besar* and *Nya Besar*. (LCC)

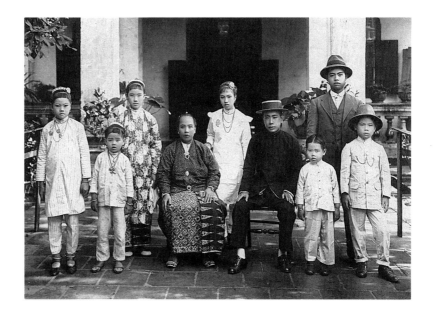

Though from the same roots, the immigrant Chinese were markedly different from the Babas. A comparison of this family with the Baba one will clearly illustrate the difference. (FRNS)

Chinese funeral observances long antedated Confucius although he is considered to have shaped the rites of death, mourning and burial. During funerals, immediate members of the deceased's family mourn demonstratively in linen sackcloth and white garments to emphasize filial piety and the family system. The sex of the deceased was made known by the decoration on top of the hearse. The lion is traditionally used for males while a white stork for females. (FRNS)

Sacrificial meals were held in honour of the deceased's spirit every seven days from death for forty-nine days. Thereafter, food and drink were offered on death anniversaries and the departed's birthday. Other important occasions for remembering the dead are the Qing Ming Festival in the beginning of the third lunar month and the Feast of the Hungry Ghosts on the fifteenth day of the seventh moon. (FRNS)

The social graces practised by nonyas were traditionally fine embroidery, skilful beadwork and culinary crafts. With the advent of western influence, it became fashionable that young ladies should also play the piano or perhaps sing. (LCC)

Inspired by the strolling minstrels of merrie England, the Baba community organized non-professional minstrel groups with ever so English names as The Cornwall Minstrels. When Al Jolson first sang in a talkie, these minstrel groups mimicked the jazz singer's style, blackened their faces and plucked out Deep Southern tunes on their banjos and guitars. (LCC)

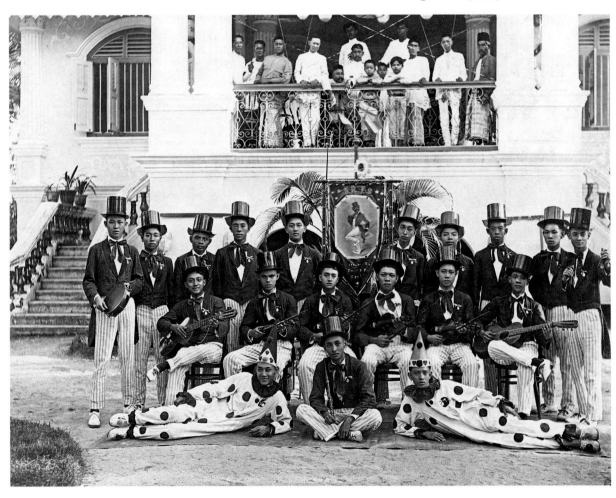

Not a portrait of amahs and their charges, nor is it a group picture of students and teachers of some Chinese School. Believe it or not this is the St Matthew's Anglican Church Choir in the 1920s. (FRNS)

Street entertainers of the White Stork Troupe. Variety is their hallmark, from recitals of the Chinese Zheng to magic shows and the inevitable gimmicky sales pitch for cure-all medicines. Modern equivalents can still be seen showing off their skills and wares near the People's Park Complex in Chinatown. (FRNS)

Stamford Raffles gave the first grant of land for the building of a Roman Catholic Church to a Malacca priest in 1822. However, no building was erected until a decade later when a place of worship was put up where St Joseph's Institution stands today. Another decade later, the Cathedral of the Good Shephard was ready for Masses to be held, making it the oldest edifice in Singapore. This portrait of the church's priests and altar boys was done in the 1900s. (FRNS)

The Malays have a word for it: *tumpang* — to be a lodger, to use another's belongings, to hitch a ride. (FRNS)

A daring thing it was in those days for a girl to pose for an advertisement pin-up even if the product was a purely medicinal ginseng health tonic. (FRNS)

A handsome Chinese couple
marry in style some time in the
roaring twenties. Their
impressive multi-tiered wedding
cake towers behind the wedding
group. (FRNS)

Following
A wedding party in various
styles of clothes outside the
Fragrant Mountain Club House.
Note the Tamil, Chinese and
English advertising posters on
either side of the group. (FRNS)

An elegant non-traditional
Indian wedding party.
Everyone, well almost everyone,
is dressed to perfection. (FRNS)

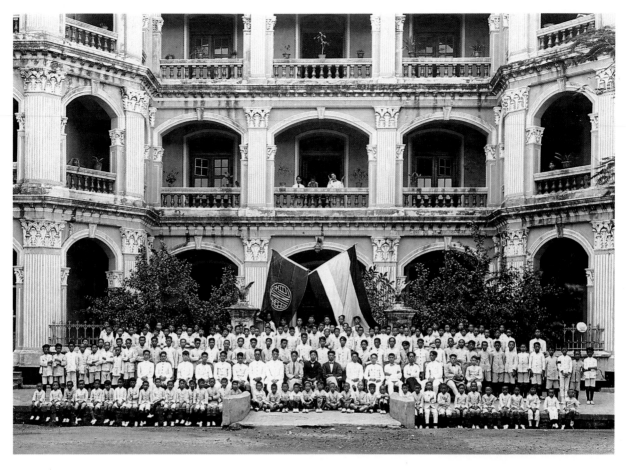

Founded in 1906 by the Hokkien community, Tao Nan School first occupied their elegant building in Armenian Street in 1910. Its 1700 students are now housed in a modern school facility in one of Singapore's highrise satellite towns. (FRNS)

新嘉坡佛教居士林慶祝阿彌陀佛聖誕歡迎圓法師演大會國民葦廬青年撮影

In the 12th century, Singapore was part of the great old Buddhist empire of Palembang until about 1360 when the Javanese Hindu Majapahit kingdom sailed against and raided its ports, including Singapore. In 1937, the members of the Singapore Buddhist Association gather in front of their premises at Blair Road to welcome the Reverend Yuan, a Buddhist missionary. Students of the neighbouring Vinayagananda Tamil School look on happily. (FRNS)

You might say that Whampoa, the Chinese who spoke English 'with the accent and idiom of a well-bred and well-read English gentleman' paved the way for a cordial relationship between the Chinese and European business communities both in trade and sport. Rugged men of the football teams from the Cricket Club and Straits Chinese Recreation Club foregather before a friendly match. (FRNS)

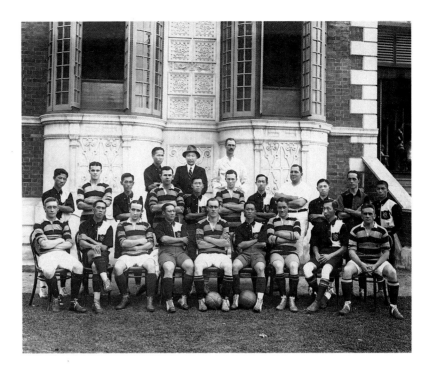

The Singapore Chinese Swimming Club water polo team during the late thirties. The pool was then just an area of water partitioned from the sea. (FRNS)

Two football teams pose for a portrait before what the young mascot thinks is a very serious match. (FRNS)

Early immigrants from South China were clannish and many associations and clubs were formed by people who originated from a common ancestral village or district. Organised for mutual protection, most clans had pugilistic teams, some of which remain today as martial arts and Lion Dance troupes.

The *Daily Times*, predecessor of
the *Straits Times* published in
1872, a comment on the police.
In the course of the article the
journalist used the most unkind
words to describe the Indians in
the Force at that time. 'Now we
know what Klings are' he wrote
self-importantly, '.... they are
weak-kneed, mendacious and
cowardly.... Their physical
weakness is equalled and
surpassed by their moral
delinquencies....' Had he seen
this admirable body-building and
fitness society, that writer
would have been persuaded to
change his choice of adjectives.
(FRNS)

Part Four:

THE AGONY AND
THE FRUITION

◄ 14 ►

ARMAGEDDON APPROACHES

SINGAPORE HAD CONTINUED TO dance when Europe erupted in 1939, for the distant rumblings of war seemed to be less menacing to its boisterous way of life than the Great Slump had been ten years before.

Then the Depression had hit Singapore hard, geared as her economy was to international trade and the export of tin and rubber. Soaring prices in the boom years of the 'twenties had led to overproduction: between 1929 and 1932 the value of rubber slid from 34 cents a pound to 5 cents a pound, and the bottom fell out of the tin market too.

One notable casualty of the slump was the collapse of the Sarkies empire. Partly, this was due to Arshak's gambling and subsidies to an army of spongers, partly because of lax control over the staff at his hotels, whose private 'mafias' discreetly siphoned off much of the income. In the end, there was a deficit of over 2.5 million dollars.

Raffles never closed, but was reconstituted as a public company in 1933 just as the depression was ending and business was on the upturn again. 'The measure of your faith in the shares you hold in Raffles must be the measure of your faith in the Colony', the new Chairman told his shareholders.

The answer was: plenty. For by now Malaya was producing nearly half the world's output of tin and rubber, much of which was exported to the USA by Singapore firms. But above all there was the great naval base costing sixty million dollars, which had taken eighteen years to build and was finally completed in 1938. As one of the most formidable concatenations of naval, military and strategic power ever put together, with 22 square miles of deepsea anchorage, oil tanks holding a million gallons of fuel, and a floating dock so huge that 60,000 men could stand on its bottom, it was designed not only to provide oil storage and dockyard facilities for the British fleet with all the paraphernalia of ship repair, but also to offer a protective back-up to Hong Kong, Colombo and even Australia. Above all, as a great imperial stake in a great imperial pivot at the junction of trade routes from India and the West to China, it was a warning to Japan.

Was it impregnable? Field Marshal Lord Roberts had warned that the history of the world would be decided one day at Singapore, and there were nagging doubts in some quarters. The magazine *Aeroplane* commented that the defence forces of Singapore were 'a laughing stock' to any intelligent Asian. But official wisdom maintained that Singapore was as perfect a fortress as geography and the mind of man could contrive. It was a guarantee that the 'arsenal of democracy' would remain secure whatever might happen elsewhere.

True, the Japanese were making belligerent noises, but Japan was 2700 miles away. Even when the Vichy-controlled administration in Indo-China allowed the construction of Japanese bases in South Vietnam, which brought their planes within 500 kilometres of North Malaya, there was little sense of danger. After all, the evidence of security was there for all to see: the officers in their blues dining at Raffles, the Other Ranks queuing at the N.A.A.F.I. or having their pictures taken by Mr Mimatsu, the Japanese photographer housed behind Raffles (who later reappeared in the uniform of a Japanese colonel). And Singaporeans were further reassured by the sight of the *Prince of Wales* and *Repulse* as they sailed proudly up the Johore Strait to the Naval Base. When Duff Cooper declared that the ships 'conferred a sense of complete security' he was echoing the general feeling, shared by the top military brass, that the Japanese were aiming their mischief against Russia, anyway.

If the tempo of life increased, it was because of the need to supply raw materials to England and to a re-arming America; there was a patriotic mood behind the bustle of planters and merchant houses to fill the holds of the vessels lining the quays of the harbour. Profit motive apart, their part in the War Effort was to justify Malaya's role of a 'dollar fortress', second only to Canada as the Commonwealth's biggest dollar earner, and concentrating on production rather than defence.

Everything was blessedly normal then, on Sunday the 7th of December 1941, as English folk made their way from St Andrew's Cathedral to Raffles for curry tiffins preceded by gin-slings or Tiger beers — eaten to the strains of Ivor Novello and Walt Disney's 'Snow White' played by the Palm Court orchestra; while others drove two miles out of town to the Swimming Club or the Sea View Hotel. The terrace of this little place — which had also been founded by the Sarkieses — was always packed on Sundays. Everyone seemed to know everyone else: there was much chaff and banter and signing of chits for rounds of drinks before the band struck up a chord. This was the signal for the pre-luncheon sing-song. Now a ritual here, it invariably ended with 'There'll Always be an England', sung lustily by every person on the premises. The syrupy song was later to be recalled as symbolizing the feelings of many people, apparently far from the war, who were so abundantly unaware of the stunning, sickening, shattering defeat that lay in store. A swan song to the old way of life!

Yes, everything was still normal as they drove soporifically home though the jumble of traffic controlled by policemen with basketwork 'wings' strapped to their shoulders to save them from waving their arms in the heat. At nightfall, the electric lights blazed advertisements for Tiger balm and Tiger beer, and while the Other Ranks in their tropical kit sought solace down in Lavender Street, a telephone call from the Cricket Club or the Tanglin Club would be enough to alert one's 'boy' that there would be twelve extra guests to dinner. Tomorrow they would go shopping at the Cold Storage and meet their friends at Robinson's for coffee. There would be a cocktail-prolongé at Raffles. The women's diaries were full of social engagements until after Christmas. All was well in the best of all possible worlds.

Until, that is, Sir Shenton Thomas were awakened by a telephone call from General Percival, commander of the British Forces in Malaya, to say that the Japanese had begun landing at Kota Bahru, on the East coast near the border with Siam. 'Well,' replied the Governor sleepily 'I suppose you'll shove the little men off.'

Which unfortunately is just what they didn't do. The British High Command was caught on the hop, just as the Americans were taken by surprise that same night at Pearl Harbour. This in its turn triggered off a series of disasters. Operation Matador, designed to frustrate such an enemy landing, was delayed until too late; systematic Japanese attacks on the RAF airfields left only 50 operational planes to counter over 500 far more sophisticated Japanese aircraft. With little or no air cover, the Commonwealth forces were progressively annihilated by the fast, enveloping tactics of their enemy, who made good use of tanks in the jungle where the British (who had not one single tank in Malaya) had always insisted that armour could never operate. But the worst blow of all was the sinking of the *Prince of Wales* and the *Repulse* off Kuantan. 'In all the war, I never received a more direct shock' wrote Churchill, when advised of the disaster in the middle of the night. 'As I turned over and twisted in bed the full horror of the news sank in upon me. There were no British or American capital ships in the Indian Ocean or the Pacific except the American survivors of Pearl Harbour, who were hastening back to California. Over all this vast expanse of waters Japan was supreme, and we were everywhere weak and naked.'

With them went Singapore's hopes. When the news came through, the Raffles ballroom silently cleared. 'It was as though not only the ships had gone to the bottom, but the bottom had fallen out of everything else as well', comments Noel Barber.

Meticulously planned and brilliantly executed, the Japanese advance through Malaya was so rapid that it had the signature of a great adventure. The feeling of invincibility made them light-headed: General Yamashita exultantly declared that since the Japanese claimed descent from gods and the Europeans from monkeys, in any war between gods and monkeys the gods must win. Certainly his lightly clad troops, many of them on bicycles, made rings around the Commonwealth defenders who were double their number but lacked their experience.

In contrast, the British High Command was hesitant and divided. A string of wrong decisions was made. Orders went astray. Communications broke down, initiatives were smothered in protocol and convention, the military and civilian authority quarrelled. It was a searing story of official ineptitude, as though the wrath of the Eumenides drove them inexorably to do the wrong things. Yet at the same time it was a story of great individual acts of bravery.

Some years previously, Bruce Lockhart wrote: 'Rome had given to the world the greatest trade empire and the longest period of peace it had ever known. But in the end its administration had been destroyed by overcentralization and overbureaucratisation by the civil service at headquarters. The same threat now threatens the British colonial administration in the East. Inertia and moral decadence precedes zoological extinction.' And Swettenham, who more than any other man had brought the Raj to Malaya: 'A masterly inactivity is today a better road to a successful official career than all the enterprise, revolution and drive in the world.' These dismal reflections were now borne out.

Firmly but eloquently, Winston Churchill ordered the army to fight to the end; there was to be no question of surrender. But once the resistance was broken, it was as if someone had pulled the plug out of a bath. The Australian official war history sums up the disaster with the pungent commentary:

> *Mr Churchill said nothing about the Malayan campaign being virtually lost at sea and in the air within a few days of its commencement; nothing about the disastrous dispersal of the army on the mainland to protect airfields now valuable only to the enemy; nothing about the Japanese monopoly of tanks, though indeed his figures did*

indicate that about half the force at (General) Percival's disposal comprised Asian soldiers. These, in the main poorly trained and inexperienced, and with many officers who were more or less strangers to their units, were pitted against other Asians who had become veterans of campaigns in China and were fighting ardently for their country instead of a subject people... Singapore had indeed been a boasted fortress, but it was not the enemy who had been deceived by the boast. To Mr Churchill himself, it had become with a shock of discovery 'The Naked Island'.

On 9 February, just two months after their initial landing, the Japanese began the final attack on Singapore, whose guns, true to form, were pointing the wrong way.* The last dance at Raffles before the British surrender is enshrined in the city's memory. There was still no idea of a fall — or at least the idea was not prevalent. A planter who was there remembers: 'How gay the ladies, the smiles and laughter, how beautiful the dresses and smart the white mess kits of the officers! I remember remarking to one of my companions: 'This must be just like the Duchess of Richmond's ball before the battle of Waterloo.'

Instead, this saddest chapter of the imperial saga ended on the afternoon of Sunday, 15 February, when General A. E. Percival, after going to church and taking communion, walked grim-faced behind a white flag carried by Lieutenant-Colonel H. S. Flower to the Japanese command post in the Ford Assembly plant at Bukit Timah. General Yamashita kept them kicking their heels for half an hour, but the negotiations lasted barely five minutes. At 6.10 p.m. Singapore surrendered — unconditionally.

---

* And when the military high command decided to site a defence point on the golf course, the secretary replied that nothing could be done before the committee had met.

Following:
A fresh, candid perspective of the British surrender at the Ford Factory is found in General Yamashita's diary.

'On this occasion,' he wrote, 'I was supposed to have spoken to Percival rather abruptly. If I did, it was because I now realised that the British Army had about 100,000 men against my three divisions of 30,000 men. They also had many more bullets and other munitions than I had.'

'I was afraid in my heart that they would discover that our forces were much less than theirs,' he continued. 'That was why I decided that I must use all means to make them surrender without terms. My interpreter was very poor. Obviously, he did not know my worries . . . . I am afraid that in my anxiety I emphasised the "yes" or "no" in English too much. The interpreter also emphasised the words very loudly when he repeated them to the British commander. This, however, did end the matter quickly and Percival agreed to my demand for unconditional surrender.' (IWM)

◄ 15 ►

THE SYONAN INTERLUDE: MISERIES AND ILLUSIONS

No battle in history was won and then lost with such absurb anti-climaxes as the battle for Singapore. In 1942 the Japanese army, smaller than the British and shorter of ammunition, had conquered the island when hundreds and thousands of allied troops surrendered. So unexpected was victory that Britons had to be pressed into helping the Japanese to stamp out fires before being packed off to Changi.

In 1945, after the atomic bomb had been dropped, thousands of Japanese soldiers, their armies intact, their magazines bursting, their stranglehold on countries all over Asia complete, laid down their arms to a puny force of allied soldiers. So unexpected was their *victory that the British had to ask their one-time conquerors to help them until reinforcements arrived on the island.*

— Noel Barber, The Singapore Story.

The next three and a half years were a period that all those who were concerned — Singaporeans, British and Japanese — would prefer to forget. Who would wish to revive such a dismal page of history?

The Japanese occupation was brutal. Soldiers and civilians alike, the Europeans were lined up on the Padang and marched off to a harsh and painful internment, where along with disease and hunger they endured daily beatings, kickings and face-slappings. The Chinese adults were all rounded up and many thousands massacred in an initial orgy of hatred before the conquerors came to understand the need for Chinese co-operation in running the economy. Indeed the Japanese attitude towards the Chinese varied. Some they treated with great cruelty, others as business partners to keep the machinery of commerce turning. And while Eurasians with direct European ancestry were interned, others were just bullied. Malays and Indians came off relatively better, though for them too it was a time of increasing misery, plagued with starvation, ill-health and unemployment. Although the Japanese preached *hakko-ichni*, the universal brotherhood of Asians, it soon became clear that they were less interested in liberating Asians than in acquiring control of Southeast Asian resources. Singapore, renamed Syonan, or 'Light of the South', was designated as the capital of Japan's new Southern Region. The island was planned to be built up as a strategic base run from Tokyo (whereas Peninsular Malaya was to become a protectorate under the theoretic rule of its sultans).

Two days after the surrender, the Japanese set up their military headquarters at Raffles College, and among other measures Raffles Hotel — renamed Syonan Ryokan — was commandeered for the exclusive use of high-ranking Japanese officers though not

THE
SYONAN
INTERLUDE:
MISERIES
AND
ILLUSIONS
231

before the staff had managed to bury a number of hotel treasures, such as the great silver trolley from the grillroom, under the turf in the Palm Court. 'Bemused room-boys, more used to the decorously overdressed British, had now to accustom themselves to the spectacle of half-naked Japanese samurai lounging in their loincloths, or less, and whirling huge broad-bladed swords around their heads while drinking in the Palm Court', notes Ilsa Sharp, adding that under the strict management of Japanese personnel they soon learnt to assemble early in the morning in the ballroom for physical training, to bow east when the national anthem was played, and above all to bow to all Japanese guests (who included General Tojo, the premier of Japan). The Raffles staff could not help noticing, moreover, that whereas their new masters preached a doctrine of anti-materialistic sacrifice for Singaporeans, they showed a distinct fondness for the good life themselves, cutting a dash in the colonial mansions and big American cars they had requisitioned, playing tennis and golf in the former British clubs, and frequenting the Turf. Robinson's and Little's, the two great departmental stores, were restricted to Japanese customers, and in many office buildings only they were allowed to use the lifts. What is more, many of the more unscrupulous Japanese made fortunes in the black market, often acting as front men for racketeers and gamblers.

As fellow Asians, the Japanese had a unique opportunity to win round the Singaporeans. But they threw it away. Far from bringing a spirit of Asian brotherhood, they spread cruelty and fear. Says Chin Kee Onn, who lived through these years of tension and tyranny: 'If Japan had less of *Seishin* and more of commonsense, the history of South East Asia would have been different.' And Tan Thoon Lip, who suffered under their regime: 'Undoubtedly her achievements were enviable, but Japan forgot to be humane.'

Some Japanese, it is true, did their best. Mamoru Shinozaki, a diplomat who had been imprisoned by the British for alleged spying activities, issued safety passes to as many Chinese, Eurasians and other Asians as he could without attracting too much attention; likewise he interceded with the Kempetai on behalf of others who had been imprisoned, and requisitioned military supplies and medicines for the sick and homeless. Had more Japanese done the same, the locals would have hated them less.

There were also some lighter moments. One of the many rules of the 'New Order' was that children passing Japanese sentries were required to bow and wish them '*Konbanwa*'. Enjoying the pun, the children would bow so low that their heads almost touched the ground, and bellow lustily '*Chium Bawah*' (a Malay slang expression meaning 'kiss my bottom'). This apparently delighted both parties: the children had a laugh once they were safely out of earshot, and the Japanese were impressed by their politness, because the lower you bowed to someone, the greater your respect. Luckily most Japanese never mastered the Malay language.

For three years the reign of terror continued. Though glimmers of hope grew as the news of Axis reverses filtered through on clandestine radios, the plight of the internees worsened during the last dreadful months of the occupation, and VE Day in Europe seemed only to herald the beginning of an endless war of attrition in the East, when suddenly that murderous extract of pure matter, the atom bomb, made all the fighting as out of date as the battle of Hastings. For the Japanese, hubris was followed by an appalling Nemesis.

For Singapore, it was the end of a nightmare. When the British troops finally landed, they found the three-mile-route from Tanjong Pagar to the Cathay building lined with people waving Union Jacks and cheering themselves hoarse. And the bedraggled survivors, shuffling out of Changi jail, were met with a welcome that brought tears to their eyes. One Englishman found his old *amah* waiting at the gate with a parcel of freshly-laundered clothes. 'They were still warm with the smell of a hot iron', he remembers. And when he entered the Cricket Club, the same boy who had always served him in the past came up smiling with a *stengah* before he had ordered it.

Remembrance of things past! The skyline of the city seemed so reassuringly unchanged, and the same old Union Jack, so lovingly hidden all those years in Changi jail, fluttered once again above fortress Singapore. In those first heady days of peace it seemed as if the whole hideous occupation had disappeared like a summer typhoon, leaving most things intact in its wake. One the few places to have altered was Raffles Hotel (where two lingering Japanese officers committed *hara-kiri*). For one thing, the entrance had been moved from the front of the hotel off the ballroom verandah to the Beach Road side, where it has remained ever since. More important Raffles, which had been maintained as an oasis of elegance by the Japanese, was now converted into a transit camp for the allied military personnel and civilian refugees emerging from Changi — many of whom openly wept when they saw the familiar facade, even though they had to sleep on the floors and the billiard tables.

Alas; the first first flush of exuberance was quickly followed by a sense of delusion. It was not just that on closer investigation the city proved to be dirty and dilapidated — the roads full of potholes, the harbour choked with wrecks — but that fresh food was almost inexistent, and even the rice ration had to be reduced to four ounces a day, a quarter of the normal pre-war consumption. Water and electricity were scarce, telephones virtually non-existent, and medical services so inadequate that many people fell back on traditional remedies, the Chinese to their *sinsehs*, the Malays to their *bomohs*.

Industry, particularly rubber and tin, was hopelessly disorganized, unemployment high, corruption universal. The black market flourished, fuelled by junior officers who made a killing selling ordnance stores. Peace did not bring an end to hunger and want, and even the official British history felt bound to comment that 'while propagandists contrasted the allied "liberation" with enemy "occupation", the distinction between the two processes was not always so clear to those who were bring "liberated".'

Indeed, subjected as they now were to the inefficiency and corruption of the British military administration, Singaporeans began to suspect that victory had brought not freedom but simply a change of masters — more benign, to be sure, but masters whose image was tarnished. After all, the British, who had been pledged to defend them, had run away and left them to the mercy of the Japanese. The humiliation of the British had shattered their faith in the protective power of the Empire and made them receptive to quite another type of creed.

Not that every coolie was seething with revolt. Far from it. But in Singapore, as in other Asian countries, the overwhelming majority of intellectuals were ready to forego the benefits of western tutelage for the satisfaction of running things themselves. And undoubtedly the communists were the heroes of the day.

Communism had first appeared in Malaya in the mid-twenties, when it became associated with the labour movement, and widened its influence during the wave of support for China in her struggle with Japan. In 1942, when the Japanese broke through Malaya, the communists took to the hills.

As members of the 'Malayan People's Anti-Japanese Army' — MPAJA, code-named Force 136 and commanded by the legendary Spencer Chapman — they had carried on guerrilla activities against Japanese troops throughout the occupation, in readiness for a British invasion planned for the autumn of 1945. Despite some British misgivings these guerrillas were decorated by Lord Mountbatten as a reward for their wartime collaboration and one of their leaders, Chin Peng, took part in the victory parade in London in 1946. Now, well armed with munitions that had been parachuted into their jungle hideouts and seized from Japanese prisoners, they emerged (by simply changing one word) as the MPABA, the Malayan People's Anti-British Army, dedicated to seizing power in Malaya and Singapore. Their prestige was so high that the moment was ripe.

The reason why they failed to stage a take-over would do justice to a Le Carre novel. For it happened that the brilliant, charismatic leader of the communists was not a communist at all, but a master spy planted by the British to exercise covert control over the Party. Loi Tak was undoubtedly responsible for the failure of communism in the crucial period following the war, and when he was finally in danger of being 'blown', this intrepid 'mole' was spirited away, taking the party funds with him, and leaving the local politburo in considerable disarray. It was no secret any longer that the Colonial Office had plans to group Peninsular Malaya and the North Borneo states into an independent Malayan Union, maintaining only Singapore as a Crown Colony.

Being caught in a quandary — for independence achieved by such constitutional means hardly suited the communists' book — the new leader, Chin Peng, decided to make good use of the MPABA's five thousand guerrillas who were training in secret jungle camps. Under the catchword '*Merdeka*', he launched a full-scale attack on the British in Malaya.

So it was that in June 1948 the people of Singapore found themselves with yet another war on their doorstep. And it was against this background that a young man named Lee Kuan Yew returned home with a double-first from Cambridge University.

Lee Kuan Yew is a fourth generation Singaporean whose great-grandfather arrived in Singapore soon after Stamford Raffles. He began his schooling at Telok Kurau English School and thence at Raffles Institution and Raffles College. During World War II, Lee narrowly escaped being a victim of an execution squad. When told to board a truck to make the death trip, he asked to be allowed to go home to collect his belongings. Surprisingly, he was permitted and wisely never returned.

The young man's education continued at Cambridge where he was active in the Malayan Forum founded by Tunku Abdul Rahman. On his return to Singapore as a qualified lawyer, he was catapulted into politics by the feeling of anti-colonialism prevalent in the early 1950s.

By 1954, the People's Action Party, now synonymous with Lee's name, was formed. Ever since it won a landslide victory in the 1959 legislative assembly general elections, the party has dominated Singapore politics.

Since then, Singapore has been part of Malaysia and is now a sovereign nation in its own right. Through it all, the man Lee Kuan Yew has never sought public recognition, yet, as surely as history has already proved, the perception and driving force of this one person has contributed greatly to the success story of Singapore. (SNPL)

◄ 16 ►

THE EMERGENCE OF LEE KUAN YEW

At the moment it is clear that the only party organized to force the British to leave, and run the country, is the Communist Party. Theirs is a tightly-knit organization making their bid for power.... It is, right now, the biggest threat to the newly established governments of Asia. How far these governments can counter the appeal and force of communism will depend on how far they are bold enough to carry out social reforms in the teeth of their own vested interests...whether they can, without the communist religion, do all that a communist state can do for the masses.

**Undergraduate Lee Kuan Yew to the Malayan
Forum in London in 1949.**

If Tom Raffles created Singapore from a tropical swamp, Harry Lee transformed a warehouse in the sun into a nation whose level of material prosperity in the East is second only to that of Japan. And he did so through a series of political manoeuvres that would have given Machiavelli food for thought.

Lee Kuan Yew was born on 16 September 1923 under the sign of Virgo and in the year of the Pig. Astrologers will deduce the significance of his horoscope, just as anthropologists will note that his Hakka forebears were noted for their arrogance, determination, energy and adventureness. Lee himself will say that he is not Chinese but Singaporean, for his great-grandfather Lee Bok Boon immigrated to the island when Raffles was still there; his family is thus one of Singapore's oldest. Grandfather Lee Hoon Leong, managing director of a shipping line trading with Indonesia, married into the Indonesian Chinese community. Lee's father, Lee Chin Koon worked for an oil company — a job that carried considerable prestige — and the Malay blood in his Nonya mother's family may account for his multiracial feelings.

Traditionally the family was British-educated, and Lee was brought up in the best colonial style: first at Telok Kurau English school, and then at Raffles Institution, where the top people in Singapore sent their sons. Cambridge should have come next, had the war not intervened; instead he entered Raffles College, which later became the University of Singapore. It was here that he first met Kwa Geok Choo, who had won the top scholarship from the Methodist Girls' School. At Cambridge, their friendship turned into love.

But in the meantime there was the trauma of the Japanese occupation. Lee was rounded up with a group of Chinese youths who were to be taken off and shot, but he managed to escape. To keep out of further harm's way, he learnt Japanese and got a job as a translator in the official Japanese news agency, Domei. Perhaps he was able to render some service to the British while he was working there, for at the end of the war he was given a priority passage on a troopship sailing for England, and after a term at the London School of Economics, which he hated, he moved to the more congenial surroundings of Fitzwilliam College, Cambridge in whose liberal atmosphere, his ideas broadened. There he read law, played golf, courted Kwa Geok Choo, by now a Queen's scholar at Girton, and joined the University Labour Club. Academically brilliant, he took a double first in law, and was called to the Bar. But his eyes were firmly set on a political career. 'The Japanese never knew what they did to a whole generation like me' was his comment. 'But they did make me, and a generation like me, determined to work for freedom from servitude and foreign domination. I did not enter politics. They brought politics to me.'

Back in Singapore, he first married Kwa Geok Choo (with an English-style wedding reception, he in a smart tuxedo and she in a white cheongsam) and with her then set up a legal practice — which his wife, herself holding a distinguished law degree, was quite qualified to run, as she soon showed. For him, the firm of Lee & Lee was to be the stepping stone to politics, the opening move in an adventure which he was to pursue with awesome single-mindedness. To keep in trim, he went on a strict diet, gave up both beer and his cherished pipes in favour of early morning press-ups and skipping, foreswore every sort of hobby, and worked around the clock. Intellectually superior to his contemporaries and a born orator, his unswerving object was to build Singapore into an independent power point in Asia, and in pursuit of this patriotic goal he was prepared to be as pragmatic as the logic of realpolitik necessitated.

Many were the problems to be faced as he embarked on his political course in 1950. For one, the Colonial Office's scheme for independence would probably make Malaya free but maintain Singapore as a British base. This could best be countered by merger with Malaya — hence his persistent slogan, 'independence through merger'. Trickier still was the tactical difficulty of winning communist support, without which he could never achieve what he wanted, yet at the same time avoid being swamped by the communists.

With a small group of personal associates, former students in England whom he had met at the Malayan Forum in London, he thrashed out his plans. If anti-colonialism was the chief issue that brought them together, along with vaguely socialist ideals of equality and justice bred from the nostrums of Harold Laski, they were all agreed on the need to rally the workers behind them. Here Lee's legal training helped. The unions needed a young barrister to justify their strike action, and this gave him the chance to catch the public eye. It also gained him the backing of student activists at the university who were supporting the strikers. By working incessantly in support of popular causes, Lee got his first boost as a leader — and became something of a nationalist hero with strong labour and student following, by the time Britain announced plans for a limited franchise election.

Now that Singapore was to have its first elected head of government, Lee and his friends realized that they needed a formal political platform. At first they toyed with the idea of joining an established party. But the only possible choice was David Marshall's Labour Front, and when negotiations for collaboration failed, they were obliged to go one better. They formed their own party, the People's Action Party.

Its electoral strategy, Lee decided, would be spectacularly leftist. Personally he was strongly suspicious of communists and fellow-travellers. But he kept this to himself. The PAP needed all the support it could drum up from leftists of all hues. Later Lee was to explain, 'Emotionally we felt more sympathetic to the communists who were sacrificing life and limb to get the British out than with the clowns and crooks who were in the open political arena'. For he knew only too well that anybody in Singapore who wanted to carry the Chinese-speaking community with him could not afford to be anti-communist. And so the PAP projected itself as a revolutionary party.

Though the PAP won only three seats in the assembly against the Labour Front's ten, Lee emerged from the 1955 election as the leading opposition member. David Marshall was simply no match for him in verbal battle, nor indeed for the British, who treated the new Chief Minister with almost open contempt and consistently frustrated his attempts to negotiate for a transfer of power. This gave Lee a double target for his oratory: the British for being obdurate, and Marshall for being ineffective. Though to be fair, Marshall — a liberal minded Anglophile and a man of considerable presence — did much to prepare the way for freedom, and come to that, for Lee Kuan Yew.

Yet if David Marshall ranted like a Shakespearean actor, the man who poured ridicule on him was undoubtedly a spell-binder. What's more, Lee's professed radicalism was no more than a ploy, for behind the scenes he was busy winning British confidence to ensure that the Colonial Office would consent to the PAP becoming the government of Singapore when the time was ripe. While publicly working hand-in-glove with the pro-communists, he was in fact urging the colonial authorities to clamp down on them. Faced with the Emergency in Malaya, the British were understandably sensitive about communism in Singapore, and Lee's assistance weighed.

It was here that Lee showed his skill as a politician. For the pro-communist elements that gave muscle to the PAP were in fact active leftist trades-unionists, with deep roots among the masses, and Lee's perennial preoccupation was to prevent control of the PAP from falling into their hands. Twice they came close to capturing the party, only to be thwarted by government action. Indeed repeated governmental intervention to ensure Lee's political survival confirmed the feeling that he had become Britain's chosen man for Singapore. And as the scent of power grew stronger, he began to change the PAP's image, highlighting its conservative respectability, while at the same time maintaining a public posture of identification with the communists. Talk of running with the hounds and the hares!

This masterful performance was aimed at the 1959 election, which Lee knew would be quite different from the earlier one that put David Marshall in the chief minister's chair. Under the new constitution Singapore was to have a hefty slice of self-government and its own prime minister. The reins of power were truly within reach.

The PAP headed a field of 14 contesting parties with so radical a platform that many western observers regarded Lee as a hard-line communist (though the British knew better). But when the PAP romped home with a landslide victory, Lee was faced with an unexpected snag: at the executive meeting to choose the prime minister, half the members voted in favour of Ong Eng Guan, the popular mayor of Singapore. It was only the chairman's casting vote that saved the day for Lee.

The new prime minister demonstrated his galvanic style from the start. On his first day in office orders went out that ministers and civil servants should be at their desks, in shirtsleeves, promptly by 8 a.m. Employers and workmen were threatened with imprisonment if they frustrated the government's policies for industrial peace. Newspapers were warned that they would be considered subversive if they published anything to sour relations between Singapore and Malaya. (The *Straits Times* promptly shifted its headquarters to Kuala Lumpur.) As a first step to create a more equal society, university lecturers and senior civil servants had their salaries cut. A virulent campaign was launched against corruption and 'yellow culture'; strip-tease shows, girlie magazines, and jukeboxes were banned. All sections of the community were given the same basic message: work for the good of Singapore. Cooperation was demanded as a proof of their patriotism.

Needless to say, these austere measures were not to everyone's taste, and on several occasions Lee was on the point of being toppled. If he won through, it was by playing one opponent against the other, often with the help of the British authorities. Commented Professor Northcote Parkinson, 'He has used the Federation of Malaya to counterbalance the Singapore trades unions. He has used the mob to intimidate the merchants and the merchants to influence the Colonial Office. He illustrates perpetually the principle that it is better to have two enemies than one.'

If Lee had kicked his goal from the left corner flag, he had known all along that a showdown with the communists was inevitable once he got into power. And indeed their disenchantment grew steadily after he became prime minister. The final break came over the question of merger with Malaya.

His aim of achieving independence for Singapore through a merger with the Federation of Malaya appealed to the British, who hoped to see the two territories fused into a single united nation. But the prospect of Singapore coming under the control of the anti-communist government in Kuala Lumpur was anathema to the leftists. Their goal was independence for a separate Singapore, in which they were confident that they would gain the upper hand. And this was precisely what alarmed Malaya's Tunku Abdul Rahman. Personally he would have preferred to keep the Federation clear of Singapore's turbulent politics. But he was even more anxious lest Singapore, upon achieving independence, should become what he called 'a second Cuba'.

For all these misgivings, a conference was called at which Singapore, Malaya and the North Borneo territories declared in favour of a merger. And predictably the signature of the pact between the Tunku and Lee had an immediate reaction in Singapore. The left wing of the PAP — the very men who had helped Lee climb to power — split away to form an opposition party, Barisan Sosialis, headed by the communist Lim Chin Siong, and took the greater part of the PAP membership with them. Yet once again skilful footwork enabled Lee to outmanoeuvre his opponents by calling for a referendum on the merger, and this was so cleverly worded that the people were simply asked, in effect, to endorse the Government's White Paper.

The Federation of Malaysia, scheduled to come into being on 31 August 1961, was in fact delayed for a fortnight in deference to the objections of Indonesia's President Sukarno, who condemned the Malaysia concept as a 'neo-colonialist plot'. Though a UN survey quickly confirmed the validity of the merger, Sukarno (hoping to unite the Malay world under Indonesian control) promptly declared a policy of armed confrontation with Malaysia, which continued until he was deposed in 1967.

But the merger soon ran into trouble of another description. As Lee strove to transform Singapore into the 'New York of Malaysia', his representatives in Kuala

Lumpur quickly showed signs of trying to dominate the Malaysian parliament. And increasingly the Malays found themselves at variance with Lee's aggressive tactics — above all his contention that no single one of the three major racial groups could claim to be more native to Malaysia than the others; in fact that the Chinese and Indian immigrants were on par with the indigenous Malays.

For their part the Singaporeans began to chafe at the strains and irritations of the merger, regarding the central government as all too conservative compared to progressive Singapore. Perhaps it was simply a clash of temperaments between the go-getting urban Chinese and the easy-going rural Malays that made the marriage so explosive. There was a good deal of mud-slinging on both sides: the Malay press accused Lee of trying to turn Singapore into another Israel and suppressing Moslems; Lee responded that Kuala Lumpur wanted to slow down the pace so that its 'medieval feudal society' could survive. 'If they think they can squat on a people, they have made the biggest mistake in their lives' he fulminated. But perhaps the sorest point was that Lee insisted on retaining his title of prime minister and acting the part.

Finally after two years of friction the Tunku had had enough. Playing a round of golf with Lee at the Royal Selangor Club he spoke plainly what was on his mind. 'There can only be one prime minister in a nation,' one can almost hear him saying as they strode down the fairway, 'and so the best course we can take is to allow you to be the prime minister of independent Singapore in the full sense of the word, which otherwise you would not.' Precisely, of course, what Lee wanted. Though when announcing the separation on TV, he openly wept. 'I don't know why Mr Lee acted like that' commented the Tunku. 'He seemed quite pleased about it.'

As indeed he had every reason to be. By a series of clever manipulations he had achieved his object; the Malaysian episode had yielded full independence.

On 9 August 1965 the Republic of Singapore was proclaimed as a member of the Commonwealth, and a month later she was admitted to the United Nations. Machiavelli, one feels, would have smiled with approval — and Raffles raised his hat.

Following:
Sir Thomas Shenton
Whitelegger Thomas: Governor
of the Straits Settlements in
Singapore till the Japanese
Occupation. (AOHD)

THE EMERG-
ENCE OF
LEE KUAN
YEW

241

◄ 17 ►

COLONIAL TWILIGHT

GOING, IF NOT GONE WAS THE voluptuous *pukka sahib* life: the impresarios of Empire, once as lofty and brittle as the deity, were departing to obscurity in Cheltenham or Hove. Going, too, was the old not-to-worry spirit of '*tak apa*', as cock-a-hoop young Singaporeans, flushed with independence and the lure of material success, swept the past under the nearest carpet. In this new climate, when all eyes were fixed firmly on the future, things that had once seemed so immutable proved remarkably vulnerable to change.

How then could the venerable old institutions survive? Raffles, for instance, the very symbol of colonial grandeur? True, the whole hotel had been refurbished after the war. Ceilings had been lowered, air-conditioning installed, and the gala opening of the new ballroom in 1948 had seemed to be tangible proof that Singapore was back to normal again. The old guard was determined that everything should be the same as it was before the Japanese invasion.

Through the years of the 'Emergency' in Malaya and the gathering of nationalist agitation, with its strikes and its riots, the illusion persisted. To be sure, Raffles was obliged to post security guards after a bomb had been found in the sub manager's office. But though the sight of road blocks outside became commonplace enough, the social graces thrived against a foreground of fashion shows, beauty parades, dancing competitions and fancy-dress balls. While Xavier Cugat's orchestra played in the Palm Court, people jumped into fountains in evening clothes, dowagers of Hanoverian queenliness exchanged felinities over coffee, planters and officers swapped tall tales about the fighting across the Causeway. As mannered as a Michael Arlen novel, Raffles was again a magnet for the rich and the powerful.

Perhaps their style was less extravagant. (Though when Prince Faisal of Saudi Arabia came in 1955, extra suites had to be improvised for his five day visit by knocking down some walls.) And the aristocracy of blood tended to be superseded by that of notoriety — movie stars, jet-setters, and itinerant politicians. Nevertheless the hotel register was again studded with celebrated names: Pandit Nehru of India, Emperor Haile Selassie of Ethiopia, Premier Sato of Japan, Pierre Trudeau of Canada, President Saragat of Italy, Prince Sihanouk of Cambodia, and even Sir Harold and Lady Wilson, to pick out just a few.

It was this romantic revival of the imperial twenties that stuck in the memory of present-day Singaporeans, and occasionally inhibited them from patronizing the hotel. Yet the irony is that the quintessential Britishness of Raffles was lovingly fostered first by its Armenian owners, and then by its Italian managers. In the early days, the Sarkieses had been synonymous with Raffles, and as the years passed, they called in fellow-Armenians to assist them. When Arshak Sarkies' extravagant generosity (along with his fondness for the Turf) finally led to bankruptcy in 1931, the hotel was taken over by a British syndicate. But it continued to be run until the Japanese occupation by an Armenian called Martyrose Sarkies Arathoon. And after the war he was succeeded by his assistant Guido Cevenini, a professional hotelier from Bologna, who inaugurated Raffles' long-standing 'Italian connection'. Following Cevenini came Mario Marchesi, and finally Roberto Pregarz.

In the fifties, the powerful Oversea Chinese Banking Corporation, with Tan Chin Tuan at the helm, bought control of Raffles. This was surely an act of faith, for like a great edifice whose foundations have been destroyed by an earthquake, the British Empire was toppling. The curtain was ringing down on the 'unending romance of our dominions'. And when independence came to Singapore, a new identity had to be found in a rapidly changing world, Raffles was to compete with the flashy glass and concrete hotels that were springing up at every corner. There was even talk of rebuilding the hotel on a site adjoining the Singapore Swimming Club.

In the end it was Roberto Pregarz, with his Italian flair for history, who turned Raffles' age into its greatest asset. Disregarding the nostrums of cost-accountancy, he restored the original high ceilings with their fans, uncovered the old ceramic tiles in the Tiffin Room, and brought back the elegant Edwardian strains of the Palm Court orchestra. He saw that it was in the hotel's past that its future lay. And in recreating the by-gone atmosphere he was seconded by his Singaporean wife Helena, who covered the walls with sketches, decoupages and tapestries on themes from Raffles' history.

Much of the place's mystique, of course, was contributed by the staff, whose long service at Raffles was a by-word — for example, a batch of employees retired recently with an average of 36 years' service, one of them having spent 51 years in his job. At the same, it cannot be denied that subversive influences could sway even such firm loyalty from time to time. In the fifties, like most labour in Singapore, the staff of Raffles was caught up in the general mood of disaffection and staged several strikes, leaving volunteers, airline hostesses and sporting-minded guests to keep the hotel running as best they could. Worse still, influenced in the sixties by the radical trades union secretary Puthucheary, the staff indulged in insidious 'work to rule' tactics, such as lunch breaks that lasted for three hours or more, which hardly improved the culinary standards.

For all this, the traditions continued from father to son. Ngiams have tended the Long Bar ever since Ngiam Tong Boon invented the Singapore Sling in 1915, along with the 'Million Dollar' cocktail (gin, vermouth, egg white, pineapple juice and bitters) mentioned in Somerset Maugham's story, *The Letter*. Few visitors have failed to sample Ngiam's heady concoctions, though not even the legendary Callenfels can have matched the feat of five guests in 1977 who downed 131 Singapore Slings in less than two hours — an average of 26 each. 'I don't know how they did it' commented Roberto Pregarz, after watching the performance. 'You are liable to feel giddy after just two.'

Recently, during the shooting of the TV film series *Hawaii-Five-O*, Robert Ngiam delighted the company by producing a variation of the Singapore Sling: he substituted vodka for gin and called it the Hawaii-Five-O, perhaps in answer to the lethal One-Five-Oh! (rum, dry vermouth, vodka, yellow chartreuse, bitters, lime and ginger ale) created by Foo Peng Chian in the Writers' Bar to celebrate Singapore's 150th anniversary in 1969.

While Raffles moved towards this signal date with aplomb, there were others who viewed the social scene with misgivings. When he came to Singapore as a university lecturer at the height of the 'Emergency', Patrick Anderson confessed himself haunted by a sense of unease: not just because there might be a communist gunman around, or that taxis and buses were burnt, identity cards stolen, and hand-grenades thrown into bars (one was thrown at the Governor, bounced off his thigh, and turned out be a dud) but rather, he felt, that 'You always seem to come up against the same things: beauty and unreality.' Beauty constantly jolted one into delighted surprise. In the Botanical Gardens, the adjectives that sprung to his mind were 'charming', 'lyrical' — Shakespearean in fact. 'They belonged to the Forest of Arden, Prospero's Island and Twelfth Night. But it is always a piecemeal affair of hints, contrasts, sparks struck out as the wheels of commerce and vulgarity grind together.'

A percipient view. For Singapore in those twilight days of empire was a city where no one quite belonged, no culture was quite indigenous. There was an interplay of different cultures between the Chinese, Malays, Indians and Eurasians, many of whom had subdivisions of their own. After all, a Hokkien was not the same as a Cantonese; a Hainanese did not think in the same way as a person from Swatow. And all spoke different dialects. It was a bit disconcerting. 'The mauve and white garlands of squid festooned across the front of a wayside eating place; the fresh wet banana leaf plates at a Brahmin restaurant, dotted with yellow and ochre curries you must eat with your fingers; the excitingly garish costumes of the Malay girls, with their marmalade-coloured batik sarongs, red or electric blue chenille scarves, plastic hair ornaments, high-heeled shoes, thick chalk-white rice powder — all these do not fit together to form a picture.'

Against such a background, the Europeans seemed no more than photographs, isolated and ephemeral — a present tense which slipped back quietly to the past. There was a certain flatness about them, a certain dowdiness, together with a few privileged eccentricities. And there was a sameness about their daily rounds. 'Morning coffee in the Cold Storage or the GH café in Raffles Place, archery or swimming or badminton when the air begins to cool very slightly, followed by the Cinema, bridge or amateur theatricals at night, with now and then dancing at Prince's or the Capital Blue Room or Raffles Hotel as a treat.'

In short the pleasant but enervating colonial round, which was already becoming a period piece (though you still come across it in some expatriate groups) when Sir Malcolm Macdonald, as High Commissioner for South East Asia, voiced his distaste for outworn conventions by refusing to join the exclusive white Tanglin Club, and indeed keeping out of Raffles as much as he could. It was he who first staged a revolt against the tyranny of formal dress, and scandalized the Colony by proposing the royal toast wearing just trousers and a shirt. The thin edge of the wedge! Yet he could not really be faulted, for when David Marshall invited Malaya's leader, Tunku Abdul Rahman, to lunch at Raffles on the occasion of his 1955 election victory, the Tunku and his entourage turned up in batik shirts, which is formal dress in Malaysia. But as time wore on the stiff British style gave way to casual local clothes, though it was not until after independence that jeans and T-shirts took over or that women discarded tight skirts and cheongsams for catsuits and pantsuits.

Now, I am told, some nostalgic glances are straying back to the days when convention decreed sophisticated sheaths for women and a Deanna Durbin look for the girls. Very fetching the young things were, too, as they swept through the tennis club and tangoed at Raffles or the Seaview Hotel, skirts held like bells by stiff petticoats; while their mums struggled, with the help of a corset and a prayer, into skin-tight evening gowns, all satin and sequins and fish-tail trains. It was still the era of the hour-glass figure, of bosoms sustained by wired-up brassieres, of dress-makers with pins and pert little hat shops in High Street and North Bridge Road; of chic twin sets from Robinsons and Whiteaways in Raffles Place, and helpful seamstresses who would knock up a cotton frock at home for ten dollars or less.

Boutiques, like levis and bikinis, were still hardly known. But among the Chinese there was a vogue for lacy kebayas worn over a batik sarong as an alternative to the high-collared cheongsams with side-slits through which, all too often, fleshy thighs would bulge embarrassingly as a matron sat down. In the fifties the high priestess of fashion was the redoubtable Doris Geddes, who held court in her salon under the arcades at Raffles Hotel, where the Tiger Tavern is today. Betty Khoo was then a small girl in a polka-dot frock with a bow at the back. But she remembers the time that Elizabeth Taylor ordered an evening dress when staying at Raffles. Alas, in the middle of a function that was being given in her honour, the gown fell to bits. 'The glitterati gasped, not so much at the exposure of Liz' great body, but the talons-unsheathed confrontation between fiery Liz and the fearsome Doris Geddes,' relates Miss Khoo. 'Liz had reportedly shrieked at Doris' shoddy workmanship — the gown had come apart at the seams. Doris, in turn, had screeched that Liz was too fat and had insisted on getting into a gown obviously too small for her. Those were the days!'

Were they really? The city was still only a fraction of the size it is today. Orchard Road, for instance, was then a hybrid thoroughfare, half European and half Chinese, lined with arcaded shophouses and highly coloured night-spots, before petering away amongst steaming foliage and nursery gardens. Opinions vary as to whether it got its name from a Mr Orchard who owned a small fruit estate at the corner of Scotts Road, or simply because the original towpath led through orchards and nutmeg plantations.

Today gleaming hotels, shopping complexes, and fast-food joints have replaced Mr Orchard's chiku trees, but up to twenty-five years ago this hedonistic strip was a mere country lane compared to what it is now. Big colonial style houses with verandahs and sumptuously kept lawns were perched up on the slopes behind, and under the magnolia bushes were colourful little shops displaying mountains of oranges and apples. Oldtimers think back affectionately to Ban Chuan's coffee shop, with its curry puffs and its sailor-bar ambience; Terry Tan says that the only other places to go in that part of town were the Princes Garni (where old-world elegance eventually succumbed to the tawdry Pink Pussycat) and the Rosee d'Or 'whose bill of fare, when the word disco wasn't even a twinkle in Rod Stewart's eye, invariably included Ahmad Daud, the crooner of the day; Rahim Hamid, Singapore's Nat King Cole; Ruby Wah of the 18-inch waist and tinkling voice, and Kartina Dahari.' You could have a night out, says Mr Tan, without the frenzy of gyrating on a postage stamp floor. And if the most upbeat tempo was when the band struck up El Cumbanchero or Tico Tico, the lavish cabaret shows at the Singapura Forum, then the only smart hotel in the area, competed sonorously with those of the Tropicana in nearby Scotts Road.

Ten cents bought a cup of coffee in one of then numerous little coffeeshops, while from the Cosy Corner restaurant (four-course luncheon: 2½ dollars) you could watch tiny yellow Ford Prefect taxis nose their way through clusters of Morris Minors and Hillman Minxes. Yamahas and even Lambrettas were still way over the horizon: the ambition of the young was to own a very beautiful bicycle, festooned with red and blue cables, a velvet saddle cover with long fringes, and polished until its spokes sparkled. Chinatown boys, dressed to kill in transparent Manila shirts and curry-puff hair styles, swished around town on these shiny mounts catching the eyes of the girls. Few then were the young men who could take their dates to a mangrove swamp on a 500cc Norton, or even drive up to the cabaret in a car: for Chinese women still got a kick to be seen riding around in a *foong cher*, or 'wind carriage', perhaps unaware until too late that their escorts regarded the automobile as a potential garconière on wheels.

Thirty years ago Singapore was more permissive, its people more promiscuous than they are today. It was not just that the rumbustious allure of transatlantic manners, the coca-cola culture as Europeans disparagingly called it, was eroding the traditional Asian reticences. Dancing cheek-to-cheek had been accepted as a social grace, so that many Chinese girls, who would have been outraged had a man tried to embrace them in public, cuddled tightly to their partners once the music struck up. In the rubber boom that followed the Korean war, a crop of semi-private night clubs whose chief object was to keep the owners well supplied with mistresses mushroomed up. By paying artistes more than they were worth, they hoped to ensnare them. The city was soon filled with gold-diggers who could hardly sing a note and who, for their part, were simply interested in what they called *tiok choi thow* — 'cutting the old vegetable's head'.

But above all the mahjong parlours became hunting grounds for affluent playboys (the very term, like *fils-à-papa*, has a period ring about it) in search of more satisfying prey than *phei-phar-chais* and taxi-girls. Certainly plenty of cash was required, for it was necessary to match dollar for dollar the not inconsiderable funds of the wives, mistresses, and daughters of rich men who were playing against them. But the time might come when the lady's cash ran out, and then the creditor could settle for something else. Likewise these parlours were places where women could find themselves a *bel-ami*. Sit Yin Fong describes how elderly mahjong-playing crones, known as *Mou Ch'at Thin* after a lascivious Chinese Empress, could be seen being massaged and fanned by young gigolos — who in this way could afford to keep a girl or two of their own on the side.

The revenue from mahjong enabled these clubs to be garishly plush. It was quite usual for players to dine and drink on the house, and often big deals were concluded over the cards. Sometimes, too, the play turned crooked. A casual code-word introduced into the conversation, or a discreet gesture, gave professional accomplices the information they needed to clinch the game. But even without cheating, mahjong masters had the skill to rake in the chips. Indeed so cunning was their manoeuvering of the cards, so tense was the action when the stakes were high, that it was not unknown for a player to die of heart failure.

To complete the squalid picture, there were the red-light districts. If Lavender Street was still a magnet for European servicemen, they were well advised to give Desker Road a miss, for this stinking back alley, where women were lined up like cattle and could be had for the price of three beers, was strictly for Asians. Equally notorious were the alleys around Sago Lane, which were known as the '$5.60 area' because of the fixed going rate: in fact anyone who innocently mentioned this figure when shopping in Chinatown would be greeted with an immediate guffaw.

Yet these degraded parts of the city which once gave it such a vicious reputation were only a stone's throw away from the cornerstone of colonial respectability. Even in the fifties it was difficult, amid such solid surroundings, to realise that time was running out for the old order of things. But before ringing down the curtain on the Raj, let us join Donald Moore at Raffles Place on a Saturday morning, even if it is so crowded with women shoppers that the only place for a mere male to escape is down the dark and gloomy steps of the ornamental lavatory.

'I don't know what Raffles would think if he were to see his Commercial Square today' mutters Mr Moore from this unlovely viewpoint. 'It used to be a serene and shady open space where merchants used to transact their business with a leisure appropriate today to governmental committees. But now the memsahibs have turned it into the busiest shopping centre east of Suez.

'There are fat mems and thin mems: mems with enormous bottoms and rolling shoulders; mems looking quite dreadful in the latest urchin cut; mems towing roaring children; smart mems who have either never had any children or who are rich enough to leave them at home to run wild with their amahs; the considerably less affluent looking mems of serving soldiers; smiling mems and dour mems; mems making a success of looking what they are not and others making a hopeless failure of it: mems who have come to buy the week's groceries and those who have come to squander money on anything that takes their fancy; bombastic mems, intelligent mems, thoughtless mems, bridge-playing, mahjong-playing useless mems; hard-working mems; hard-drinking non-conceiving mems; brittle, common mems; shop-assistant-bullying mems; mems who in five years have never been into Chinatown; mems with three servants and to whom the novelty of the situation has never quite faded; missionary mems, both dismal and jolly; American mems hiding behind Max Factor; Chinese mems displaying fat thighs; other Chinese mems displaying most shapely ones; Indian mems with bared midriffs and dazzling saris; property-owning Jewish mems; chic French mems and stolid Dutch mems.... Yes, Saturday is mems' day in Raffles Place. They hold a unique position in the Empire. It would be probably die if they left.'

Maybe Mr Moore is right in his tongue-in-cheek chauvinist way: maybe it was indeed the mems who sustained the Empire during its period of menopause, when ironically England still ruled a people who were realizing their potential. Yet in the end England kept faith to Malaya and Singapore, winning the virulent longdrawn-out war against the communists, so unaptly called the 'Emergency', before handing over her trust.

Britain left a legacy of fine buildings and world-wide trade, of goodwill and sweet-sour memories. What Singapore did with this legacy will be seen in the following pages.

Following:
Commercial buildings in the
business district of Singapore
tower above the quaint old
shophouses of Chinatown.
Urban renewal has caught up
with the Chinese precinct and
blocks of these tenements have
been bulldozed, residents
having been rehoused in
modern apartments and shops
moved to a centralized
complex.

◄ 18 ►

AN ISLAND STATE COMES OF AGE

A SINGAPOREAN BUSINESSMAN took his English friend to the revolving restaurant at the 'Top of the M'. As a youngster he had resented the British assumption that his country was not yet capable of looking after its own affairs, and he was now proud to show off the sights.

Gazing at the slowly rotating panorama of skyscrapers, the Englishman remarked that Singapore had been fortunate to take over such a remarkable infrastructure. Not a bit of it, he was told, practically everything they could see had been constructed since Independence.

'You mean to tell me that all this has been built in the last twenty years?' exclaimed the Englishman. 'How on earth was it done?'

'That's very simple to explain' smiled the Singaporean. 'The British left.'

Certainly a resident from the Somerset Maugham days would scarcely recognize the island if he returned in the eighties. After the initial surprise of landing at Changi and bowling down the park-lined expressway, the visual impact of the skyline first glimpsed from the soaring multi-curved bridge that snakes over the harbour would make him catch his breath.

Twenty-five years ago, the tallest structure in town had been the Asia building, some seventeen floors in all. Shenton Way, although already planned, was still full of scrubby patches picked over by goats, and stolid colonial-style buildings formed the bulk of the business centre.

Now a galaxy of skyscrapers lines the waterfront, and high-rises point heavenwards for as far as the eye can discern. The stately old Raffles Institution has given place to a billion-dollar complex, embodying among other things a 71-storey hotel (the world's tallest, it is said) and a swanky new marina rises toweringly from the surf where the old-timers used to bathe. Orchard Road now rivals the Ginza; Chinatown has changed, and the bumboats have been banished from their immemorial dwelling place on the river, which is destined to become a beauty spot and the hub of a mass rapid transport system running under the centre of the city. Only the Padang and Raffles Hotel remain cosily familiar, as our returning friend sips a nostalgic gin-sling in the calm of the Palm Court.

Presently he will realize, for all this, that the spectacular skyline is only a frontispiece to the dynamics of change which have transformed practically every yard of the island, and even increased its size by nearly a tenth through reclaiming land from the sea. He will find that the swamps of Jurong have been converted into Southeast Asia's most ambitious industrial project, with over 800 factories employing 100,000 workers; that the harbour has grown into the second busiest in the world, handling more tonnage than either London or New York; that without a drop of crude to call its own, Singapore has become the third largest oil refiner. And, equally surprising, that it is developing into one of the chief financial centres — a pivotal point in the melodrama of money.

As a result of all this, the gross national product now exceeds that of either India or China. Singaporeans enjoy the panacea of western-style prosperity: high employment, low inflation, excellent health, crime-free streets, an environment of helvetic cleanliness, and a standard of living surpassed in the Orient only by Japan.

How has this happened? Though Raffles set Singapore on the right course by insisting on the concept of free trade, never in his wildest dreams could he have forseen how conclusively his city would prove that economic development could flourish in the tropics. And just as Sir Stamford set his imprint on Singapore for nearly a century and a half, so the modern city state which has arisen with Phoenix-like verve in the last two decades bears irrevocably the signature of Lee Kuan Yew.

Historians dislike the idea that a single man alters history. They prefer the notion that events happen piecemeal, through incremental software integers, suffixions and adjunctives, to use current jargon. Yet in this case the Columbus concept is apt. Had it not been for Lee Kuan Yew, Singapore would have developed as a regional entrepôt while remaining a provincial metropolis along the lines of Penang, ethnically its twin. The concept of a global city is his. And so great has been his charisma, so ruthless his energy, so skillful his blend of Chinese principles and nuclear-age technology, that in a short space of time he has turned Asia's smallest nation into a mini-superpower.

More than anything else, Singapore's meteoric rise can be attributed to his personal style of government. Once it had achieved a shaky independence, Lee rallied the people to a seemingly impossible task. They must go it alone, he told them, a tiny nation beset by enemies, devoid of natural resources, a hostage to fate. For a start he shattered all serious opposition by jailing his former communist supporters. Next he broke the power of the labour unions by giving employers the power to hire and fire at will — and won around the workers with a passionate appeal for patriotism and the Chinese work ethic.

Of course there was criticism, mainly by envious outsiders. The communists portrayed him as dictatorial, capricious, wicked and vicious. The Dutch Labour Party accused him of systemically violating civil liberties. And *The Times* (who should have known better) asked what one was to make of a government that in the name of fending off a communist threat 'uses methods that are precisely common to most communist countries'. But these charges ignored the problems with which he was faced.

Lee countered his critics with the argument that emerging countries must sacrifice certain liberties for the sake of development, and in Singápore's case to prevent communist oppression. To the people of Southeast Asia, who knew what it meant, communism was neither a joke nor a public relations exercise among politicians. 'It is a very serious business with guns, subversion and terrorism and, finally, large-scale forces to overwhelm government troops and take over by force.'

Nor could other more insidious means by which they strive to achieve their aims be discounted. Antonio Gramsci, the Italian marxist theoritician, postulated that communists should seek to overthrow democratic governments by taking over the 'hegemonic apparatuses' — that is, the universities, schools, churches, trades unions, bureaucracies, publishing houses and the media in general, and thus gradually separate 'civil society' from the ruling class. Government, argued Gramsci, would then fall into marxist hands like a ripe fruit.

If this war of position is being waged throughout the western world, Lee has no intention that it should bedevil Singapore. He sees the free world becoming weaker idealogically, and worries about the effect this will have on non-marxist developing countries. At the 100th anniversary of the Hong Kong Bank in Singapore he expressed his concern at the drift. 'Politics and economics are not separable', he affirmed. 'Between Adam Smith and John Maynard Keynes, Marx and Lenin changed the geopolitical balance of Europe. Between Keynes and Milton Friedman, Stalin, Mao and Ho Chi Minh changed the geopolitical balance of the world... We are engaged in a test of stamina between the communist and the competitive non-communist systems.'

Lee's solution goes back to the Confucian philosophy that good government should be based on virtue and should operate for the benefit of the people. 'Our people started off with a very low base line. They were poor and hungry. They had the Confucian work ethic, plus the drive of migrants from India and Malaysia who wanted to lead a better life. To get a better life they had to learn to use their brains and their hands: there was no oil or uranium to be found.'

Mollycoddling was a luxury that a young state, thrusting and aglow, could simply not afford. The British had conceived a welfare state to care for people from cradle to grave, from womb to tomb. But unfortunately it had failed to lead to a society where all men and women are equal in health and opportunities. Instead they were locked in bitter class conflicts. 'They, the British, who taught us that excellence should be rewarded and honoured in order that all can benefit from the exceptional talents of the few, have now ended up by punishing the talented few to satisfy the doctrinal follies of the even fewer.'

Strong words from a socialist! But Lee foresaw that Singapore needed practical solutions to its problems, which were basically Southeast Asian ones. His philosophy of government was based on the premise that rewards should be correlated to work, and must correspond to the contribution each person made to the national well-being. 'More and more pay for less and less work must lead to greater and greater borrowing and eventual bankruptcy' he once declared. 'Our immediate task is to build up a society in which man will be rewarded not according to the property he owns, but according to his active contribution to society in physical or mental labour.'

Enlarging on the theme, he added: 'We stand for a social revolution aimed at eventually putting the economic power of the State into the hands of the people as a whole. But this does not necessarily mean public ownership. More important than owning economic power is the direction, planning and control of this power in the people's interest.'

To the acquisitive Singaporeans, always more inclined to make a fortune than to share it, Lee's pragmatic mixture of socialism and private enterprise had an obvious appeal. And his government intended to make full use of their entrepreneurial skills. 'The aim of a socialist government is economic growth with a minimum of social injustice. Private enterprise is a powerful instrument of economic growth' commented Dr Goh Keng Swee, the Deputy Prime Minister. What is more, there was no intention of making a break with the past. As a British colony Singapore had grown into the greatest entrepôt of the area, while providing the impetus that developed the tin mines and rubber estates of Malaya and Sumatra. This experience was an asset which the government wisely retained and enlarged, however tempting it might have been politically to get rid of institutions and practices that had colonial associations. 'Had we done so,' says Dr Goh, 'we could have thrown away a priceless advantage for the sake of empty rhetoric.'

Instead, they turned the biggest warehouse in Asia into Southeast Asia's biggest workshop, creating some 30 billion dollars of new wealth in the process, and jobs to go with it.

Behind this success story is a man whose dedication is total, whose integrity is absolute, whose intelligence is almost frightening. Sir Geoffrey Arthur, the Master of Pembroke, Oxford, once told me that of all the world leaders he had met during his years as a diplomat, intellectually Lee Kuan Yew was incomparably the most impressive. And though his power is supreme, it has not corrupted; scandal has never touched him. In an Asia where venality is the norm, neither he nor his ministers have ever been suspected of corruption in any shape or form. (A junior minister who once accepted a free airticket was promptly jailed.)

His life is ascetic. He neither smokes nor drinks, and eats very little. He has a mania for cleanliness and fusses over his health. He works eighteen hours a day in a modest air-conditioned office in the old Government House where the temperature is kept at a constant 72°. He used to play golf, carefully studying each stroke.* But he has now given that up as too time-consuming, in favour of a daily bout of jogging in the Istana grounds.

He is not a dictator, whatever some people in the West may think. His rule can best be described as benevolent paternalism. He conducts affairs in mandarin style, projecting a sense of machismo and inspiring the team. In Europe or the United States, he would never get away with such an omniscient posture, such singleminded drive. But in Asia people like to revere their leader; they want it so. They accept the Confucian idea that those in authority have the mandate from heaven and must be obeyed. Even at a mundane business level, employees expect words of wisdom from the boss. And so Singaporeans applaud Lee's tough measures, his iron fist in the velvet glove. The whole country looks to him for guidance.

He believes in realism, commonsense, and a system of priorities that are fed into government like a programme into a computer.

First came the Economy, since the country had to live. Experts were brought in from abroad — notably Dr Albert Winsemius, who became economic adviser for 24 years — and they counselled a policy of industrialization. So an autonomous Economic Development Board was established, and with Japanese technical assistance, bulldozers began levelling hectares of swampland and barren hills at Jurong, west of the city. Millions of dollars were spent building roads, laying out factory sites, expanding power and water supplies. Foreign investment was encouraged by generous taxation reliefs, along with the inducement of a compliant labour force uninhibited by western-style union practices, and willing to work 44 hours a week. At the same time the workers were offered up-to-date housing in an unmatched environment, for the factories were grouped around a park that includes not only a golf course and an open-air cinema, but one of the loveliest Japanese gardens outside Japan, an equally beautiful Chinese garden, and the largest bird sanctuary in the world, planned by the London Zoological Society (which, incidentally, was founded by Stamford Raffles.) To the visitor, Jurong appears to be more of a tourist 'paradise' than an industrial area producing everything from steel tubes and tyres to plywood and ceramics. There are car assembly plants, shipbuilding yards, oil

* His handicap was nine at one time, even eight.

refineries, and a supply terminal for Southeast Asia's offshore oil exploration. This is the new Singapore style, exemplified by Singapore Airlines, who boasts 'the most modern fleet in all the world' and whose standards are the envy of other carriers.

It is no miracle, insists Dr Winsemius, but simply hard-headed policy. The government had the courage to realize that it could not pursue an effective economic and social policy without creating a highly efficient economic system. That meant switching from its former theoretical left-wing attitudes to those of capitalist enterprise. 'Had that major decision not been taken,' he says, 'Singapore would have been in the same situation as many other countries — spend first, and then see whether the money can be earned. Singapore's policy has been socialism that is very pragmatic but extremely effective.' Since 1965 it has had on average the highest growth rate in the world with the exception of one or two oil countries. 'A most amazing performance. You could probably split it into two or three parts. First, achieve full employment. Second, spread it to all branches of activity. Since agriculture was out, concentrate on tourism, trade and finance. And thirdly upgrade the whole line with a reorganization to international services.'

Following economic development, Lee's next priority was the social policy, which was in fact interrelated. And here the most visible accomplishment is public housing. Like tropical vegetation, tower blocks sprouted up in communal centres all over the island. From building 10,000 units in 1965, the volume increased to 30,000 in 1976 and reached 40,000 units in 1983, which works out to slightly more than a new flat every four working minutes. The Housing Development Board's programme is auto-financing: contracts are put out to tender and paid for by the Central Provident Fund, which recuperates its outlay by selling off the flats. And purchasers are allowed to subscribe from their accumulated funds in the CPF, thus becoming property-owning citizens with a stake in the country.

'It's quite simple' says John Hill, Chief Executive of the Hong Kong Bank. 'The government takes 46% of workers' salaries — 23% deducted from pay at source by the employer, plus 23% contributed by the employer — which is credited to the individual's Provident Fund, to be withdrawn on retirement. This represents an enormous sum which can be employed for the benefit of the State. On the basis of a workforce totalling more than 1,000,000 people each with an average monthly wage of $650, it amounts to an annual figure of more than $3,500 million — and this quite apart from revenue derived from tax!

'During recent years when many countries were facing a recession, Singapore has managed to maintain full employment,' he adds. 'Admittedly questions have been asked: Who will occupy the additional 15,000 hotel rooms that are being built? Where are the tenants to lease the planned increase of 10,000,000 sq ft in commercial office space? It is difficult to see tourism expanding much over the next five years. However, this construction boom is providing the fuel for today's economy, plus the infrastructure to meet the challenges of the next two decades and beyond. One has only to look at the economic and political difficulties being faced in other Asian centres to see the justification for Singapore's development plan; and perhaps the greatest achievement of all, is to do this without incurring any international debt.'

Three-quarters of the population now live in huge blocks of flats which, to our friend who has returned after a long absence, will probably be the most surprising change of all. Soulless though these 'vertical prisons' (as Noel Barber unkindly calls them) may at first appear, there is no alternative in a country so strapped for land, and they are certainly a huge step forward in material terms from the old slum dwellings where whole families once packed into a single tiny room. Even so, people often miss the friendly bustle of Chinatown, and find it an emotional strain to be cooped up on the twentieth floor with a clutch of children to look after. But in an attempt to recreate a communal feeling, the planners have grouped these machines for living into housing estates, each with its own shops, food stalls, laundries, recreation facilities and assembly rooms within the radius of a few yards. Kids can play together, and families often find it easier and cheaper to nip downstairs for a meal than to cook and wash up themselves. In any case, television spelt an end to village life, not just in Singapore.

In education the improving instinct pursued new fields of action. The old British system was modified — after some initial experiments with American 'playway' methods — into a policy of streaming children from as early as eight years old into monolingual, bilingual and 'express' grades for the brighter ones. Examinations taken at the age of twelve now determine which secondary school a child will attend, ranging from vocational institutions for those with low marks to 'Special Assistance Plan Schools' to which only the top 10% are admitted. Entrance to university depends on Senior Cambridge 'A' levels. On an average 75% of candidates pass their primary examinations into secondary schools, and 65% from secondary schools into university. Education, unlike voting in the elections, is not compulsary. You can drop out if you wish (and perhaps become a millionaire by your own initiative) or try to join the Establishment (if your memory in the examination room is good.)

Likewise the health services have been expanded from the old British system. The hospitals at Changi and Outram Road were taken over by the government, but private hospitals such as the Mount Alvernia and Youngberg Memorial continue to function. Until now the health service was not free, except for government employees, but charged about a quarter of private GP rates. However a new Medicare system has just been inaugurated, whereby 6% of CPF contributions are deducted for national health — which, some people grumble, means that you have to pay whether you are sick or not. But now there will be no charges, at least so long as the computer says that your contributions cover the cost of the treatment. And undoubtedly Singapore offers the most sophisticated medical standards in Southeast Asia — including such things as kidney transplants.

In the early days of independence, Singapore was protected by the British bases. But in January 1968 the British somewhat unsportingly decided to withdraw, leaving its Commonwealth partner to fend for itself. The Singapore deterrent then comprised 2000 men with 1000 rifles, a left-over from the Volunteer Corps founded in 1854. Five hundred miles away the Vietnam war was being waged; nearer at home the Indonesians were making unfriendly noises.

So defence became the next urgent priority. Initially the government aimed at organizing a force that, though small, would be sufficiently powerful to deter potential attackers and give Singapore sufficient time to galvanize world opinion against the aggressor.

Headed by various Members of Parliament, there was a rush to sign up in the People's Defence Force, and at the same time a National Service Act came into being. All young men aged 18 were conscripted for a period of 2-2½ years, and a professional army was created from scratch. A decade later it comprised an armoured brigade; four artillery, three engineer, one signal, and nine infantry battalions. The Navy, based at

Pulau Brani, an island to the south, consisted of two patrolboat squadrons mounting Israeli 'Gabriel' missiles, 6 Vospor-Thorneycroft patrolcraft, 2 mine-sweepers, and 4 former USA LSTs. The SAF had a complement of 97 combat aircraft, mainly Hunter FGA/FR-74s, A-4S Skyhawks, and BAC-167Ss, along with 7 Alouette helicopters.

In the last few years these figures have increased dramatically both in numbers and sophistication. The armed forces now comprise 50,000 men in active service — national servicemen and regulars — along with 200,000 reservists, which means that 10% of the entire population can be mobilized in just 17 hours. The armed forces train in Brunei, New Zealand, and Malaysia, and plane spotters regularly catch sight of the SAF's aircraft engaged in manoeuvres.

No one seriously believes that there are any aggressive designs on Singapore. But the young republic believes in being prepared for all eventualities, to show that it is determined to defend its burgeoning way of life, and underwrite the massive foreign investment in the island. Given such overriding preoccupations, it is not surprising that culture enjoyed a rather low priority on the government's agenda. Even at the National University of Singapore, built five years ago in a stunning location on Kent Ridge overlooking the sea, the thrust was directed towards technology and economics. There was a discernible sensation that in a trading community, aesthetics were less relevant than tourist promotion. After all, you could hire musicians and artists from abroad if needs be. But recently an awareness has crept in that after the flat, the car and the TV set, should come a modicum of culture. About four years ago, the computer was programmed for the arts.

The first significant move was the formation of the Singapore Symphony Orchestra, sponsored by various business corporations. Choo Huey was recalled from Greece to conduct weekly concerts at Victoria Concert Hall, and from time to time in factory premises. Seow Yit Kin, a protegé of Yehudi Menuhin, returned to give piano recitals, and the choreographer Goh Choo San has brought over the Washington Ballet for performances. Biannual Arts Festivals are now held featuring local drama, music, dances and paintings. At the Festival of Dance, performances range from ballet and jazz to traditional dances; the Drama Festival stages different ethnic productions acted by groups of amateurs in Malay, Chinese, Indian and English. Last year's repertoire included a version of Gay's *Threepenny Opera*, reinterpreted by Max Leblond, a local lecturer, and Robert Yeo, a local poet; a scenario in Baba Malay is currently being rehearsed.

Among writers, women set the pace. Toh Paik Choo's humorous collection of market patois entitled *Eh, Goondu!* sold 3000 copies in a week; Catherine Lim, best known for her short stories set in a local context has just published *The Serpent's Tooth*, a novel dealing with human relationships; Shan Kwan Mei has made her mark as an illustrator of childrens' books with the 'Moongate' series; Jacintha Abisheganaden, a talented singer and writer who has cut a record for WEA, has bravely chosen to write a full length novel on the pop scene in the sixties. Nevertheless Alex Josey, who once handled Lee Kuan Yew's press relations, remains the dominant figure with his many books on Singapore and eclectic volumes of personal opinion.

On a more mundane level, the environment has been improved by planting millions of trees and flowering shrubs, so that for all the new concrete, Singapore remains a garden city, with an astonishing amount of greenery bursting out wherever you look. It is kept clean by tough regulations which impose fines of up to 500 dollars for dropping cigarette ends on the street, or spitting in drains. The traffic is kept flowing like a military parade, and jay-walkers risk a fine if they do not use the pedestrian crossings. There are zoning restrictions on cars at peak periods, and a unique pre-paid ticketing scheme for parking.

Lee's toughness spills over into many social areas. Singapore hangs murderers, kidnappers, illegal possessors of arms, and drug pushers, and flogs those convicted for crimes of violence as cruelly as 18th century Britain ever did, often scarring them for life. Punishment, it believes, should prevent the crime, and while many people deplore the need for such institutionalized brutality, they point to their crime-free streets and question why the West is so soft-hearted with criminals. There is no teenage mugging in Singapore.

Prompted by a barrage of slogans on the airwaves and public walls, Singaporeans are exhorted to keep their city clean, make courtesy a way of life, cut down on smoking, and stop chewing gum 'like a cow'. Rich and poor alike live obediently under an all-pervasive bureaucracy that monitors everything from the size of their families to the length of their hair, frowns on pre-marital sex and confiscates soft porn — even *Playboy* and *Cosmopolitan* do not escape the net.

Can it be that a Victorian sense of morality lurks behind Singapore's momentum into the 21st century? Well, not Victorian, (which is a chauvinistic concept) so much as a Confucian scale of values. This is Asia, after all. 'Confucianism teaches that respectful children make obedient citizens' is the Prime Minister's attitude. 'A serene and orderly world in which the Mandarins were stern but benevolent fathers who earned the loyalty and obedience of their citizen children.'

An Olympian posture to be sure, yet in human terms these Confucian ideals have been translated into a remarkable level of public comfort. 'Singapore does provide its people with a decent and very agreeable existence' comments Professor J. K. Galbraith. He attributes much of this to the excellent ethnic mixture. 'Singapore is organized — led — by the Chinese; Malays provide the traditional crafts and services, Indians are traders, lawyers, in the professions.'

Statistically the Chinese predominate with 76.7% of the population against 14.7% Malays, 6.4% Indians and 2.2% from other backgrounds. What is more, at least 57% of the community devoutly subscribe to religious beliefs, be they Christians or Moslems, Buddhists or Hindus.

How are their days spent? Somewhere in Howard Richard's notebooks I came across an account, factual if humdrum, of the routine followed by a stereotype Chinese family consisting of father, mother, and two children. They are likely to have the husband's or the wife's parents with them in a 4-room HDB flat located in one of the satellite towns. The husband has an office job; his wife is employed part-time working in either a factory or an office, or perhaps teaching or giving tuition at home. Their overall income varies between 1000 and 2000 Singapore dollars a month; they run a small Japanese car.

House-proud they are: potted plants line the window ledges, balcony and corridors. Because of the strict HDB rules, they cannot keep either a large dog or a cat, but they probably have a bowl of aquarium fish, or some song-birds in a cage. Though full-time domestic help is beyond their means, they may be able to afford the part-time assistance of a servant imported on a two-year contract from abroad. (Singapore girls shun such work — they can earn far more as waitresses or unskilled factory hands.)

Everyone wakes up at six o'clock in the morning. If he is health-conscious, the husband goes off to the local recreation park for twenty minutes of physical jerks or a bout of jogging, while his wife prepares breakfast and gets the children ready for school.

By seven they are all out of the flat. A bus calls for the children, but the parents drive to work, often sharing a car-pool. Since their classes finish at one o'clock, the children probably have lunch at school before coming home. Their afternoons are spent doing homework or receiving private tuition. Evenings are taken up with some hobbby or other — stamp-collecting is popular — or simply watching TV.

If the wife has a job she fits her time-table to that of the children. She is usually back by two-thirty to see that they get down to their books, that their homework is done. She cleans the flat, prepares the family dinner, and pops down to shop at the local National Trade Union Congress supermarket. In the evening she, too, unwinds in front of the TV — though many women attend night classes on subjects such as computer-planning, accounting, or business management, often accompanied by their husbands. In the rat-race of today, Singaporeans are always seeking means to better their lot.

'Nine to five' really means 8 to 5.30 for the man, who leaves care of the children to his spouse. But he usually lends a helping hand with the housework, washing dishes and laying the table. If his job permits, he drives his wife home during the lunch break, or takes her for a quick bite at one of the hawker food centres. He reappears in time for a leisurely dinner, though increasingly the family get-together is around the television set. Singaporeans are early birds, and by eleven everyone is in bed.

Only at the week-end is there time for some leisure. Then the whole family, in-laws included, goes off for a jaunt to the Birdpark, the zoo, the Chinese and Japanese gardens, or spends a lazy afternoon at the beach.

Who knows, they may also join in some group activity sponsored by the People's Association — which range from roller-skating, dancing lessons and instruction in the martial arts to cooking, sewing and hairdressing courses. More adventurous souls can even go mountain climbing, exploring or trekking in neighbouring Malaysia with the Venturer's Club. (One of Alex Josey's books deals with race-walking in the tropics, a competitive sport invented in Singapore.) For the higher income folk, of course, there will be golf and polo at the country clubs.

What with one thing and another, there is little time to spare. 'It's all a great rush' says A. Vengkadasalam, who came to Raffles as a bellboy in 1955 and is now Chief Receptionist. 'We always seem to be in a hurry.' For him, off days are an opportunity to catch up with some rest. But when his annual leave comes round, he may take his family on a trip to Malaysia or India. 'We just roam about from place to place, taking it easy. Life is more relaxed there than in Singapore.' But for nothing in the world would he live anywhere else.

Quek Chua Khou, who has been cashier at the hotel for 40 years, does not even consider taking a holiday abroad. 'Holidays cost money' he sighs. 'And in any case I can get to know about other countries through our guests. They tell me all about the places where they live, about the weather and the people. So why spend a lot of money in hotels that are not as good as this?' All the same, the average Singaporean family is likely to save up for a package tour to the west coast of America, Europe, Thailand, Australia, Taiwan or Hong Kong, every two or three years.

As for the youngsters, those groups of teenagers who lounge around the shopping plazas of Orchard Road and go to midnight film shows (Singaporeans are the most avid movie-goers in the world, mostly perhaps to escape the confinement of their homes), they rarely aspire to more than sipping Coke and a smoke. For anyone who craves a taste of the forbidden fruit, it is necessary to go over the Causeway into Malaysia — just as the Malaysians, for whom *Khalwat** is prohibited, are obliged to travel in the opposite direction.

Yet this docile, orderly, obedient, industrious society has a curious weakness for the status symbol. Nowhere else, except perhaps among card-carrying members of OPEC, do glossy advertisements for gewgaws with a prestige tag find more willing victims. This is not to speak of the towkays with their mandatory Mercedes, X.O. cognac, and diamond-encrusted watches, but a much broader section of the community which is categorized by sociologists as 'Homo apatheticus'.

This genus can be spotted bargain-hunting at the chic boutiques in the newest shopping complex, dancing to New Wave hits at any of the more exclusive discotheques, or just munching a burger at one of the franchised food centres that have sprung up all over the city. His hair has a greased spiky look, his clothes bear designer labels that are probably imitations, his imprint is a walkman stereo set, his girl is dressed in Japanese greys and other mod gear. So long as government policy does not prevent him from acquiring one wife, two children, a 3-roomed apartment, 4 wheels and a five-figure salary, he could hardly care less what goes on.

Indeed the authorities are becoming alarmed lest these carbon copies of the egocentric westerner blunt the keen edge of Singapore's thrust into the future. They are anxious, too, at the drift of local talent into the private sector, which offers greater material rewards than government service. In the power hierarchy, a quick head count reveals that of the top six figures, only Lee Kuan Yew himself is Singapore-born. Among the chairmen of the statutory boards, a majority of 61% come from outside.

Since the Raffles Institution was founded in 1823, and even more so since the University of Malaya came into being in 1952, Singapore has offered the best education that this region has to give. But now fewer students come to the island, and much of the home talent is tempted both to study and remain abroad.

Anxiety over the quality of leadership in the future was behind the Prime Minister's recent complaint that graduate women were producing fewer offspring than their less educated counterparts. He implied that unless the more intellectual women married, mediocracy would set in, and the downfall of Singapore would ensue.

'If we continue to reproduce ourselves in this lopsided manner,' he warned when introducing the new elitist incentives, 'we shall be unable to maintain our present standards. Levels of competence will decline, our economy will falter, the administration and society will eventually suffer.'

Never before had the leader of a fully-enfranchised society dared to tamper with the pattern of procreation in the hope of swelling the ranks of its brightest citizens, and needless to say 'the great marriage debate' sparked fierce controversy between eugenicists and environmentalists. Visions of '1984' were invoked (to the advantage of Orwell's sales) and fingers were pointed at the German Third Reich. Yet somehow Lee's elitist theories are consonant with the cerebral, high-tech dynamics that have brought

* *Khalwat* means being in close proximity with someone of the opposite sex to whom you are not married.

Singapore to its present high point of achievement. Maybe in the millenium to come, a good heart and a sharp sense of humour will prove powerless against the all-pervasive clout of the computer and the chip.

Yet I very much doubt whether Singapore will become dehumanised to that point. I suspect that Lee's purpose was above all a gingering-up manoeuvre: to rub in the message that if this tiny island is to continue expanding as a global city, it must gird its loins to stay ahead of the flock.

No doubt the old Confucian ethics will take care of the rest. They have done so for a very long time. And as the Chinese proverbs says: Man's legs can only walk. Coins roll.

Following:
The Palm Court of Raffles still captures the ambience of an elegant past.

◄ 19 ►

SELAMAT TINGGAL

THE BAGS ARE PACKED, THE shopping done. For the last time we sit in this lovely tropical garden, toasting the winter — and the book — that is ending. In a few hours, the plane will take off.

And unexpectedly, as if to highlight this moment — part wry, part regretful, part sentimental — a slice of history is being reenacted before our eyes. For the BBC has begun filming another instalment of 'Tenko' here at Raffles, and has uncannily recreated the ambience, the feel, almost the smells, of forty years back.

Over in the sand-sprinkled forecourt, officers with swagger-sticks are being jogged around in rickshas drawn by Chinese in conical hats; trim khaki-clad ATS girls mingle with the military police in voluminous well-starched shorts; a rakish Triumph Gloria two-seater snorts up with a young man in a panama hat at the wheel. As we watch, a bunch of bedraggled women P.O.Ws from Changi jail clamber out of a Bedford 3-tonner truck: upstairs on the second floor, a dormitory has been set up for them, full of mosquito nets, whirling fans, and a jumble of army packs. In the Tiffin Room below, neat groups of mems and red-tabbed officers sit waiting for the band to start playing the opening waltz of a tea-dance.

Here in the Palm Court, another scene is being rehearsed, between a fearsome matron and the Indian heroine, while safely out of range Sister Ulrich in her white nun's habit lights a cigarette. And incongruously enough, the Japs are here too — for by quirky coincidence a team of Japanese photographers are focussing their cameras on a fashion model posed at the edge of the pool.

Then suddenly, in the midst of it all, a red carpet is thrown down. Lines of Malays in blue tunics form up at the entrance, and amid a throbbing of drums and a chanting of Malay voices, the benign figure of Tunku Abdul Rahman is ushered into the ballroom for a Moslem ceremony. (Of course, I had forgotten. Today is Maulud Nabi.)

The Tunku's sensations at being confronted with so poignant a flash-back into the past can only be conjectured. But what a stylish reminder of the part this old place, like the Tunku himself, has played in the pageant of Singapore!

Au fond, is this not the secret of its mystique? A subject we never get tired of debating: it's the magic of the name, thinks Howard. Let's say nostalgia, suggests Rita. Well — romance, murmurs Amanda, the sense of romance. The human scale is right, suggests Eck Kheng, it's so grand yet it's also so homely. Colin Dudley of the BBC is more explicit: 'It doesn't rush' he tells us. 'The waiters are gentlemanly. Like gentlemen they treat their work as a service and not a job. Raffles is an oasis of peace in the mad

---

* *Selamat tinggal* is a Malay farewell.

rush of Singapore. And for the 14 million viewers of our programme it means glamour.'

Behind us, dazzling white against the heraldic green of the travellers' palms, the old dowager seems to smile, entwining us all gently in her stately dreams. She is the ultimate survivor of a lost way of life.

Yet alas, all too clearly the concrete is closing in. From my windows I have been watching the neighbouring skyscrapers edge upwards at the rate of one storey every four days, and already they tower above this grandiose old cluster of buildings that for a century has been renowned as the most luxurious hotel in the East. In 1987 Raffles will celebrate its centenary. It has already been designated as an historic monument, to be cherished in perpetuity. But what will the next century hold in store? I reflect on what the Chairman, Charles Tresise, told me a few days ago: of the plans to restore the existing buildings to their former Belle Epoque splendour by throwing open the Tiffin Room to give on to the Palm Court garden as it once did, by retrieving the great staircase from the hotch-potch of later additions that now conceal it, by returning the main entrance to the front of the Beach Road facade, where it used to be; by bringing all the rooms up to top international standards.

The gardens, he said, will be extended over the land behind to form a second palm court with a larger swimming pool, and right at the back a new tower block will be built to house the ballroom and I don't know how many additional suites. 'We intend Raffles to be the best hotel in Singapore, as it always was', Mr Tresise stressed, and there is no doubt that when these plans are carried out it will be as spectacular in the days to come as when the Sarkieses built it. I only hope that the friendly atmosphere will survive.

But now the lights have come on, bathing everything in a soft amber glow. The orchestra begins playing a Beethoven violin Romance — the second, I think. Sadly, it is time to leave.

Into Beach Road our car turns, accelerating over the great harbour bridge to give a last blazing glimpse of this tremendous city: a city whose full vibrant flavour no artist, no composer, no poet has yet managed to recapture. And as we bowl along the floodlit expressway, surely there is a farewell of trumpets in the warm scented air? Why else this lump in the throat?

Down the final straight, the car sweeps, and into the splendid finale of Changi airport. Now it is really goodbye.

The check-in is rapid, the emigration formalities even quicker. 'Come back soon!' says the officer as he stamps the passport. Silently the conveyer wafts one down to the departure bay, where on a television screen Diana and Duncan are cosily reading the news. Precisely at nine we board the great white bird, and soar off into the sky.

Though in fourteen hours' time we shall be on the other side of the globe, part of me will have remained behind, and will always stay.

'For heaven's sake,' I ask myself as the smiling Singapore airhostess comes up with a drink, 'who was it who said that there's no romance left in the world?'

Singapore, 4 April 1984

When little girls were chanting nursery rhymes like 'Lucy Locket' and 'The Brave Old Duke of York' in school, they dressed like this. (JF)

Child's play was not to be scoffed at; there were scaled down rattan furniture and delicate porcelain tea sets for little fingers. (JF)

Flying foxes or more correctly
fruit bats were once a common
sight in orchards and
plantations. The Chinese, well
known for their adventurous
palates, shot these mammals for
sport, stewed them in spices
and created an extraordinary
dish. (LKC)

Off to catch butterflies, two
mem besars are suitably attired
for their nature ramble. Both
carry complete female hunting
kits around their shoulders.
(AOHD)

How the mems used to get
ashore without getting their feet
wet. This used to be a common
sight till the late 1940s. (AOHD)

Up to the mid-sixties, troops of monkeys roamed the Botanic Gardens of Singapore. Fed by park users, they became aggressive and began to raid gardens and homes of the surrounding area. They were soon labelled a nuisance and put down en masse. (LKC)

Malay gentlemen dance the ronggeng to the beat of a *rebana* (drum). (PY)

MALAYS, SINGAPORE.

After the solemnisation of a marriage, the bridal couple mounts a decorated dias for the *Bersanding*. This 'sitting in State' is the visible demonstration to all present that the bride and groom are now husband and wife. (LKC)

A crew of the Singapore Fire Brigade, circa 1939. (JMLH)

Boys from Company 'B' of the Police Training School pose in regulation dress while non-commissioned men of an earlier era stand to attention in the ceremonial dress of 1863. (AOHD)

The Singapore Steam Laundry was founded in 1927. Nothing was mechanised then and men showed their prowess with the iron in the hand-ironing department. (AOHD)

The ting-ting man, named undoubtedly by the sound of his bell as he called his wares: sold goods ranging from perfumes to needles and pin-cushions. (JL)

Indians initially came to Singapore as temporary labourers who arrived with the built-in experience of the British. These worked in the docks, moving cargo from godown to the short service railway. (AOHD)

Built on land reclaimed from mangrove swamps, Kallang airport opened in 1937. It was, at that time, one of the most modern airports in the world. Its original grass runway was extended and surfaced with concrete by the Japanese between 1942 and 1945. (PY)

Airport, Singapore.

The sweetheart of the skies leans coolly on her plane. She was the first lady aviator of the colony and was landed in marriage to the captain of the flying club. (AOHD)

The Duke of Windsor, as
Prince of Wales, unveiled the
Cenotaph on 31 March 1922.
'We are met here to do honour
to the men who, in common
with many others from all parts
of our great Empire, died that
we as an Empire might live' he
had said at the ceremony.
'Those who passed during the
five years of war to victory,
which are symbolised by the
five steps that lead up to this
monument, we shall never
forget.' (PY)

To commemorate Raffles'
genius and foresight in founding
Singapore, his statue was
moved to Empress Place from
the Padang for the Centenary
celebrations. The Italian
Renaissance colonnade, built for
the occasion, was destroyed
after the fall of Singapore in
1942. Raffles' statue, which was
due to be sent to Japan to be
melted down, was happily saved
from that fate. (PY)

Only an extremely low tide could have permitted this steamer to slip under the low spans of Anderson and Cavanagh Bridges into the basin of the Singapore River. (PY)

To celebrate the Silver Jubilee of King George V and Queen Mary, Raffles Hotel served up a ten course western dinner. (RH)

SOUVENIR OF
THE SILVER JUBILEE

1910-1935

Her Majesty Queen Mary   *His Majesty King George V.*

JUBILEE DINNER

RAFFLES HOTEL

SINGAPORE·

6th May, 1935·

Singapore: an aerial view, 1940s. (AOHD)

Before World War Two set its strangle-hold on the East, Singapore, as part of the British empire did its part in war relief. The YWCA organised sewing circles to tailor clothes for British war victims and fund raising stamps like this one were sold. (MG)

30 August 1941, months before defeat and the sign of Victory is still being flashed on every letter posted in the Settlements. (MG)

Building
Court
drew's
edral

Municipal
Building

Cathay
Building

Central
Fire Station

Elgin
Bridge

Hill St.
Police
Station

Fort
Canning

WAR-TIME MALAYAN RECIPES

SIMPLE TASTY ECONOMICAL

BY IRIS DUMBLETON

KANG KONG

This vegetable does not look very appetising, but if cooked as directed in the recipes given, is really very tasty. It is sold by the catty, but generally in small quantities. Price about 4 cts. a catty.

IN BUYING see that the leaves are fresh and green. The kind with a cluster of small leaves and thin stalks is best.

PREPARATION. Wash, shaking in several changes of water, then pull off all the leaves, with small stems, breaking off the whole of the young tops. Cut the young parts of the stalks into short lengths then cut each into fine shreds, lengthways.

RECIPE NO. 33.

Lem'ak—with Kledek (Sweet Potato) without Oil.

See Recipe No. 31—Variation Notes.

Prepare vegetable as directed in Preparation Notes.

See Glossary for Malayan culinary terms.

DIG for VICTORY

GROW YOUR OWN FOOD

GET YOUR OWN TOOLS from

BOON SENG & Co Ltd

War was yet to come to Singapore but it was certainly on the Administration's mind. In September 1941, a book of War Time Malayan Receipes was published to help housewives meet new conditions resourcefully by making the best use of local foodstuffs. With the official publicity given to lessening dependence on imported foodstuffs, everywhere in the suburbs there were vegetables 'where in peace time there were only flower beds and tennis courts'. (JL)

Once a place where decorum and the strictest discipline had to be exercised, the parade square at Selarang Barracks is transformed into a transit camp. (AOHD)

4 — BARRACK SQ., SEPT., 1942.

While men were sacrificing themselves for the same cause of Peace somewhere on the Western Front, others, newly arrived at an arena preparing for war, came with a light heart and friendly smile. After all, wasn't Singapore Island a fortress? (IWM)

Under the stern, sullen and terrific acts of *Bushido*, the humanity of the invading Japanese was easily forgotten. Dressed in converted khakis of British troops, these infantrymen had portraits done, probably to send to mother or sweetheart in Kyoto or, perhaps, Hiroshima. (IWM)

Chinese New Year's Day 1942, 15th February, the British forces surrendered unconditionally to the Japanese at the Ford Factory, Bukit Timah. The Japanese Staff Officer, Sugita, is in the centre and Lt. Gen. Percival the British Commander is on his left. (ANM)

Dr Lim Boon Keng: a true Singaporean Chinese who served in the Legislative Council of the Straits Settlements. During World War II, he was made leader of the Chinese by the conquerors, and was unwilling participant in the milking of the Chinese community of 50 million dollars. (AOHD)

These smaller denominations of banana money soon became valueless with runaway inflation aggravated by blackmarket practices. A ten dollar bill, which depicted a banana tree (and hence the name) bought literally one banana at best. In all practical terms, money could no longer be carried in wallets and paper bags and sacks were in great demand for the purpose. (MG)

When Singapore became 'The Light of the South', many existing organisations and establishments had their names changed to include the title of Syonan. (AOHD)

A letter addressed to Syonan post-marked in Pinang and bearing a Netherlands Indies stamp overprinted with a Japanese mark. (MG)

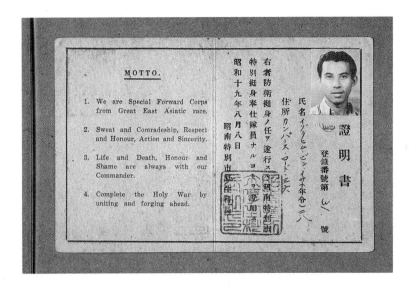

An identity card of the
Japanese Special Forward
Corp. (AOHD)

Japanese medical attendants
spray disinfectant on a beri-beri
patient. The violence of war
killed but the lack of proper
nutrition and medical care also
took countless lives in the years
of warfare. (IWM)

Many who heard the Japanese
staff sing the *Kimigayo*, their
national anthem for the last
time at the Municipal Building
after Nagasaki were not deaf to
its dignity and pathos. How
many carried this feeling of
national pride to death we shall
never know. Some favoured the
traditional *hara-kiri*, others, a
lone revolver shot and yet
others, mass suicides. The
formal surrender took place in
Municipal Chambers on 12
September 1945. (IWM)

Preceding:
As the Union Jack is hoisted
after liberation, a cheer from a
crowd of happy children below,
is sounded. For adults, it was
like a great sigh of relief. After
a brief period of military
administration, life settled to an
uneasy calm under which ran a
feeling of discontent and an
urge for self-determination.
(IWM)

With Japanese surrender
imminent and like bamboos
sprouting after a spring rain,
representatives of a host of
political organisations
demonstrate their cause. (IWM)

Displaying their patriotic fervour
after the Japanese occupation,
Singapore Muslims participate
in a victory parade. (IWM)

After the ravages of war, the British Red Cross and St. John's Nursing Services contributed to the rehabilitation work by providing 'feeding services' at various centres around the city. Here at the Prinsep Street Clinic which operated from 9:30 to 11:30 each morning, neither Mrs Irene Ooi nor her assistants have a spare moment while serving food to children. (IWM)

After three years of Japanese
occupation, during which time
the hotel entrance was moved
to this side location, the British
reoccupy Raffles as a
rehabilitation centre for released
prisoners of war. The swastika
on the lorry passing by is of
course that of a Chinese
religious sect. (RH)

Straits Times
The Percival Report

SPECIAL SUPPLEMENT — SINGAPORE — FRIDAY, FEBRUARY 27, 1941

EVENTS LEADING TO THE WAR

THE following Despatch was submitted to the Secretary of State for War on April 25, 1946 by Lieut.-Gen. A. E. Percival, C.B., D.S.O., O.B.E., M.C., formerly General Officer Commanding, Malaya.

It was officially released for publication by the War Office in London last night.

The Despatch says:—

The preparation of this Despatch on the Operations in Malaya which took place between Dec. 8, 1941, and Feb. 15, 1942, has been influenced by the fact that since the conclusion of those operations a great deal of literature has appeared on the subject.

Statements have been made and opinions expressed by writers, many of whom had but a cursory knowledge of Malayan conditions or of the factors which influenced decisions.

Often these statements and opinions have been based on false or incomplete information.

The Malayan campaign had two novel features (a) It was the first large-scale campaign for a very long time to be fought within British or British-protected territory, and (b) It was our first experience of a campaign fought with modern weapons in jungle warfare conditions.

In reading this Despatch it should be borne in mind that the knowledge which now exists was not at that time available to those responsible for the conduct of the operations, whose task it was in consequence to attempt to solve many new and novel problems.

General Remarks

Malaya is a country where troops must be hard and acclimatised and where strict hygiene discipline must be observed if heavy casualties from exhaustion and sickness are to be avoided.

The country generally tends to restrict the power of artillery and of Armoured Fighting Vehicles.

It places a premium on the skill and endurance of infantry.

As is true of most types of close country, it favours the attacker.

The form of government of Malaya was probably more complicated and less suited to war conditions than that of any other part of the British Empire.

In pan-Malayan matters the High Commissioner could not deal with the four Federated States as one entity. He had to consult each, either direct or through the Federal Secretariat. More often than not, he had to deal with ten separate bodies i.e. the Colony plus the nine States, and sometimes with the Federal Government as well, making eleven.

This naturally tended to cause delay when subjects affecting Malaya as a whole were under discussion.

The British Government had by various treaties promised to afford protection against external aggression to most, if not all, of these Malay States.

This was a factor which had to be borne in mind in the conduct of the operations.

In a country where there was so little national unity, it was natural that the Sultans should be inclined to consider the security of their own territory as of primary importance.

Prior to the outbreak of World War II there was a Defence Committee Malaya, modelled on the Committee of Imperial Defence at Home.

There were a number of sub-committees. The members of these sub-committees were as a rule partly military and partly civil.

Up to November, 1940, the three Fighting Services worked independently, the commanders of the Army and Air Force being responsible direct to their own Ministries.

The Senior Naval Officer at Singapore was originally responsible only for the sea defences of Singapore Island and for the local defence of the adjoining waters.

Later he became, as Rear-Admiral, Malaya, responsible for all the coasts of Malaya.

From July 1940 onwards, however, the Naval Commander-in-Chief, China Station, flew his flag on shore at Singapore and assumed responsibility for all the waters off the coasts of Malaya, except that the responsibility for those off Singapore Island was still delegated to the Rear-Admiral.

In October, 1940, a Commander-in-Chief Far East was appointed, the position being filled by Air Chief Marshal Sir Robert Brooke-Popham.

He was informed that the two main principles to guide his actions were (a) It was the Government's policy to avoid war with Japan, (b) Reliance for the defence of the

Another surrender, this time aboard the U.S.S. Missouri in Tokio Bay at the Japanese capitulation. General of the Army Douglas MacArthur is seen here witnessing the Japanese signatures to the Instrument of Surrender. Behind him, foreground, is Gen. Wainwright. Next to Gen. Wainwright, is Lieut.-Gen. A. E. Percival who is placing in his right-hand tunic pocket one of the souvenir fountain pens which Gen. MacArthur used and presented to him during the ceremony.—A.P. picture.

Contents

Defence Plans 2
Operation Matador 2
The A.I.F. 3
The Civilians:
The Europeans 3
The Chinese 3
The Malays 3
The Eurasians 4
The Indians 4
Others 4
Labour 4
The Air Situation 4
War Comes To Malaya 5
Singapore Raided 6
The War Council 6
Repulse and Prince of Wales 6
Kelantan Withdrawal 7
Battle of Jitra 7
Battle of Gurun 7
The River Muda 8
Fall of Penang 8
The Grik Road 8
Withdrawal from Ipoh 9
Scorched Earth 9
Civil Defence 9
Battle of Kampar 10
Slim River Battle 10
Labour Companies 11
Withdrawal from Central Malaya 11
The Johore Defence Line 11
German Ambush 12
Battle of Muar River 12
Withdrawal to Singapore 13
Causeway Breached 13
Battle of Singapore Begins 13
Empress of Asia Sunk 14
Morale 14
Landing on Singapore 14
Friday, the 13th 15
The Last Days Of Singapore 15
Capitulation 16
Surrender 16
Lessons of the Campaign 16
Conclusions 16

INDEX TO MAPS
Fighting in North Malaya 5
The Malayan Campaign 8
Singapore Island 14

Far East was to be placed on Air Power until the fleet was available.

He was further instructed that the G.O.C. Malaya was to continue to correspond with the War Office, on all matters on which he had hitherto dealt with it, to the fullest extent possible consistent with the exercise of his command.

The C.-in-C. Far East had no control over any naval forces, nor did he have any administrative responsibility, the various Commands continuing to deal with their respective Ministries in this respect.

The C.-in-C. Far East, therefore, had only a small operational staff and no administrative staff.

Becomes G.O.C.

On May 16, 1941, I assumed the duties of G.O.C. Malaya Command.

I had previously served as Chief of Staff Malaya Command (General Staff Officer 1st Grade) in 1936 and 1937.

At that time the Air Officer Commanding Far East was Air Vice-Marshal C. W. B Pulford. He had taken over command only a short time previously.

The Commander-in-Chief China was Vice-Admiral Sir Geoffrey Layton. Rear-Admiral Drew was Rear-Admiral Malaya but was shortly afterwards succeeded by Rear-Admiral Spooner.

When hostilities started the headquarters of the Army, the Royal Air Force and the Civil Government were grouped in one area, while those of the two Commanders-in-Chief and of the Rear-Admiral Malaya were grouped in another, some 10 miles or more apart.

This was far from an ideal solution, but possibly the best under the circumstances.

Had there been at that time a Supreme Command with an integrated staff probably many of these difficulties would have disappeared.

Staff Difficulties

With the increase in the garrison as the defences developed and relations with Japan became more strained, so there was an increase in the strength of Headquarters Malaya Command.

After the outbreak of war with Germany the filling of vacancies on the staff became more and more difficult as the supply of trained staff officers in the Far East became exhausted.

Regular units serving in Malaya were called upon to supply officers with qualifications for staff work until it became dangerous to weaken them any further, and selected officers were sent for a short course of training at Quetta.

The supply of trained staff officers from Home was naturally limited by non-availability and by the difficulties of transportation.

At the same time, even before war broke out with Japan, the work at Headquarters Malaya Command was particularly heavy, including as it did war plans and the preparation of a country for war in addition to the training and administration of a rapidly increasing garrison.

"Local War Office"

In addition, the Command was responsible for placing orders to bring up to the approved scale the reserves of all supplies and stores, except as regards weapons and ammunition.

In fact, Headquarters Malaya Command combined the functions of a local War Office and those of a Headquarters of a Field Force.

Authority for the raising of new units and for all increases in establishments had to be obtained from the War Office.

With the pressure of wartime business it will be appreciated that delays occurred, some of which had serious consequences.

In 1941 sea voyages from the United Kingdom were taking 2-3 months so that there was a long delay in filling staff vacancies from Home, even after approval had been given.

In consequence, the strength of Headquarters Malaya Command was usually much below establishment.

Resources Strained

When war with Japan broke out there were less than 70 officers at Headquarters Malaya Command, including the Headquarters of the Services.

This is about the war-time establishment of the Headquarters of a Corps.

Our resources were thus strained to the limit.

It should be realized that the G.O.C. Malaya did not have a free hand in developing the defences of Malaya.

In principle the defences were developed in accordance with a War Office plan which was modified from time to time in accordance with recommendations made by the G.O.C.

By the beginning of 1941 the overall estimated cost of the War Office scheme had amounted to slightly over £6 million, and actual expendi-

Friday, 27 February 1948, seven years after General Percival made Hobson's choice and surrendered Singapore, his dispatch to the Secretary of State for War was published. (JL)

Perfect 10: Mr and Miss Singapore, 1949. (HLEE)

A bevy of YWCA belles pose for a formal portrait, apparently before a picnic outing. (AOHD)

'I hope teacher doesn't realise that I have my shoes on.' As is now, physical as well as intellectual development was the concern of the education system. (AOHD)

Primary school children perform 'When I was a Lady' during an annual school concert. Let it be said plainly that the 'ladies' were not really ladies but little gentlemen cleverly disguised. (AOHD)

An eclectic mix of instruments combine to form the basis of this school orchestra. Young talent was not overlooked, as is well illustrated by Goh Soon Tio's nurture of Lee Pan Hon from childish musician of Chinatown towards international recognition. (AOHD)

Cub scouts, boy scouts and sea scouts looked forward to jamborees and campfire nights, when it was time for cheeky skits, robust troop yells and hearty fire-side singing. (AOHD)

While the British community called theirs fetes, locals, evolving a Singaporean identity used the tag 'Food and Fun Fair' for fund-raising carnivals. This one was held at the Raffles Girls' School, the sister school of the institution Raffles founded for the education of 'the higher classes of the native population'. (FRNS)

This brawny shot-putter has come a long way from her cloistered sisters of another age who were once much restricted by ancient Chinese traditions of modesty and coyness. (FRNS)

Winners at the Annual Sports Day could expect little polished cups prettied up with ribbons in the school colours. (AOHD)

The search for knowledge starts early in Singapore. Here, children spend time among the books of the Junior Library on Stamford Road. (NTLY)

Photography, even in its infancy, was a popular hobby. Many clubs and associations had photographic groups which pursued the art. (FRNS)

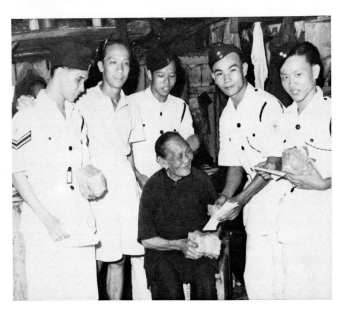

Members of the Singapore Red Cross visit and attend to old folk living in a cubicle in the upper stories of the shop houses of Chinatown. The environment is dark and squalid, and rows of cramped bunk spaces have access from narrow corridors. (FRNS)

THE · FIRST · CITY · FATHERS

The first City Fathers as seen by true Singaporean cartoonist T. H. Peng. Singapore received her charter on Saturday, 22 September 1951. (JL)

City Day cartoon. (JL)

Considering the idiom of today, the headline chosen for this City Day edition is most unfortunate. But it was a happy day and after T. P. F. McNiece received the royal charter from Governor Sir Franklin Gimson, smiles and handshakes were seen everywhere. The greeting of the day was certainly 'We are real citizens now'. (JL)

The Pepsi Cola Float in the grand and joyous City Day Parade on 22 September 1951. (HLEE)

While downtown theatres showed movies from the Golden Age of Hollywood, backyard and rural open air cinemas flashed action-type dramas on stretched bedsheets and painted canvas. (LKC)

The *Khatam Quran* is no longer an integral part of the Malay wedding ritual today. Brides and grooms, in earlier times, were required to recite passages of the Holy Book to show that they knew the Quran. Here, the bride's younger brother participates in the ritual, thereby fulfilling the obligation which he would otherwise be required to perform at his own wedding. (JMLH)

Hadrah groups, chanting religious songs to the rhythm of drums, accompany Malay grooms to meet their brides. Carried in procession are also *Bunga Mangga*, brightly coloured plumes, which indicate the presence of the bridegroom. (JMLH)

Could this tiger at Kallang airport be a direct descendant of the legendary 'lion' of Singapura? (JMLH)

Following:
The music was early rock and roll, Italian, sentimental, Hawaiian; the bands, self-styled, self-taught and up-to-the-minute. This one, led by Baby Low attempts to capture the range of their repertoire in their modish name. (BLKW)

Not to be outdone by imported prams pushed by other amahs, this one had this two-seater built. The whiskey crate seat is, of course, unoccupied. (AOHD)

Before scholls and Japanese slippers were cross-strap slip-ons like those worn by most of these children, 1950. (MG)

A STRAITS TIMES PUBLICATION COMMEMORATING

THE CORONATION OF
Her Majesty
QUEEN ELIZABETH II

PRICE ONE DOLLAR

Coronation Day 1953, when a
generation of Rule Britannica
children celebrated with
parades and special concerts.
'Britannica' from Bukit Panjang
Government School is flanked
by her mates dressed as a
fitting entourage. (AOHD)

Singapore in 1953 resounded
with much enthusiasm during
the coronation celebrations of
Queen Elizabeth II. The *Straits
Times* put out a special
commemorative supplement,
and Her Majesty's portrait
appeared on everything from
stamps to lapel pins and car
emblems. (JL)

With the night sky spangled with firework colours, a mighty sea dragon, all 150 metres long and lit by 8000 lights, glided along the sea off the esplanade to bring to a magnificent climax the Coronation celebrations. (GH)

Twenty deep around the Padang, crowds watched the 3,500 participants in the city's Coronation Day Parade. On that bright morning of 2 June 1953, Governor Sir John Nicoll, inspected the troopers which included demure maidens carrying Coronation parasols and smart men of the First Singapore Regiment Royal Artillery in their songkoks and red ceremonial sarongs. (GH)

Costume parties are always colourful and a favourite among the hob-nob of society. Malcolm Macdonald, then Special Commissioner in Singapore, attends one dressed as a clown. (LWTC)

Wong Peng Soon, Singapore's champion badminton player of the 1950s, executes his famous backhand. This photograph was made by Loke Wan Tho, film magnate and keen amateur bird-life photographer. (LWTC)

The cream of society got together to stage fashion and live tableaux depicting women around the world for two evenings in August 1952. Proceeds were in aid of charities and a sequel was organised four years later and called 'More About Eve'. (LWTC)

China

Model: MISS LYDIA TAI

YANG KUEI-FEI, the most famous beauty of China, lived during the reign of Emperor Ming Huang of the T'ang Dynasty, Eighth Century A.D. Chosen as one of the court ladies, she soon became the Emperor's favourite. They spent happy days together, gathering around them the best poets and musicians in the country. Many were the songs and poems written about Yang Kuei-fei's beauty. However, the country was neglected and the border tribes were making raids upon the outlying district. Finally there was a rebellion in the army and the men marched upon the palace. The Emperor was forced to lead the troops and Yang Kuei-fei was put to death.

Dry or not, the ring-side seats at the Great World boxing stadium would be full of eager fans yelling for a K.O. The 'Worlds' of Singapore catered to all tastes in public entertainment. (JL)

Great World, Happy World, Gay World, New World: brightly lit grounds, sounds of entertainment, roundabouts, the jolly noises of side-shows, and traditional music add up to a veritable anthology of staple recreation in the 1960s. (EUP)

Chinese traditions having been put second to western style childrens' birthdays were celebrated with a chorus of 'Happy Birthday', a cream cake and gifts made in England. (MG)

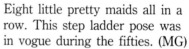

Vernon Martenez: student, choreographer, designer, producer. He was, in the fifties the first young man to organise and stage a musical extravaganza in the Victoria Theatre. (FRNS)

Eight little pretty maids all in a row. This step ladder pose was in vogue during the fifties. (MG)

The hard life of a boatman doesn't change, unlike the skyline of the city port he serves. (EUP)

The street markets of Chinatown teemed with activity in the morning hours. So wide was the range of food and goods sold. There, you'll find light Chinese pastries, snake meat, ginger roots, buddha's palm, jade, plastic toys, paper masks ..... (EUP)

He sells doormats, egg whisks, every type of broom, graters, colanders, and a great variety of spoons. His is, in short, the mobile hardware store. (EUP)

INDIAN MAGICIANS AND SNAKE CHARMERS. SINGAPORE

Although they did not perform the famed Rope Trick, Indian travelling magicians lived up to their image and reputation as snake charmers. (LKC)

Some British traditions, like the New Year Regatta carried on well into the fifties. Sea sports drew crowds and hawkers joined in to heighten the carnival atmosphere. (JL)

AN INTERVAL AT THE NEW YEAR SEA SPORTS, SINGAPORE

The setting and health standards may have changed but Singaporeans, young or old, have not lost their passion for hawker food. (EUP)

Devout Muslims pray five times in a day. On Fridays, only men proceed to mosques to offer their prayers. (EUP)

A Malay woman in *baju kurong* and *sarong* with her Chinese friends in *samfu* and *cheongsam*. Besides textile shops, fabric was sold by door-to-door saleswomen who showed sample swatches and took orders for the latest in rubia, voile or lawn. (EUP)

Before DC 10s and Big Top Jumbos, were propellered planes aboard which predecessors to today's 'Singapore girls' began a tradition of attentive service. (AOHD)

Up to the early 60s, travel by boat was still popular. The P & O line still cruised the region and families, as of old, gathered at Keppel Harbour to bid friends and relatives a good voyage. (MG)

Western dance in Chinese decor was the formula successfully employed by the Southern Cabaret at Eu Tong Sen Street. (EUP)

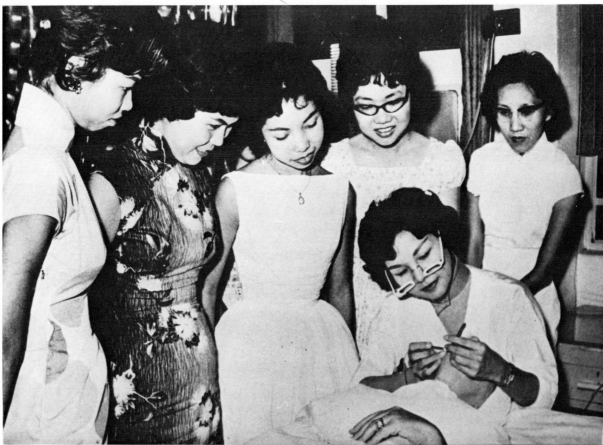

With the advent of 'high technology', audio visual equipment was becoming a useful tool in schools; a great leap forward from Bernard Shaw's Pygmalion voice machine. (NTLY)

Worried looking children face the needle of health care officers. Most, if not all, infectious diseases have been effectively curbed by innoculations and control of the environment. (NTLY)

Her publicity material could well have proclaimed her 'London trained', bringing eager disciples to learn the latest in beauty culture. (NTLY)

A photographer takes a parting shot of Toa Payoh Village. This was one of the first major public housing areas which the Housing and Development Board, newly established in 1959, transformed beyond recognition. (AOHD)

These SIT flats formed what was once considered a 'great, modern' housing estate. (EUP)

A headstart for mass
participation sports. Joggers
race through a new housing
estate to promote fitness and
perhaps raise funds through a
thoroughly Singaporean
phenomenon — the jogathon.
(AOHD)

Following left:
During the seventh moon of the
Chinese calendar, hungry ghosts
return from Hades to be treated
to feasts given by filial
descendants and entertained by
street operas. (AOHD)

Following right:
Johnny Aruzoo, the Elvis
Presley of Singapore, doing his
thing at an RAF 'Beggars
Party'.

Reclaiming land from the eastern coast of Singapore has not only given 225 sq mile Singapore much needed man-made acreage for building but also a superb recreation belt. Fringed by immaculate beaches which these strollers on old Changi beach in the fifties would not recognise, the East Coast Parkway boasts of campsites, tennis centres, windsurfing clubs and golfing facilities. (AOHD)

A commemorative gift from the residents of Malacca Street, this giant broom was used as a symbol during the launching of a campaign to make Singapore litter-free. (AOHD)

Following:

Strings of exploding fire-crackers once carpeted streets and homes with lucky red paper during Chinese festivals. Pyrotechnics were banned when they caused loss of life and property through accidental fires. Not to be left luckless, the Chinese now hang dummy cracker decorations while bursts of tape recorded cracker sounds can be put on at whim. (AOHD)

Singapore's imposition of a S$500 fine for littering has created an international impression of almost legendary proportions. The stiff measures have brought results. Singapore is now the cleanest city of Asia and perhaps, the world. Back in 1968, when the campaign was launched, community volunteers participated in the big clean-up. (NYSP)

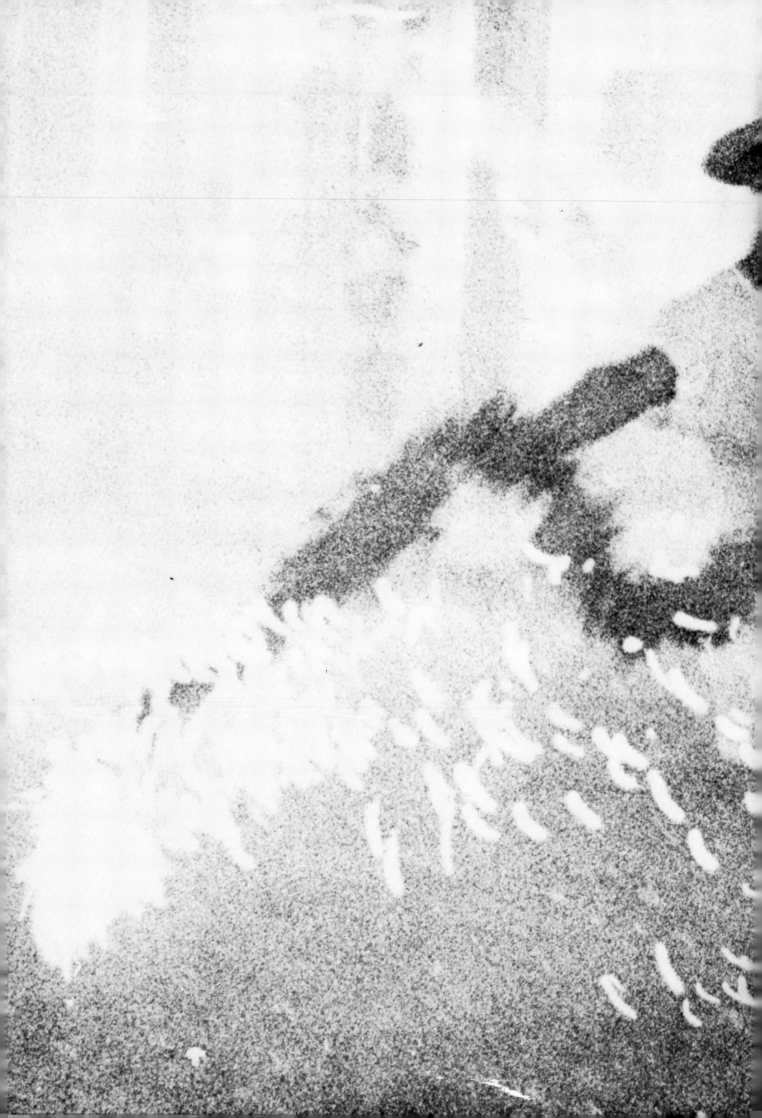

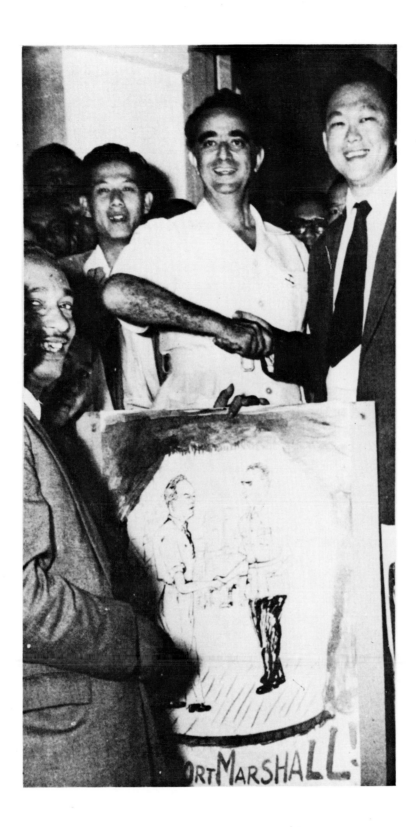

Proceeding with deliberate caution, David Marshall brings the Singapore General Assembly to amend and pass a motion calling for 'self-government' instead of 'independence'. The motion carried and the debates over, Lee Kuan Yew extends Marshall a victory handshake. (RH)

The Federation of Malaya in
August 1955 was on the road to
independence. The struggle in
Singapore had just begun.
Tunku Abdul Rahman Putra,
prince and Chief Minister
designate of Malaya meets
David Marshall, Singapore's
Chief Minister at Raffles. (RH)

David Marshall's platform for the 1961 Anson by-election was complete independence, the abolition of the Internal Security Council and the withdrawal of the British military presence. He was therefore, certain to have the support of pro-communists. Marshall won, on a Workers' Party ticket by 546 votes. Two years later, in the first general election as part of Malaysia, David Marshall, stood as an Independent, polled 416 votes and lost his deposit. (NYSP)

Cheered by a crowd of jubilant multi-racial supporters, Lee Kuan Yew is chaired on his victory in the June 1957 Tanjong Pagar by-elections. The elections were the direct result of a challenge thrown to Lee by David Marshall in Parliament weeks earlier. (WR)

Communists effectively infiltrated Chinese-language schools in 1954. Not only were classrooms penetrated but also alumni and teachers' organisations where emotive issues of Chinese education and culture were exploited. (WR)

Of the 284 students registered for examinations at Kwang Hwa Chinese School on 27th November 1961, much less than half were willing and able to pass the human boycott barricades and take the paper. (NYSP)

The lions of Singapore once stood their positions on either end of Merdeka Bridge, now part of Nicoll Highway. These once-upon-a-time landmarks can still be seen along the driveway leading into the National Stadium (EUP)

On 16th September 1963, (the Prime Minister's 39th birthday) Singapore joined Malaysia. (NYSP)

Women police trainees were taught various skills to prepare them for duty. Happily, their knowledge of judo was rarely put to use though, as this picture shows, they were able to throw another's weight around. (NTLY)

Riots and political unrest plagued Singapore from the mid-fifties to the early sixties and the riot police were in top form both in actual operations and squad drills. (NTLY)

It is ironic that a platform of non-communalism in Malaysia suggested by the PAP should have resulted in an eruption of racial strife for Singapore. On 21st July, 1964, on Prophet Mohammed's birthday, a peaceful religious procession somehow turned ugly and violent. Singapore became the scene of pitched battles and for days after, people of all races kept a self-imposed curfew. (NYSP)

Addressing multi-racial flat
dwellers a week after rioting
broke out, the Prime Minister
reiterated the message given
earlier in a radio broadcast:
'The vast majority of our people
want to live in peace with each
other ..... We shall make it
clear that lawlessness does not
pay. But more important,
harmony between our
communities must be
preserved.' (NYSP)

Reaching out to the Indian Sikh community, Prime Minister Lee wears a turban during the Tamil New Year and Baisakhi Day celebrations. (NYSP)

In 1960, the fires of political change had been lit but had not yet settled to a steady glow. Malaya had shed colonialism, Singapore achieved self rule, but on the road ahead was merger and independence. Here, during May Day Celebrations of 1960, the cry was 'Merdeka — Freedom!' (NYSP)

Alex Josey's golfing partner, Mr, Lee Kuan Yew, watches intently as he sinks a short putt with a five iron. Both gentlemen had, at one time, handicaps of eight. (JOSEY)

Sir Stamford Raffles: I founded Singapore.
Sir Andrew Clarke: I pacified The Malay States.
Sir Frank Swettenham: I Federated them.
Sir John Anderson: I created Greater Malaya.
The Dreamer: There must be a next step somewhere.

If the Dreamer were to awaken in modern Singapore, he would surely realise that some were not content only to dream.

National flags flutter to greet
the first President of the
sovereign democratic and
independent republic of
Singapore. (NYSP)

On introducing Yusof bin Ishak
as the Yang di-Pertuan Negara
of Singapore, Premier Lee Kuan
Yew's remarks were apt. 'It is
not,' he said, 'his high birth
which has commended him for
this high office, for he is a
commoner. It is only that he is
one amongst us whose deep
understanding of the hopes and
fears of our people, and whose
natural dignity, ensure that the
duties of his high office will be
discharged honourably and
well.' (NYSP)

His Excellency, the Yang di-
Pertuan Negara, Inche Yusof
bin Ishak, reads his speech at
the opening of the Third
Session of the Singapore
Legislative Assembly, 31
October 1961. (AOHD)

Military bands were part of the colonial tradition. Here bandsmen, not in their ceremonial best, rehearse for moments of pomp. (RB)

British naval personnel drink to the health of the Queen in what seems to be a traditional ceremony in Sembawang Barracks. (RB)

When the British military presence began to be withdrawn in 1971, shopkeepers in Changi and around British camps worried about their future. There was also, naturally, the more important concern of building up a effective fighting force to replace the withdrawing troops. (AOHD)

The British troops having withdrawn, left Singapore to provide for her own defence. However, in terms of recreation within army barracks, the influence of billiards has left its mark. Here, Encik Othman Wok, a Cabinet Minister, tries out the new table presented to the Infantry Regiment. (AOHD)

In the mid-fifties, the British
government proposed to draft
young Singaporeans for military
service. On May 13th,
protesting youths gathered at
Fort Canning to reject the
proposal. However, the British
were adamant, which resulted in
island-wide strikes. In 1962,
Chinese students gathered to
commemorate what had become
popularly known as the '513'
movement. (NYSP)

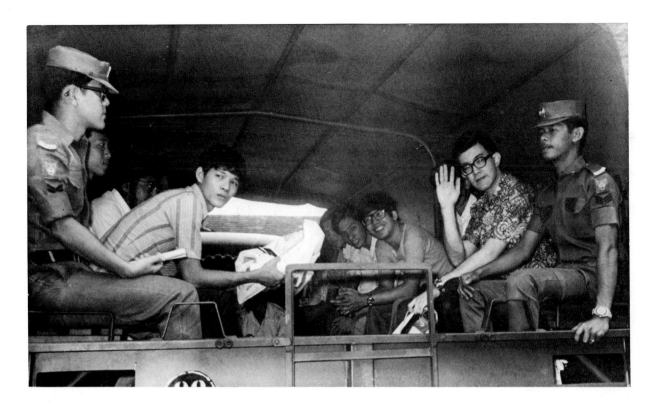

Singaporean males on reaching
the age of eighteen years face
the draft into compulsory
military service for the duration
of 2½ years. No one fit to serve
is excluded. Here, President
Sheares' son, Edwin, begins his
stint of military life in 1972.

Benjamin Henry Sheares carried
the presidency of Singapore
with great aplomb and quiet
dignity. He was a world
renowned gynaecologist who
served the nation in his
retirement years till his death in
1981.

The Chinese community called it Chen Choo Pasar or Pearl Market because it was situated at the foot of Pearl's Hill. After the huge fire which destroyed the stalls, the People's Park Complex was built on the same site. (PY)

Just as it was popular during *pukka sahib* times, the Esplanade or Queen Elizabeth Walk remains an enjoyable place for a stroll. That is, if half of Singapore does not have the same idea. (PY)

The Asia building, the tallest landmark in the commercial district remained so even till the late sixties. The building boom of the next decade threw up skyscrapers which dwarfed it completely. (PY)

Though hidden by high rise office blocks today, the circular New Market is very much the lunch hour hub of the business centre of Shenton Way. (PY)

1972, and few women seemed to be interested in politics or was it the heat that kept them away from the PAP election mass rally held at the foot of Cavanagh Bridge? (EUP)

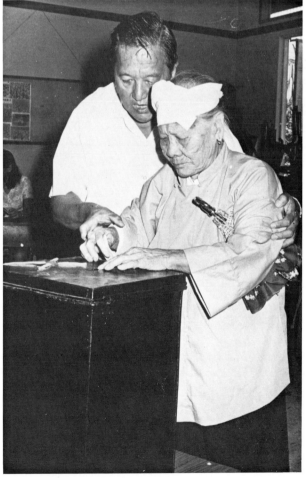

The epitome of civic consciousness, this old woman puts age and ague aside to exercise her right to elect her government. (EUP)

The Singapore Government is determined that the power of the press will not be used by any foreign sources against Singapore's interests. In discussing the subject of freedom of the press, a westerner was overheard telling his Singaporean friend, who had claimed that local journalists often towed the party line, that the standard of reporting in Singapore was better balanced than many believe. (AOHD)

Mass weddings were not a recent innovation but were organised even in the late fifties. This one has a travel agency as co-organiser; undoubtedly special honeymoon rates were part of the package. (SNPL)

Since its inception in Singapore in 1974, television has, as in the world over, won a habitual following. Who has not wondered who shot J.R., gossiped over Hong Kong soaps and chatted about the potrayal of national service life in The Army Series? (AOHD)

The dance styles of the three major ethnic groups of multi-racial Singapore blend in this cultural presentation: Malay, Indian and Chinese drums throb in unison while many hued sarongs, saris and silken ribbons flutter in a kaleidoscopic dance. (AOHD)

The idea of turning Singapore into a 'Garden City' was first mooted in 1972. Each year thence, tree planting days are organised to give public housing estates and the city a greener setting. (AOHD)

Children amuse themselves at a playground near a block of flats built by the Housing Development Board. HDB estates are ubiquitous; over 80% of Singaporeans live in them. If everything goes according to the plan laid out by the government, every citizen will own a place to live in by the end of the century. The estates are designed with a great deal of forethought. Shops are within walking distance, buses service the area, 'green belts' are allocated and children have a place to play.

Two old-timers shoot the breeze in Chinatown. They are surrounded by a bird-cage, Chinese lanterns and other odds and ends. The swivel chair indicates that one of the men might be a barber.

These young men relax after a game. There are various sports centres in the city and exercise, be it in the form of football, squash, basketball, swimming, aerobics or taiji, is greatly encouraged. Football is the most popular spectator and participation sport.

An elderly man with a bundle rides a trishaw. He is a Muslim as is over 15% of the population. Scenes like this were not rare some years ago when trishaws were a common mode of transportation. And now these three-wheelers are being revived, to keep up with the popular demand for them as a tourist attraction.

Heaps of prawns, fresh from the sea, await selection before they are fried with noodles and dished out in platters. Stalls like this provide cheap, nourishing food and one does not have to go very far to find them. Often they are grouped together to form hawkers' centres so that a wide variety of food is found all under one roof.

A kiosk selling an array of periodicals and sundries. Some magazines, published locally, are of a high standard. These shops are there at every turn.

A cafeteria located in one of Singapore's newest and smartest shopping malls. These glittering concrete and glass structures house chic boutiques, salons, franchised restaurants and shops selling electronic goods. Resplendent with fountains and escalators, these shopping centres attract throngs of tourists and teenagers, among others.

One of most popular beaches in Singapore runs along East Coast Parkway. The area has been turned into a mini resort with seafood restaurants, sports centres, holiday chalets and barbecue pits. Hordes of weekenders turn up with all the appropriate equipage: mini-compos, sun-shades and beach balls. Scores of ships lie in anchorage bearing testimony to the fact that Singapore is the second busiest harbour in the world.

A laden bumboat or *tuakow*,
lies anchored in the Singapore
river. The fine old colonial
buildings in the background
lend an atmosphere of
timelessness. Recently the river
was cleaned up and the boats
allotted a new resting place.
Now the river, as seen from
Elgin Bridge, represents a
clean, graceful sweep.

A stunning sunset witnessed
from the Benjamin Sheares
Bridge. The tall skyscrapers
that line the Central Business
District are representative of
the great technical advances
that have taken place in the
last couple of decades.